DB2

Answers!
Certified Tech Support

ABOUT THE AUTHORS

Richard Yevich, RYC, Inc.

Richard is an internationally recognized consultant, lecturer, and teacher, known for his expertise in enterprise information systems. He specializes in large warehouse and distributed relational systems across multiple platforms, and in establishing proper design to achieve high performance and high availability. Richard is widely published and has written columns for several magazines. He is a regular guest speaker at conventions and user groups in the U.S., Australia, Japan and Europe, and has won best-speaker awards for many of these. He is one of the authors of *Data Warehouse: Practical Advice from the Experts,* published by Prentice-Hall, in 1977. Richard was formerly a senior consultant with Codd and Date, Inc. He is a member of IBM's DB2 and S/390 Sysplex Gold Consultants programs.

Susan Lawson, Yevich, Lawson & Associates, Inc.

Susan is an internationally recognized consultant, teacher, and lecturer specializing in database performance, VLDBs, and data warehouses. She has been working with DB2 for 12 years with a strong background in system and database administration. She was formerly an IBM Data Sharing advocate for the Santa Teresa Laboratory where she provided technical expertise for DB2 Data Sharing customers. Susan also has been published in several magazines such as *IDUG Solutions Journal* and *DB2 Magazine*. She is also a member of IBM's DB2 and S/390 Sysplex Gold Consultants programs.

Klaas Brant, KBCE, B.V.

Klaas is the founder of Klaas Brant Consulting and Education, and has worked with DB2 for more than 12 years specializing in DB2 internals and performance tuning for both applications and subsystems. He has done extensive work in creating administration, tuning, and backup/recovery strategies, and has published and lectured worldwide on DB2. Formerly an associate with Codd & Date, Inc, Klaas has worked closely with the R&D team of a leading DB2 software vendor to create new products and to enrich existing products. He is an IBM-certified DB2 Database Administrator and DB2 Application Developer. Klaas is a member of IBM's DB2 Gold Consultants Program.

Sheryl Larsen, RYC, Inc.

Sheryl is an internationally recognized researcher, consultant and lecturer. She is known for her extensive expertise in SQL, and in achieving performance through the proper application of SQL in standalone and distributed environments. Sheryl has over 14 years experience in DB2, has published many articles and authored DB2 courseware as well as several popular DB2 industry posters. Sheryl is a member of IBM's DB2 Gold Consultants Program.

DB2

Answers!
Certified Tech Support

**Richard Yevich, Susan Lawson,
Klaas Brant, Sheryl Larsen
RYC, Inc.**

Osborne/**McGraw-Hill**

Berkeley • New York • St. Louis • San Francisco
Auckland • Bogotá • Hamburg • London
Madrid • Mexico City • Milan • Montreal
New Delhi • Panama City • Paris • São Paulo
Singapore • Sydney • Tokyo • Toronto

Osborne/McGraw-Hill
2600 Tenth Street
Berkeley, California 94710
U.S.A.

For information on translations or book distributors outside the U.S.A., or to arrange bulk purchase discounts for sales promotions, premiums, or fund-raisers, please contact Osborne/**McGraw-Hill** at the above address.

DB2 Answers! Certified Tech Support

1234567890 AGM AGM 90198765432109

ISBN 0-07-211914-4

Publisher
Brandon A. Nordin

Associate Publisher and Editor-in-Chief
Scott Rogers

Acquisitions Editor
Megg Bonar

Project Editor
Betsy Manini

Editorial Assistant
Stephane Thomas

Copy Editor
Andy Carroll

Proofreader
Rhonda Holmes

Indexer
Valerie Robbins

Computer Designers
Ann Sellers
Michelle Galicia
Gary Corrigan

Illustrators
Beth Young
Robert Hanson
Brian Wells

Series Design
Michelle Galicia

To Pam for her constant support and the advice to 'go for it!'
To Charles without whom there would be no book and no
RYC. To Lee who gave me the final 'kita.'

Richard Yevich

To my loving parents, my devoted husband, and a
terrific brother; to my porch pals Mike and Diane; to
Larry Hubbard who over 11 years ago helped me choose
a career path between artificial intelligence and DB2.

Susan Lawson

To my wife Irene; my five kids: Roxanne, Nicolien, Floris,
Erik, and Martijn; and my dear friends Yvette, Linda,
and Paul for their never-ending support.

Klaas Brant

To God, for my second chance in life, Marty, for your vi-
sionary encouragement and love, Tori, for diverting my
attention to the precious parts of life, and Kel, for being a
sister like no other. In addition, this book would not exist
without the help and support I received from the following
friends and family while I was recovering from a violent
crime: Ginger, Nanine, Richard, Janine, Susan, Charles,
Nic, Lisa, Dave, Sandy, Craig, Marty Sr., Leanne, Steve,
Mike, Lori, Tom, Mom and Dad.

Sheryl Larsen

COMPANY PROFILES OF THE CONTRIBUTORS

RYC, Inc.

Headquartered in Austin, Texas, **RYC, Inc.** provides on-site consulting, advanced education, and on-line tools to assist businesses in designing and improving the largest and most complex databases in the world. RYC's areas of expertise include data sharing, complex SQL, Sysplex, parallel processing, high-performance design, and database architecture strategies for operational databases, warehouses, and VLDBs. The principal consultants at RYC are internationally known experts in their specialties who provide practical advice based on experiences with real-world projects.

RYC specializes in high–volume, high–availability relational databases for both operational and warehouse environments, and concentrates on practical improvements that can be made to current database environment while ensuring that a foundation is built for the next release. RYC helps to plan and implement tomorrow's information strategies based on today's database realities, and works with many companies whose business demands force them to utilize everything their DBMS has to offer. From RYC's foundations in VLDB's, 24 × 7 availability, data sharing, sysplex, and parallel processing, RYC leverages its experiences to assist businesses in resolving problems associated with large and complex databases, by teaching advanced database techniques for DBAs and developers, by designing architectures and models for high-performance databases, and by supporting the database professional with online reference tools. Please visit RYC on the web at **www.ryci.com** for more detailed information.

KBCE, B.V.

Klaas Brant Consulting & Education B.V. (KBCE) specializes in the implementation of complex projects that require database technology such as client/server, data warehousing, database marketing, ERP and inter/intranet connectivity. KBCE offers consulting, training, software and services, specializing in IBM DB2 on OS/390 and Windows/NT. More information can be found on our web site: **http://www.kbce.nl** or requested via e-mail to info@kbce.nl

Yevich, Lawson & Associates, Inc.

Yevich, Lawson & Associates, Inc. is a company specializing in database solutions for DB2, MS SQL Server, Oracle, and Sybase. YL&A provides experienced database consultants for long-term database consulting as well as short-term assistance. Consultants with YL&A provide a client with years of database skills in a variety of areas such as system analysis, database design and implementation, performance tuning, and SQL coding.

Contents @ a Glance

Contents

ix

Acknowledgments

I wish to thank Megg, Betsy, and Stephane at Osborne/McGraw-Hill, without whose patience and gentle but relentless pressuring, this book would have never made it to press. Thanks also to Andy for his careful and amazingly thorough copyedit. A very special thanks to Charles Golson, who put the entire effort together and guided all of us through the process. There are many others who put up with and nurtured the authors during the effort and they all deserve a special thanks. Kathy Komer deserves a ton of praise for her constant review of the material. A very special recognition goes to Susan (co-author) for her tireless work over hundreds of hours in making this happen. Also, last but not least, thank you Roger Miller for your gentle pushing, guidance, and always being there to answer all our questions. All bets are off!

Richard Yevich

Introduction

Have you ever been in a class or a presentation and seen or heard a performance expert demystify a topic and enlighten you with a bit of valuable information that you have never seen before, only to find out that this information is undocumented, or unexplained? Where can you find such information? In this book we have taken our combined DB2 experience totaling over 56 years and have documented many tricks of the trade, including our own.

There are many questions asked everyday regarding how DB2 works and what the best options are for optimal performance. Over several years, we have accumulated a collection of the questions we are most frequently asked covering many areas—application programming, basic and advanced SQL, object creation, database design, and monitoring and tuning for performance, among others. We have compiled questions and answers regarding DB2 on the OS/390 platform and DB2 on Intel (Windows 98, and NT), OS/2, and Unix platforms, and we present them here in this book.

The old standard answer of "it depends" just doesn't cut it for people with very technical questions who are looking for help. Although no one answer can provide the ultimate solution for every problem, this book offers a solid place for you to start. We address these frequently asked questions by relaying to you what we have successfully implemented and have seen work in several client environments. Keep in mind that what works for some may not work for everyone. "Try, tune, try again" is a standard quote for performance tuning, and several tuning tips in this book will require the same attention. However, you will find that the tips presented here are very practical and will be very useful in tuning your environment and in answering your most frequently asked questions. In fact, there actually may be some questions and answers in here that some of you may not have come across . . . yet!

On a final note, we have tried to present the most accurate and current information, and have provided figures and screenshots to illustrate the material. Due to changes in versions and recent releases, however, it is possible that you may encounter some differences in accuracy or results. Even so, we are confident that the information we present here will show you the way.

Susan Lawson and Richard Yevich

Chapter 1

Top 10 Frequently Asked Questions

Answer Topics!

- Denormalizing tables for performance
- Using multiple buffer pools
- Using a subquery in the SET clause of an UPDATE statement
- Including multiple tables in a query
- Deciding when to partition a tablespace
- Using Java with DB2
- What the negative affects are of having only one plan for all packages
- Using VARCHAR columns
- Connecting a Windows-based PC to a DB2 host
- Accessing DB2 from a REXX program

Top Ten FAQs @ a Glance

There are a few questions that are asked about DB2 all the time. Some of them are actually based on facts that have changed since the early days of the product, and some are based on myths and misinformation, which tend to get passed on year after year.

The four most common questions concern denormalization, bufferpool use, partitioning, and VARCHAR column use. The detailed answers included in this chapter will dispel the following myths:

Myth 1 Denormalization is usually needed for performance reasons.

Myth 2 It is okay to always use only one bufferpool.

Myth 3 It is okay to wait to partition until the row count gets overly large.

Myth 4 VARCHAR columns should always be used.

Besides these myths, several other important questions always come up today, especially about Java, Windows to OS/390 connectivity, the size of SQL statements, and so on. This chapter gives you the top ten questions and answers.

 ### 1. When should I denormalize my tables for performance?

There are trade-offs to be made when normalizing tables. While the rules of normalization tell us to break tables apart in order to avoid redundancies and inconsistencies, there may be performance implications if these normalized tables are regularly being joined together. In the past, if there were tables being joined together on a regular basis, you would have considered denormalizing them (joining them together in one table) in order to avoid the overhead of the join process during each SQL execution.

However, since the early 1990s, DB2 has evolved sophisticated joining methods and improved performance. Denormalization should not be needed for performance reasons today. If it appears necessary for this reason, there may be problems with the overall table design. There may also be a few rare cases when denormalization is necessary, such as in a read-only data warehouse environment.

 ### 2. How should I use multiple bufferpools?

For the OS/390 platform, it is highly recommended that you have several bufferpools with objects separated according to their type of processing and residency characteristics. This allows for more precise tuning and sizing of each bufferpool. For example, it is ideal to keep objects that have random access in bufferpools separate from objects that have a lot of sequential access. Some general rules of thumb for bufferpool separation on OS/390 are listed in the following example:

BP0: Use only for the DB2 catalog and directory exclusively.

BP1: Use only for the DSNDB07 work tablespaces exclusively.

BP2: Use for vendor utility objects.

BP3: Use for sequential tablespaces.

BP4: Use for sequential indexes (nonmatching scans).

BP5: Use for random tablespaces.

BP6: Use for random indexes.

BP7: Use for code and reference tables.

These can be broken down further, based on update and residency requirements. It might be necessary to have a separate bufferpool for regularly updated tablespaces with high updated-page re-reference and another for highly updated tablespaces with little or no updated-page re-reference. The whole concept is based on granularity according to characteristics. The finer the granularity, the better the performance, assuming that there is enough memory to support the breakout.

For non-OS/390 platforms, multiple bufferpool strategies depend on the amount of memory available. If the total buffer space is less than 10,000 4KB pages, and specialized tuning knowledge is not available, use only one bufferpool.

If your system is not constrained by these conditions, consider separate bufferpools for the following:

● Temporary table spaces
● Data accessed repeatedly and quickly by many short update transaction applications
● Certain applications, data, and indexes that you want to favor
● Tables and indexes that are updated frequently
● Tables and indexes that are frequently queried but infrequently updated
● Data accessed by applications that are seldom used

 Note: *Watch the guideline for DSNDB07 work files; SYSPLEX query parallelism has an impact because it can use the work files of any subsystem on which any part of the query runs.*

 Note: *Watch the guideline for DSNDB07 work files in DB2 Version 5 because stored procedure result sets have an impact on bufferpool size and use.*

 ### 3. Can I use a subquery in the SET clause of an UPDATE statement?

Yes. A special kind of subquery, called a scalar subquery, can be used in the SET clause of an UPDATE statement in DB2 UDB. A scalar subquery, by definition, can only retrieve one value as the result (one row of one column). The following query is an example of an UPDATE statement using a scalar subquery:

```
UPDATE T1
   SET COL2 = (SELECT SUM(COLX)
                  FROM T4 WHERE COL7 > 30)
       , COL3 = 90
WHERE COL1 = 'ABC'
```

 ### 4. How many tables can I include in a query?

A maximum of 15 tables can be included in a query in DB2 OS/390 through Version 5. In DB2 UDB, the limit is based on available storage. In DB2 OS/390 Version 6, this limit has been raised to 225 tables. This limit applies to every table reference, regardless of where it appears in a full SELECT statement. In a join, the 15-table limit is being removed in DB2 OS/390 Version 6, and this change is being delivered through an APAR to Version 5.

 ### 5. When do I need to partition my tablespace?

There are several advantages to partitioning a tablespace:

- For large tables, partitioning is the only way to store large amounts of data (DB2 OS/390 Version 5 permits 254 partitions up to 4GB each, and Version 6 permits 254 partitions up to 64GB each). Nonpartitioned tablespaces are limited to 64GB of data.

- Partitioning will allow you to take advantage of query, CPU, and sysplex parallelism. Even defining a table with one partition will allow a query involving a join to enable CPU parallelism.

- You can take advantage of the ability to execute utilities on separate partitions in parallel. This also gives you the ability to access data in certain partitions while utilities are executing on others.

- In a data-sharing environment, you can spread partitions among several members to split workloads.

- You can also spread your data over multiple volumes and need not use the same storage group for each dataset belonging to the tablespace. This also allows you to place frequently accessed partitions on faster devices.

However, even with all the advantages of having partitioned tablespaces, you must keep a few disadvantages in mind when deciding about partitions. For instance, currently you cannot use the ALTER statement to add partitions to your table. Also, more datasets are normally opened for partitioned tablespaces, and a tablespace scan for a partitioned tablespace may be less efficient than one for a segmented tablespace (unless the SQL is coded to allow the optimizer to use page-range scans).

6. Can I use Java with DB2?

Yes, everywhere. Java is a supported language for all versions of DB2. Java can be used for application systems, applets for Web interaction with DB2, and DB2 stored procedures (even on OS/390). There are also many special features that enable Java to work with DB2 as well as all other languages do.

There is JDBC, which is a SQL interface for Java that uses dynamic SQL. This allows Java from any platform to use dynamic SQL through the JDBC interface and be run on any other platform.

There is also SQLJ, which is a SQL interface for Java that uses static SQL. This performs at a higher throughput level than JDBC because the SQL is precompiled and the access paths have been determined before the Java program is run.

In addition, on OS/390, IBM is providing a high-performance Java compiler to translate the Java byte code into machine language. There are application development environments that support the use of Java and the DB2 interface, such as VisualAge for Java.

7. Are there any negative effects of having only one plan for all packages?

The all-in-one approach is another one of those myths. The basic problems for having a single plan for an environment are the following:

- **Lack of ability to monitor and tune:** If you are getting an SMF record for every transaction in CICS (TOKENI or TOKENE), you might be able to manage using only one plan, but the task is much harder. If you are getting the rollup, then accounting data is not useful.

- **More storage in EDMPOOL:** If you specify RELEASE(DEALLOCATE) for plans with a large number of packages, the space in EDMPOOL is expanded greatly. This will generally take storage away from other potential uses.

- **More CPU to manage the storage, longer chains:** This is probably less of a problem than the other items, but the EDMPOOL storage increases may force you to use RELEASE(COMMIT) where you could otherwise use RELEASE(DEALLOCATE). With only one plan and one set of parameters, some tuning options are precluded.

A good, solid, general guideline is to have a plan per each batch program, and to have plans containing packages for online applications grouped by some common function/process.

 ## 8. What are the guidelines for using VARCHAR columns?

In general, the use of the VARCHAR (variable character) datatype is only preferred to the CHAR (character) datatype if the amount of space to be saved is significant (only in the tablespace, not in indexes). The use of VARCHAR should be for columns whose values vary considerably in length. The following are some points to keep in mind about the use of VARCHAR columns:

- Do not use VARCHAR columns unless modeling shows that it provides a benefit.
- Do not use VARCHAR columns for DASD savings.
- If an EDITPROC is in place for DASD compression, VARCHAR is not needed for space savings.
- If you are using DB2 compression (hardware only, please), VARCHAR is not needed for space savings.
- Consider putting the variable data into a separate table, linked via primary/foreign key indexes.
- Consider using multiple rows of fixed length with a sequence number instead of VARCHAR to allow textual data of any length to be handled.
- Consider using a fixed-length column instead of VARCHAR for most uses, and put the overflow in another table. This works when the data is usually near the same length.

 Note: *Do not expect these seven design tactics to come from logical design. These are physical design issues.*

 Caution: *VARCHAR has a 2-byte overhead per value and will require some additional processing. It is also messy to handle in some languages.*

 9. How do I connect to a DB2 host from a single Windows-based PC?

This is a very common request and it may be the most common connection in the DB2 world. IBM has a product called DB2 Connect, which can provide this kind of connection for several different configurations. For a single Windows client to connect to a DB2 host, there is the DB2 Connect Personal Edition.

DB2 Connect allows clients to access data stored on database servers through DRDA (distributed relational database architecture). The most common of these connections is for a Windows client (95, 98, or NT) to connect to an OS/390 DB2 server. DB2 Connect supports APPC connections between DRDA clients and the DB2 servers. DB2 on OS/390, as of Version 5, also supports TCP/IP in a DRDA environment. DB2 clients, through the appropriate CAE (Client Application Enabler), can use many supported protocols to establish a connection to the DB2 Connect gateway. This does require the proper CAE to be installed on the client. However, the CAE is not a DRDA Application Requestor but DB2 Connect does provide DRDA application requestor (AR) functionality.

Besides the DB2 Connect product from IBM, there are other middleware products from other vendors that also provide this type of functionality.

 10. Can I access DB2 from a REXX program?

Yes, but it requires a special interface that will not be provided to the REXX language until sometime during the summer or fall of 1999 (when IBM is scheduled to provide REXX for DB2, including REXX stored procedures). Until that time, there are many REXX DB2 products from established vendors, and there are also many REXX DB2 products that are both shareware and freeware. Most of the latter are available on the Internet.

Chapter 2

Environment

Answer Topics!

Environment @ a Glance

This chapter on the DB2 environment answers questions related to the installation and ability to use DB2. Questions about installation parameters, default values, installation problems, and general database environment management will be answered. After releases have been installed, questions arise concerning whether or not programs and data have been affected and about additional maintenance. This chapter covers questions about release migration, vendor maintenance for releases, and the Y2K compliance of DB2 versions and maintenance releases.

On all platforms, security is not only a major concern but the implementation of security and authorizations always raises questions. Questions surrounding both group level and user level security issues are covered along with their use and some problematic concerns.

Another issue of the DB2 environment is solving the problems around the implementation and maintenance of security. Naming standards are another environment issue that is covered in this chapter.

INSTALLATION

What default DB2 installation parameters should be changed?

Almost all installation parameters in all versions of DB2 (DSNZPARMs for OS/390, as shown in Figure 2-1; configuration parameters for UDB, some of which are shown in Figure 2-2) are not acceptable defaults, especially for production environments. Before installing DB2, you should carefully read the DB2 Installation Guide and get to understand the purpose of each parameter. Then do some detailed planning before you start the installation. Chapter 5 has several detailed questions and answers on some of the more critical parameters and their usage.

```
DSNZPARM -- DB2 OS/390 Subsystem Parameters

Parameter              Parameter              Parameter
---------              ---------              ---------
ABEXP                  EXTSEC                 RGFESCP
ABIND                  GRPNAME                RGFFULLQ
ALCUNIT                HOPAUTH                RGFINSTL
ALL/dbname             IDBACK                 RGFNMORT
ARCPFX1                IDFORE                 RGFNMPRT
ARCPFX2                IDTHTOIN               RLF
ARCRETN                INBUFF                 RLFAUTH
ARCWRTC                IRLMAUT                RLFERR
ARCWTOR                IRLMPRC                RLFERRD
ASSIST                 IRLMRWT                RLFTBL
AUDITST                IRLMSID                ROUTCDE
AUTH                   IRLMSWT                RRULOCK
AUTHCACH               LOGLOAD                SECQTY
BINDNV                 MAXARCH                SEQCACH
BLKSIZE                MAXDBAT                SEQPRES
BMPTOUT                MAXKEEPD               SITETYP
CACHEDYN               MAXRBLK                SMFACCT
CACHEPAC               MAXRTU                 SMFSTAT
CATALOG                MEMBNAME               SRTPOOL
  "                    MON                    STATIME
CHGDC                  MONSIZE                STORMXAB
CMTSTAT                NUMLKTS                STORPROC
COMPACT                NUMLKUS                STORTIME
CONDBAT                OUTBUFF                SYSADM
COORDNTR               PCLOSEN                SYSADM2
CDSSRDEF               PCLOSET                SYSOPR1
CTHREAD                PRIQTY                 R2
DDF                    PROTECT                TCPALVER
DEALLCT                QUIESCE                TRACSTR
DECDIV3                RECALL                 TRACTBL
DEFIXTP                RECALLD                TSTAMP
DEFLTID                RELCURHL               TWOACTV
DESCSTAT               RESTART/DEFER          TWOARCH
DLDFREQ                RESYNC                 TWOBSDS

DLITOUT                RETLWAIT               UNIT
DSHARE                 RGFCOLID               UNIT2
DSMAX                  RGFDBNAM               URCHKTH
EDMPOOL                RGFDEDPL               UTIMOUT

EDPROP                 RGFDEFLT               WRTHRSH
```

Figure 2-1   Listing of the DSNZPARMs for OS/390 as of DB2 V5.1

What release of DB2 should I have installed for year 2000 compliance?

In order to be year 2000 compliant, you need to at least have installed Version 3 of OS/390, Version 2.1.1 of Common Server, or Version 5 of UDB. Version 2.3 of OS/390 is *not* year 2000 compliant, and it also is no longer officially supported by IBM. Although the initial plan was to drop the support for Version 3, IBM has decided to continue the support until the year 2000, because many users who are still running Version 3 or earlier versions do not have sufficient time before year 2000 to upgrade. By January 1, 2000, IBM will support many releases of both OS/390 and UDB—quite a unique situation. Remember that even though these later releases of the DB2 database management system are year 2000 compliant, you might need upgrades of other system software or changes made to your applications.

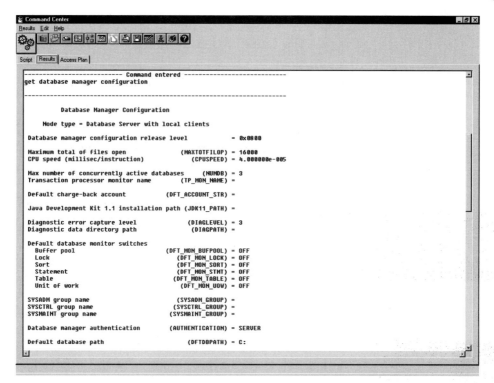

Figure 2-2 Configuration screen showing some of the UDB V5.2 parameters

What should be the initial setting for bufferpools?

There is no solid answer for defining the initial sizes of bufferpools; the most appropriate size is dependent on your workload. If your bufferpools are too small, there can be a great deal of overhead when pages are moved in and out of the bufferpools, resulting in bad application performance. On the other hand, if your bufferpools are too big, the pages will remain resident in the bufferpool long enough to be referenced, and your bufferpool could begin paging, which will cause performance to degrade. With a pool that is too large, lock and latch wait times might increase due to bufferpool queue management processes, which also increase CPU overhead.

The question on initial bufferpool sizing during installation is a difficult one, because at the time of installation you might not have a full understanding of the application workload

against the objects to be placed in each of the bufferpools. In the past the sizing was crucial, because once DB2 was started, the size could not be changed dynamically. You can now issue the ALTER BUFFERPOOL command to shrink or increase your bufferpool sizes or alter the properties (thresholds) of the bufferpools. A good initial setting for a small to medium OS/390 system would be a total size of about 120MB for all bufferpools. There is much more on the sizing of bufferpools in DB2 OS/390 and UDB in Chapter 16.

What should be the initial settings for the EDM pool?

The initial sizing of the EDM pool at installation time is also a question without a solid answer. The biggest problem is that the EDM pool size cannot be altered once DB2 is started, although there is a plan to change this in a future release. To alter it, you need to change the appropriate DSNZPARM (EDMPOOL) and then recycle (stop and restart) the DB2 subsystem.

The EDM pool holds cursor tables (CTs), package tables (PTs), database descriptor blocks (DBDs), copies from the CTs and PTs for each user called skeleton cursor tables (SKCTs) and skeleton package tables (SKPTs). It also contains the authorization cache for plans and packages, and skeletons from frequently used dynamic statements (if dynamic statement caching is turned on). If your EDM pool is too small, you will suffer performance problems, or even worse, you can experience EDM pool failures resulting in failing applications. Be sure to review your EDM pool size before any large, new applications go into production.

EDM pool usage should be around 70 percent, and you can view this through an online monitor or statistics reports. Several online monitors will also show you the hit ratio of requests for objects against the times the objects were already located in the EDM pool. It is ideal to have a hit ratio of 85 percent or more in a busy system. If you are going to take advantage of dynamic statement caching, you will have to increase the size of your EDM pool. A good starting size for an EDM pool for small to medium systems is between 40MB and 80MB.

 Tip: *DBD can be kept small by using the MODIFY utility regularly, which purges old recovery data from the DBD.*

 Tip: *You can reduce the size of a plan by using*
CACHESIZE(0) during binding if the plan is granted to
public. The space required in the EDM pool also depends
very much on the workload and bind parameters, such as
RELEASE(DEALLOCATE).

What is the difference between workstation install and TSO install?

DB2 Installer, an option with DB2 OS/390, allows an install of DB2 from an OS/2 or Windows/NT workstation. It uses a graphical interface to complete installation tasks. This function is delivered on the same CD-ROM with DB2 Visual Explain. The workstation install is a front-end that replaces part of the traditional install. However, many system programmers who install DB2 still prefer the TSO install because the interaction with the jobs produced by the install panels is easier and more familiar.

What should be my work file settings?

DB2 work files are located in a temporary database normally called DSNDB07 (it will be different if you use a sysplex data-sharing implementation of DB2, since each subsystem needs to have a unique name), and it should be large enough to overflow temporary space needed by the Relational Data System (RDS). The size and number of these work files is very dependent on the workload in the subsystem, but these temporary work files can be extended while the system is running, though this will require an outage in order to use the extensions.

A system with data warehousing applications will require more temporary space than a normal OLTP (On-Line Tele-Processing) system. Nevertheless there are some general guidelines. Always make sure that there are several tablespaces (work files) defined in the temporary database, separated as much as possible over controllers and channels. It is better to have five medium to large size tablespaces instead of one large one, with five being a good starting number. Some of the larger installations have as many as 40 work tablespaces on 40 different DASD volumes. Also, make sure that the defined temporary tablespaces cannot

take extents. Extending the physical datasets behind the temporary work files is a painful process, and future queries might use the badly organized extents in the future. To avoid this problem, use SECQTY 0 when you define the tablespaces. If the volumes are sized correctly and the memory allocated to the sort work areas is correct, then using a SECQTY of 0 will only prevent runaway queries from continuing.

How many active logs are needed?

At a minimum, you will need three dual logs, but preferably more. When DB2 switches logs and starts archiving, things can potentially go wrong. DB2 will retry at the next switch to archive all logs that need archiving. If there are no empty logs, DB2 gets very nervous when the last log fills up (DB2 will issue many warning messages). If there are no logs left to write to, DB2 comes to a halt until the necessary archiving is performed. That is why you need a minimum of three. You need dual logs because a single log introduces a single point of failure, whether or not you have disk mirroring.

What are the functional differences between UDB products?

There are two basic groups of DB2 software engines: the midrange to large system engines, and the Unix / NT / OS/2 engines. The midrange to large system group includes the OS/390 version, an OS/400 version, and a VSE/VM version; the Unix / NT / OS/2 system group includes versions for OS/2, Windows NT, Windows 95, AIX, HP-UX, and Solaris, with others planned. The Unix / NT / OS/2 engine is the newest member, and it benefits from more modularization. There are multiple products based on the engine for the Unix / NT / OS/2 environments, which for reference in this context we will just call UDB. The reason for the multiple UDB products is the many different platform types, from simple servers to SMP (symmetric multiprocessing) machines, MPP (massively parallel processing) machines, and clusters. There is not a basic difference in the database engine, because the underlying kernel is the same. It is the outer wrapping that supports the enhanced platform functions that is different.

The product list for UDB includes:

DB2 UDB Personal Edition
DB2 UDB Workgroup Edition
DB2 UDB Enterprise Edition (EE)
DB2 UDB Enterprise—Extended Edition (EEE)

DB2 UDB Personal Edition

The DB2 UDB Personal Edition has the same engine and the same basic functions as all the other products, except that it cannot accept requests from a remote client and it is only available on the Intel platform (Windows 95, 98, NT and OS/2). It is licensed for one user, but can be used as a remote client to a DB2 UDB server where one of the other products is running, as shown in Figure 2-3.

DB2 UDB Workgroup Edition

This product contains all the functionality of the Personal Edition and it can also accept requests from a remote client. The DB2 Workgroup Edition is also only for the Intel platforms and was designed for LAN environments, providing support for local and remote clients, as shown in Figure 2-4.

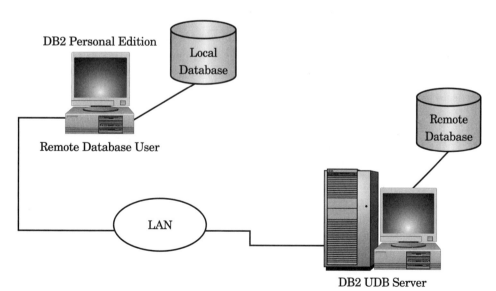

Figure 2-3 DB2 UDB Personal Edition

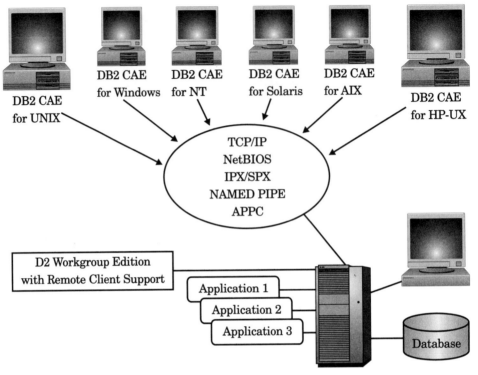

Figure 2-4 DB2 UDB Workgroup Edition

DB2 UDB Enterprise Edition

This product contains all the functions in the Workgroup Edition, plus it provides for host data connectivity by including DB2 Connect Enterprise Edition (described at the end of this answer). DB2 Enterprise Edition was designed to run on single processor machines as well as on SMPs. This edition runs on both Intel and UNIX environments and is shown in Figure 2-5.

DB2 UDB Enterprise—Extended Edition

This product contains all the functions of the Enterprise Edition and also provides the ability to partition a database across multiple independent computers (nodes) of the same platform. It supports databases that exceed the size capacities of the Enterprise Edition, which would be limited to a single machine. Enterprise Extended Edition (EEE) runs

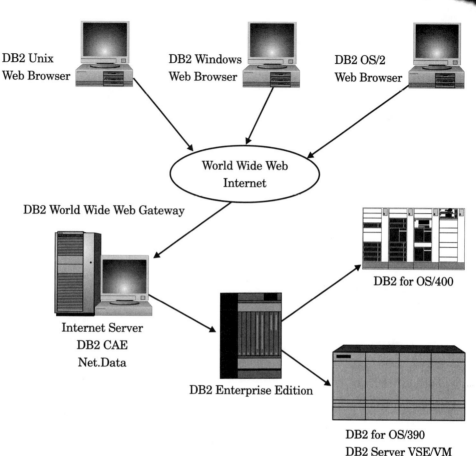

Figure 2-5 DB2 UDB Enterprise Edition

on single machines, including SMPs, but also runs on clusters of machines, including clusters of SMPs.

DB2 Connect Personal Edition, DB2 Connect Enterprise Edition

The DB2 Connect series of products allows clients to access data stored on database servers supporting DRDA (Distributed Relational Database Architecture). It supports the APPC (Advanced Program-to-Program Communication) protocol to provide support between DRDA Application Requesters and DRDA Application Servers, and also supports TCP/IP in a DRDA environment. The DB2 Connect gateway

allows any of many supported network protocols to be used for the DB2 client to establish a connection. While the DB2 Connect Personal Edition is only for the Intel platform, to provide access to host database servers, the DB2 Connect Enterprise Edition provides for multiple clients to access host databases.

Other DB2-Related Products

There are other products for developing applications and systems for DB2: DB2 Personal Developer's Edition, and DB2 Universal Developer's Edition. There are also two components available: SDK (software developer's kit), which is shipped in the Developer's Editions; and CAE (Client Application Enabler), which is the runtime client.

MIGRATION AND MAINTENANCE

 When migrating up multiple releases, what is a good "burn-in" period for each release?

If you decide to migrate up multiple releases in one weekend, or a similar short period, you need to start DB2 with the newly applied release, and have it running for a while before continuing with the next upgrade.

After you have migrated your system, be sure that you take good backups of all your system-critical data, including two image copies of your catalog. There are generally several DSNZPARM changes and default value changes that might require adjustments to the subsystem definitions, bind parameters, and object defaults. Changes should only be made that will not prevent an automated fallback if that should become necessary. It is also very important to run some update processing to certify that the installation works correctly (use the IVP procedure supplied or your own test processes). Also make sure that DB2 has archived the logs at least twice (this can be done by using the commands to force a log switch on OS/390, although UDB has no such command yet). Then shut down DB2 normally and continue with the next upgrade. Never just start DB2 in maintenance mode and shut it down immediately, since this would not uncover any problems in normal use.

Can I skip releases when migrating from one OS/390 DB2 release to another?

No, you cannot. IBM has supplied upgrade procedures with every release that will migrate (alter) the catalog from release X to release $X + 1$. There are no procedures to migrate the catalog from release X to release $X + n$ (where $n > 1$). Some people do multiple migrations in one go (over a weekend, for example). You can debate whether this is wise, but it is possible. If you do multiple migrations at once, it is important to remember that a fallback procedure could take a very long time because you may need to fall back multiple times.

It is possible, however, to install a new release as a separate subsystem, and then migrate existing databases and objects to the new subsystem. This will prevent any automated fallback to the existing system, and in many ways it can be a benefit, as it potentially cleans up many of the dead definitions in the catalog and directory.

Caution: *If you do not follow the correct migration procedures, you could get yourself in trouble. Fallback (the procedure that will bring you from release $X + 1$ to X) may not work, and for IBM it becomes difficult, if not impossible, to diagnose your system.*

What are tolerance PTFs on OS/390?

The tolerance PTFs are also known as fallback PTFs. Every new release of DB2 introduces new facilities and structures. DB2 makes sure that these new facilities (features) are flagged in the catalog with special flags. If you have used these new facilities and you do a fallback (moving from release X to release $X - 1$) the affected objects will go into a restricted state. The affected objects are not usable until you migrate to the new release again.

The code needed to recognize the new facilities and put them in restricted state is brought into the "old" release with the tolerance PTFs. Also, system objects, such as archive logs, can be different after a migration and fallback. The old release should be tolerant so it will recognize this situation and be

able to deal with it. Only after the tolerance PTFs have been applied can a migration can safely be done. Applying the tolerance PTFs is often called positioning for the new release.

How often should I apply maintenance to any DB2 family member?

The longstanding rule of thumb—of applying maintenance every six months—is no longer valid. This is especially true with the newer releases of DB2 on all platforms, due to the many enhanced functions. For example, additional code has been added to Version 5 for OS/390 since the general availability release (approximately 80,000 new lines of code). This new code added additional functionality and new features, and it made some very important fixes. It is wiser to have maintenance no further behind than 2 or 3 months.

What is DB2 OS/390 early code?

The early code is a part of the OS/390 operating system that performs subsystem services for DB2. One of these services is processing the console commands and starting DB2 as a subsystem. The early code is loaded into OS/390 at IPL time, and needs to be at the same level as the highest DB2 release running on this OS/390.

Can I run multiple releases of DB2 OS/390 together?

Yes, you can run newer and older releases of DB2 together at the same time; however, you have to be certain that the early code is of the highest release. This should not be a problem since the code is always compatible with earlier releases. The early code (ERLY) is a piece that integrates into OS/390 and performs subsystem services, such as initiating the necessary started tasks when you issue the –START DB2 command.

Your new DB2 goes into new APF (Authorized Program Facility) non-linklist datasets. You have to point your job STEPLIB to the new DB2 system, for all new DB2 started tasks and all related jobs. You'll also need to create a new TSO procedure that has the new DB2 libraries as STEPLIB; otherwise you will run into trouble with the DSN command processor. If you are heavily into TSO, be careful with

STEPLIBs because they can cause a performance problem in TSO. An alternative is setting up special CLISTs or REXX procedures that use ISPF LIBDEFs or use ALTLIB. By doing so, you can access the old and new releases from the same TSO session.

Can I skip the catalog integrity queries after a migration on OS/390?

Yes, and no. The catalog integrity queries are provided to make sure that the catalog migration will work smoothly. You could choose to do the catalog queries prior to the actual migration process, to save time during the migration. However, Version 5 can now create indexes to help speed up the catalog integrity queries, and this makes the decision easier since it will not take as much time to perform the queries.

Caution: *The catalog integrity queries are not the same as DSN1CHKR. The queries look for logical inconsistencies (indexes on nonexistent tables, for example). DSN1CHKR looks for physical inconsistencies (broken links or invalid pointers). Although a logical error is normally the result of a physical error, this is not always true.*

Is a mass rebind needed after software maintenance is applied to any DB2 system?

Generally speaking, a mass rebind (REBIND on OS/390 or DB2RBIND on UDB) will not be needed after software maintenance is applied, unless IBM has a fix that requires a rebind after the fix is applied.

Many fixes in a software maintenance influence the behavior of the optimizer. This means that after the fixes are applied, the optimizer may be able to select a better access path or the execution of a plan or package may be more efficient. This would be true for newly created plans or packages but not for existing plans or packages. To ensure that existing plans pick up the new fixes, a mass rebind is often recommended. However, numerous organizations cannot do a mass rebind in their DB2 subsystem in a single weekend, so it is not likely that IBM will code fixes that insist on a mass rebind.

> **Caution:** *A rebind forces the optimizer to reevaluate the access path. The optimizer might even select bad access paths, in terms of performance, if the statistics are incomplete or the data is not in optimal shape. By performing a mass rebind you could introduce very unpleasant surprises.*

> **Tip:** *You could, of course, rebind plans or packages that would benefit from the fixes. Wildcards could be very useful in OS/390 (for example, REBIND(ABC*), while in UDB you would have to perform individual rebinds on the plans or packages selected.*

 ## Is fallback always possible?

No, fallback is not always possible. If facilities or features of the new release are used, then after a fallback, objects involved can be put into a restricted state. A good strategy is to set a target date after which a fallback will not be done, and new facilities and functions can safely be used.

SECURITY

When does DB2 OS/390 use the current SQLID, and when does it use the composite of the primary and secondary IDs?

The DYNAMICRULES bind parameter was introduced to influence the way security is checked for dynamic SQL statements. If you use a GRANT, REVOKE, or CREATE for an unqualified object, if you implicitly qualify a table, view, index, or alias, or if you use DML SQL and the statement is executed dynamically from a plan or package that was bound with DYNAMICRULES(RUN), then DB2 will use the authorization ID of the application process and the SQL authorization ID (CURRENT SQLID) for authorization checking. If DYNAMICRULES(BIND) is used, DB2 processes dynamic SQL statements with the same rules used for embedded or static SQL statements. At execution time, DB2 will use the plan or package authorization ID for authorization checking. Any use of unqualified table, view, index, and alias names in dynamic SQL statements will be implicitly qualified with a value of QUALIFIER specified at bind time, or the authorization ID of the plan or package owner will be used.

What is the relation between DB2 and RACF?

DB2 as a resource can be protected by RACF (Resource Access Control Facility). This is not a very good choice because you will see massive access to the RACF database to check if the user has access to DB2. If the security in DB2 is set up correctly, this check will not need to be performed. Within DB2 you normally use your userid as the primary ID, and use the RACF groups that you are assigned to as the secondary ID. This is done in the exit routines DSN3@ATH and DSN3@SGN which can be the same. Also, these routines can filter or add secondary IDs depending on the input or the groups they find in RACF. Sample assembler code for the exit routine comes with DB2. Physical objects in DB2, such as tablespaces, indexspaces, and active and archive logs can be protected by DB2, and doing this is a good idea.

Tip: *If you didn't already have the RACF groups in storage (an RACF option) then DB2 might be a good reason to start with that. Otherwise you will see excessive access to the RACF database. The downside of this approach is that you need to refresh the in-storage list if the user is connected to new groups.*

What is an "install" SYSADM?

The SYSADM authorization level has a different meaning in OS/390 than it does in UDB. The SYSADM in UDB has the authorizations of the OS/390 SYSADM and the OS/390 "install" SYSADM. For this reason, you need to understand the difference in the levels as implemented in OS/390.

In the OS/390 install panels and appropriate DSNZPARMs, you can define one or two install SYSADMs. They have more authorization than the normal SYSADMs. For example, they can access DB2 after it has been started in MAINT mode. A very good reason to use the install SYSADMs only, and never grant SYSADM to anyone, is the fact that

the granted SYSADMs cannot be revoked easily, without a cascading effect in DB2. This means that if you are not careful, you could drop a lot of objects in DB2 when you revoke a granted SYSADM. For an install SYSADM, you can remove the userid from the DSNZPARM and that user looses *all* powerful rights without the cascading effects. There is more information on this topic later in this section, but as should be evident, the OS/390 "install" SYSADM and the UDB SYSADM basically have the same levels of authorization and control.

Tip: *An install SYSADM can also be a RACF group. This will move the security problem to RACF, which is where it belongs.*

 ## Is a SYSADM authid (authorization ID) dangerous?

Yes, the SYSADM ID can be very dangerous. However, you do need one or two very powerful users to tune and administer your DB2 subsystem. A SYSADM has very powerful rights in both the OS/390 subsystem and the UDB instance in which it is given, and if it is assigned to inexperienced people it could lead to severe system problems. Minimize the use of granted SYSADMs, and in OS/390 only use install SYSADMs if possible.

Tip: *If you are concerned about the fact that a SYSADM has full SQL DML access to the data in all database tables, there is an alternative called SYSCTRL in both OS/390 and UDB. The downside is that you often need the full SQL DML access.*

 ## Can a SYSADM authorization ID be revoked without cascading effects on OS/390?

Yes, a SYSADM ID can be revoked without cascading effects. There is a little trick to doing so. Make sure that the SYSADM you want to revoke is in the DSNZPARM as an installed SYSADM. Then REVOKE the SYSADM authorization. Since DB2 knows that installed SYSADMs have no implicit authorizations granted, it will not attempt any cleanup with the disastrous cascading effect. After this, remove the ID from the DSNZPARM. Of course, all implicit granted authorizations still exist, but the user no longer holds the SYSADM authorization.

Tip: *Do not grant SYSADM authorization to personal userids. Either use functional IDs that can be passed from person to person, or use only "install" SYSADMs. This is the best option, since "install" SYSADMs get no implicit grants. Remember that the install SYSADM can be a secondary ID.*

Does dynamic SQL always use user security in OS/390?

No, dynamic SQL does not always use user security. The bind parameter DYNAMICRULES controls the level of security used for dynamic SQL. The value can be RUN or BIND. The RUN value is the default, and DB2 uses the same user security as it always has in the past. The BIND value means that for all dynamic statements the composite set of IDs of the binder will be used; not that of the executor of the plan or of the package at runtime. The exception to this rule is a dynamic prepare/execute statement for which DB2 will use the security of the owner of the plan or package.

What authorization does a database administrator (DBA) need?

In order to create, alter, and drop DB2 objects, you need at least the level of DBADM authorization on the database where the objects to be manipulated are defined. In OS/390, you can grant an RACF group as DBADM and connect the DBA(s) to that group. If you create objects, then you should fully qualify them. If you issue grants or revokes, you should set the current SQLID first. If the DBA needs to be removed, detach the userid from the DBA RACF group.

Tip: *Besides DBADM, there are also other group IDs that hold less authorization and might be suitable for junior DBAs on OS/390, such as DBCTRL.*

 ### Where do OS/390 secondary authids get defined?

Secondary authids are unique to DB2 on OS/390 (at least through the release of DB2 Version 5 UDB for Unix / NT / OS/2). Secondary authids are defined in the security exits: DSN3@SGN and DSN3@ATH. There is a flowchart in the system administration guide that explains when which exit will be called. The exits can share the same code as long as both entry points are available.

IBM supplies a sample assembler code that will query RACF and set the secondary authids according to all RACF groups the user is connected to. Some non-IBM security packages can work differently. Consult the vendors of these packages for more information on when secondary authids are set.

 ### Can I control DB2 completely from RACF on OS/390?

No, you cannot completely control DB2 RACF because it has its own security setup. Once you are inside DB2, it has its own security administration and checking. There are two security exits that can set the primary and secondary IDs, which normally use the userid as primary ID and all RACF groups the user is connected to as the secondary ID. RACF can be used to control the access to DB2 (which is normally not needed and causes much overhead in RACF), and it can protect the physical object that DB2 uses.

 ### What are the benefits of using OS/390 secondary authids, and how do you set them up?

Secondary authids are used by DB2 to do security checking. Normally, secondary authids are RACF groups set by the DSN3@ATH or DSN3@SGN security exits of DB2. These exits have full control on what they include or exclude in the authorization list. The default sample from IBM takes all RACF groups as secondary authids and the userid as primary ID. The security normally will try all authids until it finds one that passes the security test. For static SQL, this is done at bind time. For dynamic SQL, this is normally done at runtime, unless DYNAMICRULES(BIND) is used during the bind process. You can use the secondary authids for security processing in DB2 (GRANT/REVOKE). If all authorizations for DB2 are only assigned to the secondary authids, then externally from DB2 you can control if the user has the authorization or not, since using secondary authids externalizes the security to RACF where it belongs.

> **_Caution:_** _The maximum number of secondary authids is 245. However, the overhead involved in checking the authids is heavy. Minimize the number of secondary authids in the security exits, or sort them so DB2 finds a quick hit. This would be possible, for example, if the exit used a naming convention._

How does DB2 handle DCE security?

DB2 can use DCE (Distributed Computing Environment) security services to authenticate remote users. With these services, remote end users can access DB2 by means of their DCE name and password. This same name and password is used for access throughout the network so that users do not have to maintain a separate RACF password. DCE uses an authentication technology with encrypted tickets that contain authentication information for the end user.

NAMING STANDARDS

Why do I need a naming standard?

You do not need a naming standard to get DB2 operational. It will work perfectly without naming standards. However, if you have one, you will benefit a great deal from it. For example, it is very nice that in a message that gives you an object, you can quickly determine what kind of object you are talking about or who to contact in case of errors due to the way it is named. The naming convention becomes extremely useful when you use wildcards in commands in DB2 or in tools for administrating DB2. In general, by having a good naming standard, the administration of DB2 will be easier and more productive.

What is a good naming standard?

A naming standard is good if you can determine the type of object from the name presented. By using a common naming format, you can use wildcards for searching and easily get a group of objects that physically belong together. One thing to remember is that the database name shows up in the dataset names for all physical objects. When you want to use wildcards for searching outside of DB2, you can then start at the database level.

For example, you could have all object names start with *XYPPP*, where the characters have the following values:

- X is either T (Test) or P (Prod)
- Y is the object type, one of D (Database), T (Tablespace), I (Index), and so on
- PPP is the project number

The rest of the naming standard could be up to the DBA.

Can I have multiple naming standards in one DB2 subsystem?

Yes, multiple naming standards can be implemented in the same DB2 subsystem because DB2 does not require a specific naming standard. For example, if there are multiple customers or development groups on one DB2 subsystem, they may use many different naming standards for their objects. Of course, from a system administration point of view, you would like to have everyone using the same naming convention.

Why don't my VSAM dataset names match the DB2-defined names for indexes?

The method for naming the physical objects behind DB2 indexes on OS/390 is to use the first eight characters of the defined name used in the DDL. If the DDL-defined name is longer than eight characters, it is possible that the first eight characters will not be unique. If this happens, DB2 uses random characters in the eight positions allowed by VSAM for the underlying index dataset, in order to make it unique.

Chapter 3

Data Storage

Answer Topics!

Data Storage @ a Glance

The underlying storage system for DB2 OS/390 physical objects is nothing more exotic than traditional VSAM linear datasets. However, there are a few new twists in the implementation and usage of these datasets and their content when using them to support DB2 tablespaces or indexspaces.

How DB2 formats and uses pages has always been a gray area; depending on the type and implementation of the chosen operating system, there are several issues surrounding dataset management, such as placement and control mechanisms that are answered in this chapter.

Over the years, objects have become extremely large both on the OS/390 platform and the smaller UDB platforms (Unix or NT). The introduction of LOBs (large objects) in the smaller UDB platforms brought several new objects to manage and more complex issues for the DBA to deal with. DB2 OS/390 Version 5 introduced the LARGE tablespace, allowing a 1TB table to be implemented; Version 6 will allow for a 16TB table. These types of large objects have several interesting complications associated with their implementation and support.

Compression is used for a couple of reasons in DB2. You can compress data so that more rows fit onto a page, allowing you to store more data and also allowing for better performance when reading data into bufferpools. In some instances, however, compression may not be the optimal choice, depending on the usage of the data. Several common questions surrounding the techniques used to achieve compression are answered in this chapter.

This chapter will answer questions that have been asked over the years regarding the use and placement of the underlying VSAM datasets, the format and use of pages, as well as dealing with recent complications and issues that have been introduced with large objects. It will also cover issues concerning datasets and pages in the UDB Unix and NT platforms.

GENERAL INFORMATION

Is DASD space always reclaimed after a delete on an OS/390 segmented tablespace?

No, only mass deletes (deletes without a WHERE clause) will immediately reclaim the segments (DASD space) belonging to that table on which the deletes occurred. Running the REORG utility on the segmented tablespace will reclaim the segments deleted in other ways. For example, when a normal row delete would cause the last row to be deleted in a segment, the segment is not reclaimed because of the overhead required to do so.

What is strict tablespace clustering on OS/390?

The announcement letter of DB2 Version 1.2 contained a new clustering type: strict tablespace clustering. This new type never became available for users, but it is used by the catalog. The idea is that many related tables are put in a simple tablespace, and clustering is maintained by key. If a page is retrieved in order to retrieve a particular row, there is generally no physical I/O required to retrieve the related data, because it should exist on the same page. The optimizer greatly benefits from this facility. This is one of the many reasons that the catalog has not yet been converted to a segmented tablespace. Strict tablespace clustering is used in some rare applications where the strict clustering is maintained by application programs.

In DB2 UDB, does it matter performance-wise what devices I place my data on?

Yes, the placement of data across devices can affect performance in many ways. There is always a benefit to having multiple paths to data. Also, since all processing is moving towards parallelism, spreading data over multiple containers over multiple devices increases the amount of parallelism that can be used in retrieving and processing the data.

What is the difference between SMS and DMS in DB2 UDB?

The difference between SMS (system-managed storage) and DMS (data-managed storage) is described below.

SMS:

- After the table is created, containers cannot be added.
- Data, indexes, and LOBs for a table must be stored in one tablespace.
- The space where the containers are defined is not preallocated and will grow when data is added.

DMS:

- Containers can be added to a tablespace by using the ALTER TABLESPACE statement.
- The data can be in one tablespace and the indexes and LOBs can reside in other separate tablespaces.
- Space for containers can be preallocated and must be allocated when the container is created.

How do I add new containers to a tablespace in DB2 UDB?

You can add new containers to an existing tablespace when you alter it. When an ALTER is performed to add new containers, the database manager will redistribute the tables in the tablespace over all of the containers, including the newly added one(s). When adding several containers, it is recommended that you add them all at once in order to avoid repeatedly incurring the overhead of the redistribution of the tables over the containers. To achieve maximum performance during this operation, define each container on separate disk devices so that the data can be accessed in parallel.

```
ALTER TABLESPACE MYTABSP ADD
    (FILE 'd:\mytabsp\newspace.dat' 50000)
```

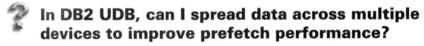

Tip: *Adding a container by using ALTER on a tablespace can only be done if the tablespace is defined using DMS space.*

In DB2 UDB, can I spread data across multiple devices to improve prefetch performance?

Using prefetch will allow for data and index pages to be copied from disk into the bufferpool before they are required, allowing for I/O time to be minimized. If data is spread across separate individual devices, the performance of the prefetch operation will become more efficient, especially when tables are accessed by queries processing large quantities of data. This can be done if the tablespace was defined using DMS storage, and if there are multiple device containers defined on separate disk devices.

How do I determine the number of pages in each level of an index?

The way to determine the number of pages in each level of an index is through a tool such as DB2 Estimator, which breaks down the index by levels, showing the number of pages on each level. The number of pages per level can be calculated by using formulas in the DB2 manuals, but doing so is time consuming, and since the DB2 Estimator is a free product for DB2, using it is the preferred method.

Tip: *The DB2 Estimator from IBM is free and can be downloaded from the Internet. The DB2 Estimator supports the IBM-maintained versions of DB2. It was used to model one of the large, operational data warehouses in existence before the data warehouse was created.*

What are the guidelines for the number of tablespaces per database?

In an ideal world, even where you need to manage thousands of DB2 objects, you would have one database per tablespace—this would keep the DBDs small, and any DDL maintenance necessary for the objects in the database would have no concurrency impact on objects in other databases. This is the preferred method of implementation, and it works best in 24×7 environments. In general situations, we look for a middle ground—the recommendation for performance and storage management would be from 10 to 20 tablespaces and associated objects per database. (See also Chapter 6 for more information on this subject.)

DB2 PAGES

What are pagesets?

There are two types of pagesets in DB2: data pageset, which contains the VSAM linear datasets for a tablespace; and index pagesets, which contain the datasets for indexspaces. There are three types of pages in a pageset: header pages, data pages, and space map pages. If the tablespace is compressed, there are also dictionary pages.

What actions cause a zero page condition to be produced?

A zero page is a page with all zeros, normally found at the end of the pageset or at the end of a segment. Zero pages can also exist after the last dictionary page. There are several actions that can cause a zero page condition.

- Any tablespace can have zero pages at the end, between the last data page and the next track/cylinder limit.
- A segmented tablespace could have a zero page in the last pages of the last segment.
- A compressed segmented tablespace could have zero pages between the last dictionary page and the first data page.

Once a page has been formatted, it will remain formatted and can become empty due to row deletion, but it will never become a zero page. However, canceling a job can produce zero pages under certain conditions. This can occur if several applications are in contention for the same page, possibly trying to insert in clustering-key order. If page-level locking is used and the applications are in contention for the same page, the inserts will not wait on locks. Instead, they will spread the rows onto multiple pages. If one of the applications cancels after locking a page but before formatting it, and another application has already formatted the following page, a zero page can be left by the canceled application.

What are broken pages?

When DB2 updates a page in the bufferpool, it uses a technique called a broken page.

This process works as follows: There are two flags on a tablespace page—one in the page header (top of the page) and one at the bottom of the page. When an update starts, the top flag is flipped, causing the page to be "broken," that is, the two flags contain different values. DB2 performs all the updates on the page, which can include reshuffling of rows to move all the free space to the bottom of the page (referred to as either inter-page reorg or page-in-motion). After DB2 is done, the bottom flag is flipped, too, and the two flags are equal again. The page is now "unbroken." Broken pages cannot be selected by the write-engines to be written to disk; they should only exist in the bufferpool and should never occur on disk.

How are pages formatted in the DB2 UDB environment?

The page layout for DB2 UDB is very similar to the page layout in DB2 for OS/390. The pages are 4KB in size. After accounting for a page header and RIDs, that leaves about 4020 bytes available for data on the page.

What is the space map page and how does DB2 use it?

On OS/390, there is always at least one space map page, stored in the first few pages of a tablespace dataset. The space map contains a bitmap and by using special algorithms, DB2 can quickly determine if there is space available in order to insert data on a target page. If the tablespace is segmented, the space map also contains the segment map. In the segment map, the tables are mapped to the segments using the OBIDs (object IDs) of the tables. The segment space map is also used by mass deletes to empty the segments. The space map will cover a certain number of pages. Additional space map pages can occur throughout the tablespace.

 ## What are object IDs (OBIDs)?

DB2 assigns a number to every created object (table, tablespace, database, and so on). This number is stored in several catalog tables. Internally, DB2 does not use the long character names and instead uses the OBIDs to keep track of objects. Not only are the OBIDs used in the physical objects themselves, but they are also used in the DBDs containing the objects created in a given DBD. This way, DB2 knows the ownership of the rows when it processes pages. The OBID is also used when DB2 looks at space maps to identify which segments belong to which tables.

Tip: *The DSN1COPY service aid can translate OBIDs while copying.*

 ## What is an off-page (relocated) row?

If a row contains VARCHARs (variable character columns), there is the possibility that after an update to the VARCHAR column, the row will no longer fit on the page. In this situation, DB2 will move the row to another page, leave the index pointing to the original location, and place a pointer on

the original page pointing to the new location. The row is now called an off-page or relocated row. If the row is updated again in the future and has to move again, the original pointer is updated, so there will be no pointer-chains.

Off-page rows can also result from updates on compressed rows (see "What would cause the OS/390 catalog statistics NEARINDREF and FARINDREF to grow if I am not doing inserts?" earlier in this chapter).

Why should I preformat my DB2 pages?

In DB2 Version 5 for OS/390, the PREFORMAT option was included in the REORG and LOAD utilities. This option will allow you to preformat pages, allowing for faster insert processing by avoiding the overhead of having to preformat pages during the insert process. This option is very useful for heavy insert applications where the ratio of the number of reads to the number of inserts is low and tablespace scans are not used (if a tablespace scan occurred it would have to read all of the empty, formatted pages). There may be a bit of extra overhead for the REORG or LOAD utility, but it has been found to be minimal.

How does DB2 compression affect the layout of a page?

DB2 compression is a row-level compression handled by using a compression dictionary. Data in a row is compared to a compression dictionary, one byte at a time. If an entry is found in the dictionary, it is replaced in the row with a pointer to that entry. Also, a bit is changed in the row prefix to indicate that this particular row is compressed. If there are no entries in the row that have an associated entry in the compression dictionary, the row is not compressed. Also, if data in the row is replaced by a pointer to a dictionary entry, there is a slight possibility that the row could become longer; if this occurs, it is also not compressed.

The diagrams in Figure 3-1 show what a page would look like before and after DB2 compression. The left page format simply shows the row prefix being pointed to by the ID map. The page diagram on the right shows the same thing but with the flag bits set by compression in the row prefix. The '0' bit

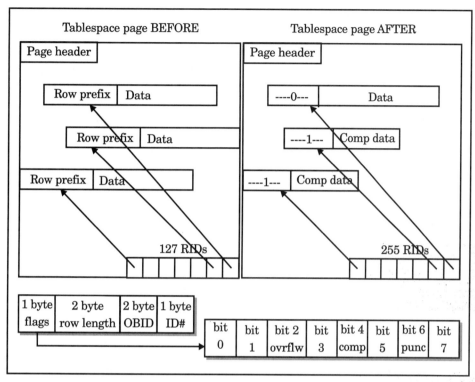

Figure 3-1 Tablespace page changes during compression

means the row was not compressed, and the '1' bit means it is a compressed row. On the left at the bottom there is a diagram of the row prefix, and the flag byte is shown in greater detail at the bottom right. The overflow bit, the compressed bit, and the punc bit are shown in their proper positions.

DATASETS

 ## What is the relationship between DB2 and VSAM?

DB2 uses IDCAMS to allocate the tablespaces and indexspaces. The allocated space looks like a VSAM linear dataset but it does not match that format exactly. DB2 uses DFP functions, the access method that VSAM uses at a very low level, to read, write, and extend the datasets. The datasets are no longer VSAM because the CI (control interval) information is missing. Also, DB2 uses the full 4KB page.

 ## Why do I sometimes have empty secondary extents?

For the first allocation of a secondary extent of a pageset, DB2 uses a special algorithm. It does not wait until the primary extent is completely filled; it will asynchronously allocate and format a new extent when the primary extent is almost filled. Therefore, when an application fills the primary extent to the trigger level, but then stops inserting, you will see a completely empty secondary extent. This asynchronous allocation is done only for the first secondary extent. If the dataset continues to be extended, allocation of each new extent is a synchronous process causing increased wait time for the application.

 Tip: *Remember that secondary extents are not necessarily good; in certain situations they can cause serious performance problems. As a general rule, when a pageset goes into extents, take action to make sure the data fits into one extent in the future.*

 Caution: *Do not use the defrag option that DF/SMS or other space-management tools offer. Although these tools place the data in one extent again, it is not in a reorganized state, and during the next REORG the data might not fit into the allowable space.*

 ## Why are all extents not the same size?

This is often seen in environments where mass inserts are done using INSERT SQL statements with the SELECT clause. When DB2 knows the result set of such a select, it can sometimes overflow and request a slightly larger secondary extent than necessary. There is no cause for alarm in this situation. When the primary extent can not be allocated as one chunk, the primary extent is allocated as multiple (up to five) chunks of random size.

How do I control the physical placement of my datasets?

If you want to physically place a dataset on a specific volume, there are two options. One is to create a storage group that is non-SMS and point to the volume that you want to use. The other option is to use the IDCAMS utility to allocate the dataset (user-defined tablespaces) on a specific volume.

How do I control where the results of a REORG are placed?

When a REORG is run and the object is under the control of STOGROUPS or SMS, the output of the REORG is placed back into the same STOGROUP but not necessarily on the same volume. This can defeat the purpose of the dataset placement. However, when the underlying datasets are user defined, the same physical dataset space is overwritten, or reused for the output of the REORG.

Note: *There is a change delivered in a supplemental fix to V5 and as a feature in V6 on OS/390 that will solve this problem. It is called REORG REUSE and will allow placement of the output of a REORG to REUSE the same space when using STOGROUPS or under the control of SMS.*

How can I break up an NPI (non-partitioning index) into multiple datasets?

With DB2 Version 5 on OS/390, we have the option to define a non-partitioning index using multiple datasets. This is performed using the new PIECESIZE option on the CREATE INDEX statement. By using "pieces," you divide up the non-partitioning index into several independent datasets, depending on the piece size specified. This will help eliminate contention against the non-partitioning index in terms of insert, update, and delete processes. A piece can be defined as small from 256KB up to 4GB.

 ## How are extents taken when a "piece" of an NPI is full?

When a load is performed and the non-partitioning indexes are using PIECESIZE, the entire piece will be filled up to the amount specified in the PIECESIZE definition during the creation of the NPI. DB2 will use the primary space quantity and as many secondary extents as necessary to fill up to the piecesize. During later processing, when an extent is necessary, the extent will be taken at the end of the non-partitioning index.

 ## What should the primary quantity for a "piece" be?

To set the primary quantity space-definition for a piece of a nonpartitioning index (NPI), you first need to set the size for a piece of an NPI. To choose a PIECESIZE value, divide the size of the NPI by the number of datasets that you want; this is different for every NPI in every application, and is based on I/O configuration, the sizes of the DASD devices, and the size of the NPI.

Once the number of pieces and the PIECESIZE is determined, you can define the proper primary and secondary space quantities. The PIECESIZE should be evenly divisible by the primary and secondary quantities, or else there will be wasted space in the NPI.

Based on user experiences, it is best to define the primary quantity equal to the PIECESIZE, keeping the secondary quantity relatively small, since it should never be used.

 ## Should I use DF/HSM for DB2 datasets?

Although DB2 will recognize the use of DF/HSM and wait for tablespace datasets to be recalled, this is normally not a preferred way of working. You might consider DF/HSM for tablespaces that are not used for a long period (for example, infrequently accessed QMF objects). Some installations do their log archiving to disk and use DF/HSM to migrate them to cartridge. There are special facilities in the RECOVER utility to detect and deal with this situation. Even with these facilities, the RECOVER utility will not be very fast—the datasets have to be recalled in order to use them. Also be careful; there are situations in which recall can not be guaranteed, and recovery of data might fail.

Where should my DSNDB07 work files be located?

There should be a number of DSNDB07 work files, all large and of the same size. There should be as much separation of these as possible; at a minimum, each one should be located on a separate DASD volume.

Is it safe to use DF/SMS DEFRAG to eliminate secondary extents?

No. Although it will work, you can easily get into trouble when running utilities that will reallocate the space. You could suddenly find that a tablespace that used to fit into one extent will be scattered all over in many extents or, even worse, doesn't fit in the maximum number of extents anymore.

Can OS/390 DB2 datasets be managed by SMS, and is this the best choice?

SMS (system-managed storage) can be used with DB2 to manage database objects' physical storage. As a general rule, SMS can and should manage DB2 datasets. This rule assumes that the DASD management staff fully understand SMS and its interaction with DB2, and that they work with the DBAs to identify critical objects that will potentially need I/O separation. Some of the largest installations of DB2 use SMS to manage all the DB2 object storage.

What is the recommended size and number of datasets for the DSNDB07 work files?

It is recommended that you define several datasets for the work files, and that you size them with a large primary quantity with no secondary extents. The reason for this

is that you do not want to have the datasets going into extents when you have a runaway query. It is also best if you can allocate the datasets on separate devices with separate channels.

There is no fixed recommended number of datasets, as the number is based on the size and number of concurrent queries, the size of materialized result sets, the size and number of joins, sorts, and group bys, and the size of the sort pool. In most situations, a good starting number would be five work files, on five different DASD devices and channels. The highest number we have seen in use is 44 work files on 44 DASD volumes.

Once defined, the work files should be monitored, as every change to DB2 and to application code can cause a differing amount of storage to be used.

LARGE OBJECT STORAGE

 ### If I defined my tablespace as LARGE, how does it affect the format of the RID (row ID)?

In Version 5, DB2 OS/390 introduced the LARGE keyword on the CREATE TABLESPACE statement, allowing a tablespace to have up to 254 partitions of 4GB each (1TB tablespace), and in Version 6 to have up to 254 partitions of 64GB each (16TB tablespace). When a tablespace is defined as LARGE, the RID takes on a larger format; it is extended by one byte to allow for addressing the larger number of pages that can be stored in a LARGE tablespace.

 ### When should I use the LARGE tablespace option?

The LARGE tablespace option can be used not only if you want to store large amounts of data, but it can also be very useful if you require more than 64 partitions. For example, one company uses 156 partitions to maintain rolling weekly warehouse data in each partition for a period of 3 years, while another needs 24 partitions to maintain 2 years of monthly data. Even if the amount of data does not exceed the 64GB limit and require a LARGE tablespace, the varying number of partition numbers allowed can use the 4GB limit

in Version 5 and the 64GB limit in Version 6. The need for flexibility of use, as well as size, dictates when you should use the LARGE tablespace option.

What are LOBs?

LOBs (large binary objects) are data types used to store large objects, such as medical records (x-rays, for example), videos, pictures, audio messages, fingerprints, and so on. There are three general types of LOBs:

BLOB   Binary large object
CLOB   Character large object
DBCLOB   Double-byte character large object

Each LOB column can be up to 2GB in length. In DB2, the implementation of LOBs is actually a superset of the capabilities of long VARCHAR and long VARGRAPHIC data types.

Are there any naming convention considerations for LOBs?

There are guidelines for naming objects, especially in the OS/390 implementation. These are shown in the example in Figure 3-2. In this example, just follow one column to get a feeling for the importance of the naming conventions. There is a column called LEGAL BRIEF, which is a character LOB column. Since the data is stored in a LOB table, that table name for this particular column is called BRIEF TAB, which is stored in a LOB tablespace called BRIEFTS. By naming columns in this fashion, or with a similar name, there is an established conistency.

What is a ROWID, and how can I use one?

The ROWID exists in DB2 Version 6 on OS/390 and is being added to UDB soon. It is the mechanism for handling LOBs. An LOB column in a table contains information about the LOB and does not hold the LOB data. This data is stored in other containers or tablespaces. In the table that defines the

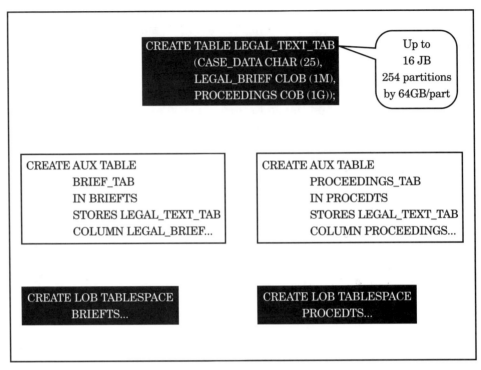

Figure 3-2 An example of LOBs and a guideline for naming

LOB column, there is also a column called a ROWID. DB2 uses this data to point to the LOB data in the LOB storage object. The ROWID is a variable-length character string 40 bytes in length.

If SQL selects a row from an LOB table, the ROWID can also be selected. Since the ROWID implicitly (not explicitly) contains the location of the row, it can be used to navigate directly to the row (in a direct UPDATE statement, for example). This type of access method is called direct row access, and it bypasses using an index or a tablespace scan. Although there are cases where using the ROWID to directly access the data might not work, such cases are predicted to be extremely rare. In the case of a failure with direct row access using the ROWID, DB2 will select an alternate access path.

When a query that uses direct row access is bound, a normal access path is picked. This is the access path that will

be used in case of failure of direct row access. Although not normally a consideration, using the ROWID for direct row access with disallow parallelism for that query. If a query qualifies for direct row access and parallelism, direct row access will be used. If direct row access were to fail, the fallback would not be to parallelism but to the optional access path selected at bind time.

Another use of the ROWID would be as the partitioning key.

The value of a ROWIS is a random, in the range from low-values to high-values (hex "0000..." through hex "FFFF..."). Therefore, if you are using a ROWID as the high-level column of a partitioning key, you can have linear distribution over the partitions in a partitioned tablespace.

How are fragments resulting from the manipulation of LOBs (large objects) maintained in DB2 UDB?

Fragments resulting from the manipulation of LOBs are maintained through the use of a corresponding recipe for the locator. Recipes are manipulated, whenever possible, instead of the actual LOB data. You can think of a recipe as being an item holding pointers to the actual data. Recipes can actually hold other recipes. This is all done internally to prevent the actual manipulation of LOB data.

How are locators used with LOBs in DB2 UDB?

Locators are used to avoid the cost of having to move large objects from the database to the application (which is a very resource-intensive process, because LOBs can be up to 2GB in size) and having to store the object in the application. A locator is used in the application program to represent the LOB without the object actually being moved to the application program. The locators are manipulated instead of the actual object, which still resides in the database. These locators are defined in the SQL declare section of an application program. A simple analogy would be to think of the address of a house as the locator for the actual physical structure. If an SQL query was used to find all the houses (LOBS) that contain families named JONES (in the LOB detail), the result set returned would be a list of addresses (locators).

Are there any performance considerations for large objects in DB2 UDB?

Yes. There are a few items you should take into consideration when defining and using large objects in UDB.

- For large objects over 1GB you will need to create the table using the NOT LOGGED option for the column so that changes will not be logged.
- Define the large object in a separate partition that is specially tuned for handling a large object.
- Avoid materializing large objects.
- Make use of LOB locators (see the previous question).
- Try to only access the portion of the large object that is needed by the application process (for example, use SUBSTR).

What is a long tablespace in DB2 UDB?

A long tablespace is used for storing large objects, and these tablespaces must be defined in DMS format. You specify that a tablespace is long during its creation.

```
CREATE LONG TABLESPACE largetbs MANAGED BY DATABASE
USING (FILE 'd:\largetbs\tsspace.dat' 50000)
```

Tip: *Separating large objects from other objects will help improve the clustering of the table.*

What are extenders?

Extenders are primarily a set of APIs and other definitions that specifically fit a particular type of LOB. For example, there would be pieces provided to enable the manipulation and imagery of video binary LOBs.

There are image extenders, audio extenders, video extenders, and text extenders. There are other extenders that will be delivered for DB2 in the future, such as fingerprint and GIS series. Each extender normally defines a distinct UDT (user-defined datatype), a set of UDFs (user-defined functions), and triggers. There is a large amount of

information about the properties of an LOB that is captured and maintained. Extenders provide all the pieces necessary to enable complete object-oriented applications.

COMPRESSION

 ### What types of compression are best for DB2 OS/390?

DB2 has an option to compress tablespaces. The main reasons for doing this are to allow more rows on one tablespace page, therefore bringing more rows into DB2 when requested; to minimize the I/Os necessary to process the data (more data per I/O); and to reduce the resources required to store the data. The penalty you pay, of course, is the overhead of the compression and decompression of the data. The compression algorithm used by DB2 requires overhead during compression but very little overhead during decompression.

Do not use compression if you do not have the hardware assist in OS/390 (microcode to support the compression and decompression algorithms). Many organizations believe that hardware compression is automatically delivered by DASD or that the RAID devices provide an alternative, but this is untrue. Internal DASD hardware compression ensures that minimal physical disk space is used.

Also, remember that index compression is not provided by DB2, and indexes benefit more from the hardware compression provided by DASD or RAID devices. Normally it does not hurt to have the disk compression as well as software compression for tablespaces. The overhead is not noticeable, and the gain is significant. The new DASD RAID devices normally compress data by a 4 to 1 ratio (25 real cylinders emulate 100 logical cylinders). When you use DB2 compression, which puts more data on a single page, the ratio on the RAID devices drops an average of 2 to 1 (25 real cylinders emulate 50 logical cylinders). These two methods of compression cannot be compared, as they provide entirely different benefits.

 Tip: *Use compression carefully on tablespaces that have regularly repeated tablespace scans because of the overhead of decompressing again and again.*

Do I have to rebind my packages after compression is turned off?

Yes. If you turn compression off for a tablespace, any plans or packages that were dependent on those objects will have to be rebound. The rebinding is necessary because when compression is turned off (or on), the number of rows per page will change; this will affect the calculations used by the optimizer in determining access paths because fewer rows will be transferred per I/O. Plans and packages should also be rebound if the percentage of rows compressed changes significantly, as this can also affect query optimization.

How do I measure the effects of compression?

In order to measure the benefits of compression, you can look in the DB2 catalog. The following fields show the compression statistics collected by the RUNSTATS utility.

- In the catalog table SYSTABLEPART, the column PAGESAVE shows the percentage of pages saved in either the tablespace or the partition. A change in the value signals the potential need for a DICTIONARY REBUILD. A downward trend means the dictionary is less effective.

- In the catalog table SYSTABLES (table level) and the catalog table SYSTABSTATS (partition level), the column PCTROWCOMP shows the percentage of rows that are compressed. This is used by the optimizer during access path selection. It helps determine CPU cost.

Can compression have any effect on the organization of data?

When performing updates, there are two situations that can cause data to become disorganized and to cause increases in the NEARINDREF and FARINDREF statistics:

- Updates to variable character columns in a table
- Updates to tables in compressed tablespaces

There are only two conditions that can potentially cause an increase or decrease in the length of a row. But here, we are only concerned with the conditions that cause an increase in the length. The row's length might increase in size due to an increase in the length of a variable-length column. When compression is used, it can also cause an increase, rather than a decrease in the length of the row. In either situation, the updated row might not be able to fit on the current page. When this is the situation, it is relocated on a page that has the space required. On the original page, a pointer takes the place of the row and points to the RID (row ID) on the page now storing the data. If that page is within 32 pages of the original page, the NEARINDREF count would increase. If it is not stored within 32 pages, the FARINDREF count would increase.

Do I get a 4 to 1 compression ratio if I am using both RVA and DB2 compression?

The new DASD RAID devices normally compress data by a 4 to 1 ratio (25 real cylinders emulate 100 logical cylinders). When you use DB2 compression, which puts more data on a single page, the ratio on the RAID devices drops to an average of 2 to 1 (25 real cylinders emulate 50 logical cylinders). For more information on this topic, see the question "What types of compression are best for DB2 OS/390?" earlier in this section.

Why is the percentage of compressed rows greater after a REORG than after a LOAD?

The percentage of compressed rows after a REORG is greater due to several reasons. The way that the compression dictionary is built during the execution of the REORG always provides the best possible dictionary, and this will always be a better dictionary than the one built by the LOAD utility. Also, after a table is compressed there is normally data maintenance (inserts, updates, deletes), which do not necessarily match the existing dictionary. As these updates accumulate in the table, the percentage of rows actually compressed goes down.

Chapter 4

Catalog and Directory

Answer Topics!

Catalog and Directory @ a Glance

The DB2 catalog and directory act as central repositories for all information about objects, authorizations, and communications regarding the support and operations of DB2. They are somewhat different with each of the DB2 family members, but the catalog performs the same general function. The catalog is composed of several DB2 tables and can be accessed via SQL. The catalog contains details about DB2 objects obtained from the DDL (Data Definition Language) when an object is created or altered, or from DCL (Data Control Language) when an authorization is granted on an object or group of objects. The OS/390 catalog will also contain information about communications with other DB2 and non-DB2 databases through the use of the Communications database (CDB), which contains information about VTAM and TCP/IP addresses.

The DB2 directory, an OS/390 component, is not accessible via SQL, but it does contain vital information regarding the operation and maintenance of the DB2 subsystem and objects.

Descriptions of both the DB2 catalog and directory are contained in this chapter as well as explanations of their usage, including some of the most frequently asked questions regarding maintenance, access, and the physical placement of objects. Also, there are queries included for executing some of the most common reports that extract object and authorization information from the DB2 catalog. These report results can be used for design reviews, troubleshooting, and integrity checking.

SUPPORT AND MAINTENANCE

Is there a performance impact if my DB2 catalog resides in SMS multivolume datasets?

If the catalog for a heavily used production subsystem is in SMS multivolume datasets, there is a potential for performance problems. It is recommended that large contiguous datasets be used for heavily accessed, critical DB2 resources. DASD multivolume, multiextent datasets take more time and I/O as opposed to a single-volume, single-extent dataset. DB2 can handle the multivolume datasets for system datasets with any secondary allocation, but it is not advisable in terms of the critical performance needed by the catalog.

How do I know when to reorganize my DB2 catalog and directory on OS/390?

By using the same techniques for determining when to reorganize application tablespaces and indexspaces, you can also determine when to reorganize the DB2 catalog tablespace and indexspaces. First, ensure that statistics are kept current by using RUNSTATS so that decisions for reorganizations are based on current numbers. A reorganization would also be necessary if the objects are in extents, or if unused space needs to be reclaimed.

On OS/390, DB2 catalog reorganizations have only been possible since Version 4, due to complicated list structures and internal hashing in the catalog, and the RECOVER utility was previously the only option for reorganizations against the indexes. If the catalog is not reorganized on a regular basis, the performance of both user and system queries against the catalog could begin to degrade. All of the tablespaces in the DSNDB06 database can be reorganized.

On OS/390, DB2 directory reorganizations are important, because the directory contains critical information regarding internal DB2 control and structures. These are important to DB2 processing because they affect application plans and package execution, utility execution, and database access.

Keep in mind that there are relationships between the DB2 catalog and some of the DB2 directory tables. For

instance, you would want to reorganize the directory table DBD01 when you reorganize catalog table SYSDBASE. Directory tables SCT01 and SCT02 would need to be reorganized with SYSPLAN and SYSPACKAGE, respectively.

How and when should I add indexes to the DB2 catalog tables?

With DB2 Version 4 for OS/390, we were provided with the opportunity to create our own indexes on the DB2 catalog to assist with performance and object reporting queries that access the DB2 catalog. What type of access is being performed against the catalog and which tables are being accessed will dictate which table would benefit from an additional index.

Can I use SQL against the DB2 directory, and what information does it contain?

The DB2 directory is used to store information regarding the operation and housekeeping of the DB2 environment, and it cannot be accessed by using SQL, as the DB2 catalog can be accessed. It contains information required to start DB2, and there are activities and utilities in the DB2 environment that actually do the updating and deleting of table entries in the DB2 directory. The DB2 directory contains five tables, and a description of each is given below.

SPT01 This table is referred to as the skeleton package table (SKPT), and it contains information about the access paths and the internal form of the SQL for a package at bind time. Entries are made into this table during bind time (BIND PACKAGE), and entries are deleted when a package is freed (FREE PACKAGE). This table is loaded into memory at execution time (along with the SPT02 table described next).

SCT02 This table is referred to as the skeleton cursor table (SKCT), and it contains information regarding access paths and the internal form of the SQL for an application plan. Entries in this table are made when a plan is bound (BIND PLAN), and deleted when a plan is freed (FREE PLAN). This table is also loaded into memory at execution time.

DBD01   The information in this table is referred to as DBDs (Database Descriptors), which are internal control blocks. Each database in DB2 has one DBD for its objects (tablespaces, indexes, tables, RI constraints, and check constraints). Updates to this table are made when a database is created or updated. This information is accessed by DB2 in place of continually using the DB2 catalog. This allows for faster, more efficient access to this information. The information in the DBD01 directory table is also contained in the DB2 catalog.

SYSLGRNX   This table is referred to as the log range table, and it contains information from the DB2 logs regarding the RBA (Relative Byte Address) range for updates. This allows DB2 to efficiently find the RBAs needed from the DB2 logs for recovery purposes. A row is inserted every time a tablespace or partition is opened or updated, and it is updated when the object is closed.

SYSUTILX   This system utilities table stores information about the execution of DB2 utilities, including the status and the steps during execution. This information is used when a utility needs to be restarted. Information in this table is added when a utility is started, and the entry is removed when the execution has ended.

 ## Should I run RUNSTATS on the DB2 catalog?

Yes, RUNSTATS should be run frequently on the DB2 catalog, depending on the amount of DDL (Data Definition Language), DML (Data Manipulation Language), and other activities that are occurring which will insert and delete rows in DB2 catalog tables. DB2 cannot appropriately optimize queries against the catalog without having RUNSTATS current on the tablespaces and indexspaces. The same principle applies here as with DB2 user-defined objects; a current view of all DB2 objects is required to determine the need for and frequency of reorganizing catalog tablespaces and indexspaces.

 ## How do I increase the size of the DB2 catalog datasets?

There may be instances in which the DB2 catalog datasets go into extents, causing additional overhead in terms of I/O against the catalog. In these situations, the catalog space should be increased. This is performed by running the RECOVER utility on the appropriate database, or the REORG utility on the appropriate tablespace, using DFDSS, or HSM. These last two choices are really shortcuts that can offer immediate relief to the problem.

There is a specific order to recovering catalog datasets, due to relationships and dependencies in the catalog. This order is as follows:

1. DSNDB01.SYSUTILX
2. DSNDB01.DBD01
3. SYSUTILX indexes
4. DSNDB06.SYSCOPY
5. SYSCOPY (3) indexes (IBM only)
6. DSNDB01.SYSLGRNX
7. SYSLGRNX Indexes
8. DSNDB06.SYSDBAUT
9. SYSDBAUT (3) indexes (IBM only)
10. DSNDB06.SYSUSER
11. DSNDB06.SYSDBASE
12. SYSDBASE indexes (IBM only)
13. SYSUSER (3) indexes (IBM only)
14. All other catalog and directory tablespaces and indexes
15. Catalog indexes (user-defined)
16. System utility tablespaces, such as QMF
17. Communications database
18. Object and application registration tables
19. Resource limit specification tables
20. User tablespaces

To quickly combine all the space into a single extent there are two alternative approaches. When you have the space elsewhere, you can use the utility DFDSS to copy it to another location which combines all the space used into a single primary extent. The DB2 subsystem needs to be shut down to perform this and this approach should only be used as a temporary measure, and only when the normal procedures cannot be followed.

Also, you can use HSM to perform a simple migrate and restore which will remove any extents. This also requires the DB2 subsystem to be shut down.

When do I execute the CATMAINT utility?

The CATMAINT utility should only be executed during a release migration and can only be executed by the INSTALL SYSADM authorization ID. The purpose of the CATMAINT utility is to change the DB2 catalog structure by creating new tables and indexes and altering existing ones. It must be able to complete all necessary changes (execute until completion), or it will not be successful.

Can I use the REPAIR utility against the DB2 catalog or directory?

You can use the REPAIR utility against the DB2 catalog or directory; however, it is not really recommended that you do so. You can run the REPAIR LOCATE on the DB2 catalog, but the datasets supporting the DB2 catalog and directory are not in the same format as normal DB2 datasets.

What are the benefits and drawbacks of using a shadow copy of the DB2 catalog?

Having a shadow copy of the DB2 catalog can help with contention against the catalog if there is heavy access or inquiry against the catalog from programmers, developers, DBAs, and vendor utilities. A shadow copy can help to reduce bottlenecks caused by these types of inquiries. One complication associated with having a shadow copy of the catalog is synchronization. In order to be sure that the queries against the shadow catalog are getting current information, the shadow needs to be kept up to date through a refresh process.

Should I allow everyone (developers and users) access to the DB2 catalog, or should I create views for them to use?

The DB2 catalog does not contain any user data, and access to it can be fairly open. However, on OS/390 views can be developed for use by programmers, developers, or users to give them a report of information on objects for a particular project. This often is helpful, since obtaining useful information from the DB2 catalog often requires several tables to be joined together. If concurrency is an issue, limiting access only to certain views, and therefore certain tables, may help. On UDB, a set of user views is part of the product in a schema called SYSCAT.

How can I reduce contention against the DB2 catalog?

You have a few options for reducing contention against the DB2 catalog:

- Use a shadow copy of the DB2 catalog
- Limit access to optimized, canned queries or views
- Schedule operations such as execution of Data Definition Language for off-peak periods
- Schedule catalog-intensive utilities for off-peak periods
- Make sure that the catalog is reorganized on a regular basis, depending on activity affecting the catalog
- Keep RUNSTATS current so dynamic queries use the latest statistics
- Be sure that all indexes on the DB2 catalog are type 2

When do I use the DSN1CHKR utility?

The DSN1CHKR utility on OS/390 is used to check for broken links in the DB2 catalog and directory. It will not repair the broken links, but simply report on which ones are broken. The utility can be run with either the FORMAT or DUMP option to find the links in a given tablespace, and then to indicate if there are any broken links or if there are orphan links. It will then print the page with the inconsistent link. By using the FORMAT option, you can view formatted DB2 pages. The MAP

option on the DSN1CHKR utility will also help with diagnosing broken or orphaned links because it will print the records of a RID (Row ID) chain, starting with a given beginning RID and then following the pointers through the links.

When should I manually update the statistics in the DB2 catalog?

There are a few statistics in the DB2 catalog that can be modified for query performance. This can be done to simulate production statistics in a test environment to get a feel for how queries will optimize in the production environment. It can also be done to influence access paths. This topic is covered in detail in Chapter 11, Advanced SQL.

Can I selectively delete recovery information from SYSCOPY?

No, you cannot selectively delete recovery information from the SYSCOPY catalog table on OS/390. The DB2 MODIFY utility removes records from the SYSCOPY table at a given point in time. If you have, for example, a damaged cartridge, you cannot selectively remove this information regarding the dataset(s) needed for recovery. If you catalog your image copy (which is the best option), you can uncatalog the image copy. Not finding it in the catalog, DB2 will instead fall back to the previous image copy recorded in the SYSCOPY table.

For those users who would like to be able to clean the SYSCOPY table selectively, (for example, remove all quiesce points (RBAs) older than 7 days, but leave all other utility information resident) there is a means for accomplishing this through the help of ISV software. DB2, itself, does not support this (yet).

CATALOG INFORMATION QUERIES

How do I find out if an authorization has been granted multiple times to the same userid?

The following query will produce a report that displays, by object, any duplicate authorizations where a privilege has been given to the same authorization ID by different users.

```
SELECT 'PLANS', GRANTEE, NAME, COUNT(*)
FROM SYSIBM.SYSPLANAUTH
GROUP BY GRANTEE, NAME
HAVING COUNT(*) > 2
-- MULTIPLE GRANTS OF SAME PLAN AUTHORIZATION
UNION
SELECT 'PACKAGES', GRANTEE, NAME, COUNT(*)
FROM SYSIBM.SYSPACKAUTH
GROUP BY GRANTEE, NAME
HAVING COUNT(*) > 2
-- MULTIPLE GRANTS OF SAME PACKAGE AUTHORIZATION
UNION
SELECT 'TABLES', GRANTEE, TTNAME, COUNT(*)
FROM SYSIBM.SYSTABAUTH
GROUP BY GRANTEE, TTNAME
HAVING COUNT(*) > 2
-- MULTIPLE GRANTS OF SAME TABLE AUTHORIZATION
UNION
SELECT 'SYSTEM', GRANTEE, NAME, COUNT(*)
FROM SYSIBM.SYSRESAUTH
GROUP BY GRANTEE, NAME
HAVING COUNT(*) > 2
-- MULTIPLE GRANTS OF SAME SYSTEM AUTHORIZATION
UNION
SELECT 'DATABASE', GRANTEE, NAME, COUNT(*)
FROM SYSIBM.SYSDBAUTH
GROUP BY GRANTEE, NAME
HAVING COUNT(*) > 2
ORDER BY 1,3,4 DESC
-- MULTIPLE GRANTS OF SAME DATABASE AUTHORIZATION
```

How do I find if foreign keys exist without indexes?

In order to find foreign keys that do not support indexes, several tables in the DB2 catalog must be joined together. It is recommended for performance, in terms of referential integrity operations, that foreign keys have corresponding indexes. The following query will allow you to determine if there are foreign keys existing without these indexes.

```
SELECT SR.TBNAME, SR.RELNAME
FROM SYSIBM.SYSRELS SR, SYSIBM.SYSTABLES TB
    WHERE SR.TBNAME = TB.NAME
        AND TB.DBNAME = 'DB2DB001'
```

```
AND TB.CREATOR = 'DBA1'
    AND NOT EXISTS
        (SELECT *
        FROM SYSIBM.SYSFOREIGNKEYS FK,
            SYSIBM.SYSINDEXES IX,
            SYSIBM.SYSKEYS SK
            WHERE SR.RELNAME = FK.RELNAME
            AND SR.TBNAME = FK.TBNAME
            AND SR.TBNAME = IX.TBNAME
            AND IX.NAME = SK.IXNAME
            AND FK.COLSEQ = SK.COLSEQ
            AND FK.COLNO = SK.COLNO
            AND FK.COLNAME = SK.COLNAME)
ORDER BY SR.TBNAME,SR.RELNAME
```

How do I find out which values are allowed in each tablespace partition?

The following query will allow you to view the values allowable for each partition of all partitioned tablespaces within a given database. The LIMITKEY field from SYSTABLEPART actually contains the values allowed in a given partition as they were defined in the CREATE INDEX statement when the partitioning index was defined.

```
SELECT T.DBNAME, T.NAME, P.PARTITION, P.LIMITKEY
    , P.CARD, P.FARINDREF, P.NEARINDREF, P.FREEPAGE, P.PCTFREE
    , P.COMPRESS, P.PAGESAVE, DATE(P.STATSTIME)
FROM SYSIBM.SYSTABLESPACE T, SYSIBM.SYSTABLEPART P
WHERE T.DBNAME = 'DB2DB001'
AND T.NAME = P.TSNAME
ORDER BY T.NAME
```

How do I check the logical consistency of my DB2 catalog?

DB2 comes with a set of queries to check the logical consistency of its catalog. The queries can be found in the SAMPLIB dataset in member DSNTESQ. This member provides queries that check the catalog consistency, CREATE and INSERT statements to create and populate a copy of the DB2 catalog, and queries that can be run during migration.

These catalog consistency queries do not take the place of DSN1CHKR, and you should run the DSN1CHKR before these logical consistency queries to ensure the physical correctness of the DB2 catalog. If you do not want to run these queries against your production catalog, then the statements are provided for creating a copy of the DB2 catalog. If you only want to run a few select queries, there is a grid to tell you which catalog tables will be used in the event that you are creating a copy catalog and only want to create the tables necessary for execution. The queries can by executed in SPUFI, DSNTEP2, or they can be cut and pasted into QMF queries.

The following is an example of one of the logical consistency queries from DSNTESQ:

QUERY25   Each index key column must have a row in SYSCOLUMNS. This query will check for this condition, with expected results being no rows returned. If rows are returned from this query, it may possibly mean that an improper recovery or copy was done that caused the data inconsistency.

```
SELECT IXCREATOR, IXNAME, COLNAME, COLNO
FROM SYSIBM.SYSKEYS KY,
   SYSIBM.SYSINDEXES IX
WHERE IXCREATOR = CREATOR
AND IXNAME = NAME
AND NOT EXISTS
   (SELECT *
   FROM SYSIBM.SYSCOLUMNS CL
   WHERE CL.TBCREATOR = IX.TBCREATOR
   AND CL.TBNAME = IX.TBNAME
   AND CL.NAME = KY.COLNAME)
```

How do I find out which tables and associated indexes are in each bufferpool?

Information about objects in a bufferpool can be found in the catalog tables SYSTABLESPACE and SYSTABLES.

```
SELECT
TS.BPOOL,TS.DBNAME,'TABLESPACE',TS.CREATOR,TS.NAME,
   TB.CREATOR,TB.NAME, TS.NACTIVE, TB.NPAGES, TB.PCTPAGES
```

```
FROM SYSIBM.SYSTABLESPACE TS, SYSIBM.SYSTABLES TB
WHERE TS.NAME = TB.TSNAME
UNION ALL
SELECT IX.BPOOL,IX.DBNAME,'INDEX      ',IX.CREATOR,IX.NAME,
    TB.CREATOR,TB.NAME, IX.NLEAF, TB.NPAGES, TB.PCTPAGES
FROM SYSIBM.SYSINDEXES IX, SYSIBM.SYSTABLES TB
WHERE TB.NAME = IX.TBNAME
ORDER BY 1,2,3,4,5
```

 ## How can I obtain information for each index partition?

To select information from the DB2 catalog for detail statistics about each index partition, you will need to join SYSINDEXES, SYSINDEXPART, and SYSINDEXSTATS. The following query will give you details, such as leaf distribution, free space, cluster ratio, and cardinality of each partition, for all indexes in a given database.

```
SELECT IX.IXNAME,IX.PARTITION,IX.PQTY, IX.SQTY, IX.LEAFDIST,
    IX.FAROFFPOSF,   IX.NEAROFFPOSF,IX.FREEPAGE,
    IX.PCTFREE, IX.CARDF,IT.KEYCOUNT,I.COLCOUNT,
    I.CLUSTERING, I.CLUSTERED, I.FIRSTKEYCARDF, I.FULLKEYCARDF, IT.NLEAF,
    IT.NLEVELS, IT.CLUSTERRATIO, SUBSTR(CHAR(I.STATSTIME),6,5)
FROM SYSIBM.SYSINDEXPART IX, SYSIBM.SYSINDEXES I,
SYSIBM.SYSINDEXSTATS IT
    WHERE IX.IXNAME = I.NAME
        AND IX.IXNAME = IT.NAME
        AND IT.NAME = I.NAME
        AND IX.PARTITION = IT.PARTITION
        AND I.DBNAME = 'DB2D0001'
ORDER BY IX.IXNAME, IX.PARTITION
```

How can I find out what columns the indexes in my database are composed of?

In order to get a report with all of the columns belonging to an index, listed by table for a particular database, three catalog tables need to be joined together. You will need

SYSTABLES to select the tables for a given database, joined to SYSINDEXES to obtain the index information for each table, joined to SYSKEYS to get the columns defined to each index. The following query performs this task:

```
SELECT I.TBCREATOR, I.TBNAME, I.NAME,
    I.UNIQUERULE, I.CLUSTERING, I.COLCOUNT, K.COLSEQ,
    K.COLNAME, K.COLNO, K.ORDERING
FROM SYSIBM.SYSINDEXES I,SYSIBM.SYSTABLES T
    ,SYSIBM.SYSKEYS K
        WHERE I.TBCREATOR = 'DB'
        AND I.TBCREATOR = T.CREATOR
        AND I.TBNAME    = T.NAME
        AND T.DBNAME    = 'DB2D0001'
        AND I.NAME      = K.IXNAME
        AND K.IXCREATOR = 'DB'
ORDER BY I.TBNAME, I.NAME, K.COLSEQ
```

Chapter 5

Subsystems
and Instances

Subsystems and Instances @ a Glance

- Subsystems (OS/390) and instances (UNIX, Windows, OS/2) deal with the various parameters and configuration settings for running DB2.

- There are literally hundreds of parameters across all the DB2 platforms, and many of these need not be changed. Some of these must be changed and need to be set according to specific guidelines depending on processing requirements.

- This chapter will deal with the general settings and parameters for all platforms.

- Questions are answered pertaining to the sizing and number of subsystems and instances, mixing workloads in a single instance, and setting and using specialized features. Some of the more critical questions deal with dispatching priorities, logging, and the number and sizing of buffer pools.

GENERAL INFORMATION

How many OS/390 DB2 subsystems should I create?

Not too many! Because DB2 is a subsystem (an extension to OS/390), the overhead created by the OS/390 system is considerable. Nevertheless, there are good reasons to start an additional DB2 subsystem. These could be business reasons, such as SLAs (service level agreements) or availability hours, or they could be technical reasons, such as the resource usage of a single DB2 system or the need for specific tuning. The maximum number of DB2 subsystems executing on OS/390 depends on the hardware configuration of your machine (the storage and number of processors) and on the software configuration (for example, other workloads or page dataset configurations). A normal OS/390 should be able to run between 2 and 8 DB2 subsystems; 3 or 4 DB2 subsystems per OS/390 system is a nice average. Normally the person who is in charge of OS/390 tuning will help determine this number.

Caution: *It is possible that if you create a new DB2 subsystem, several settings in OS/390 (for example, ECSA) will need to be changed. If this is not done, all running systems could suffer bad performance or even system outages. Always plan carefully when creating a new subsystem and monitor its environment closely in the first few weeks.*

What is the maximum number of DB2 subsystems OS/390 can support?

There really is no maximum that OS/390 can support, but you have to limit the number of DB2 subsystems in order to keep the OS/390 running well within the limits of the hardware configuration, such as memory constraints. When you have DB2 running on an OS/390 subsystem, it will use lots of resources (such as storage). You should have a valid reason to start a new DB2 subsystem and be careful so as to not overload the OS/390 system. DB2 was designed to handle large workloads and mixed workloads. Therefore, creating a new subsystem for a new customer or new project is not

necessary (unless you need to set different goals in the Workload Manager for this customer or project, or the application has specific tuning requirements). Several organizations have separate DB2 subsystems for Test/Development, Volume Test, and Production.

At what priority should DB2 and its associated address spaces be executing on OS/390?

The best general recommendation for OS/390 address space dispatching priorities would be for the IRLM address space to be placed above IMS, CICS, and DB2, with DB2's MSTR and DBM1 address spaces placed above CICS. This recommendation would result in the following:

1. OS/390 Monitor with IRLM capabilities
2. IRLM
3. DB2 performance monitors
4. DBM1
5. MSTR
6. CICS

If the IRLM is not at the top of the dispatching priorities, the DB2 locks will not get set and released without causing excessive wait time. Also, if the IRLM is not above DB2 at DB2 startup, a warning message is issued.

If a performance monitor is being used that can analyze problems in the IRLM, then dispatching IRLM higher than a DB2 and/or OS/390 monitor could be a problem. If a performance monitor can't get dispatched ahead of IRLM, you will not be able to find or analyze the problem. It is important to pay attention to the dispatching recommendations of the maker of the various performance monitors. Each have one or more address spaces and always recommend specific dispatching priorities.

Note that under OS/390, the DPRTY parameter is no longer valid, and all priorities have to be set using the OS/390 parameters in either the IPS/ICS table, or the program priority table. If the IPS/ICS table is used to define relative priorities, then the priorities can be changed dynamically.

 ### When should the I/O scheduling priority be changed, and what should the settings be?

On OS/390, DB2 can schedule single-page synchronous read and write I/Os, sequential prefetch, list sequential prefetch, and sequential detection using the application address space's I/O scheduling priority. In order to use this facility, OS/390 I/O priority scheduling must be enabled by specifying IOQ=PRTY in the IEAIPSxx member of SYS1.PARMLIB. Also, the IOP parameter must be used to set the I/O priority for the address space of a performance group. The IOP parameter is in the IEAIPSxx member of SYS1.PARMLIB. When these settings are used, the I/O scheduling priority for asynchronous write I/Os is determined by DBM1 address space. This is the strategy that is used when it is necessary to favor OLTP systems over other address spaces for I/O processing.

 ### What is the easiest way to add another instance to my UDB server?

Using the Control Center is the easiest way to do everything in DB2, OS/390, UNIX, Windows, or OS/2. To add a new instance in UNIX, Windows, or OS/2, start the Control Center as shown in Figure 5-1. By using the right mouse bottom over any of the items on the hierarchical display produces a menu of functions. In this case, Add was selected to bring up the Add Instance window for adding another instance.

After the instance is created, select the new instance and again click the right mouse button to bring up a menu of options for the new instance. This is shown in Figure 5-2.

 ### Why are OS/390 DB2 address spaces sometimes non-reusable?

If an address space has cross-memory communication and cross-memory services do not clean up normally, then OS/390 will issue the message: IEF352I ADDRESS SPACE UNAVAILABLE. This message indicates that the address space will not be reused by OS/390 until the next IPL. This situation can occur if DB2 is not normally terminated; however, there is no reason for panic. Always make sure that DB2 is properly terminated using the –STOP DB2 command.

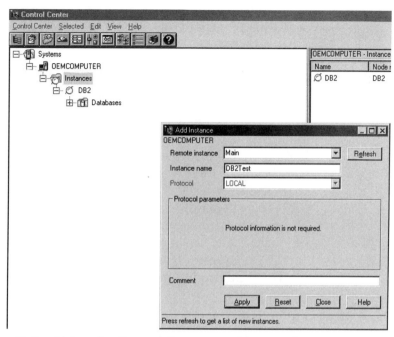

Figure 5-1   Using the Control Center to add a new instance

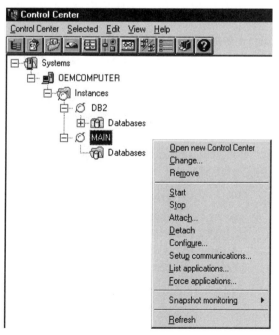

Figure 5-2   Menu of options for an instance

Can I mix a production and test workload in one DB2 subsystem or server?

Normally, you would want to isolate the production workload into a separate DB2 subsystem. The reasons for this include performance, security, and SLAs that are normally different from those assigned to test environments. Also, in test, new applications tend to behave poorly because the proper tuning had not been performed yet. This could disturb production workload and have a negative effect on its performance. Also, there are several DSNZPARMs that will have to be tuned differently depending on whether it is a test or production environment. However, some companies combine test production and use a single subsystem to volume test and certify the system. However, this is not an advisable thing to do. Text and production should always be separated.

! **_Caution:_** _Be careful about giving your objects (databases, tablespaces, etc.) the same names in multiple subsystems. You could easily forget to which DB2 subsystem you are attached and drop or alter the object in the wrong environment._

Can I have a test and a production DB2 UDB workload on the same physical machine?

Yes. Through the definition of instances, which are logical database servers, you can have two completely independent database servers on the same physical machine.

How does DB2 know that hardware compression is available?

When DB2 starts, it will look at an OS/390 control block called CVT (communications vector table). If the CVTCMPSH indicator bit is turned on in CVT field "FLAG2," then DB2 will use hardware compression. System programmers can investigate the CVT using IPCS.

Should I have one or more bufferpools using any of the DB2 engines?

Each DB2 database needs at least one bufferpool. Using only one bufferpool was once a very good idea, since there were not many options: memory was constrained, and methods for tuning and sizing bufferpools were not refined. Since bufferpools can now be individually tuned and it is possible to have several bufferpools, having only one bufferpool is a bad idea. This applies to all DB2 platforms. Using the wrong number of bufferpools forces objects with differing access and update characteristics to share a single resource, which is very detrimental.

 Can DB2 for OS/390 be used as a very large (ASCII) server?

Yes, DB2 Version 5 has a new feature allowing for it to be a server for ASCII data. Normally everything in OS/390 is designed to be in EBCDIC format. However, many enhancements were made to DB2 Version 5, including dynamic statement caching and ASCII support, so that it could be used as a server for large ERP packages, such as SAP, Peoplesoft, or Baan.

The ASCII support was specially designed so that translation does not need to be performed when the data is transported into an ASCII environment, such as Unix. When DB2 is used by a Unix application server (such as the SAP implementation), no DB2 connect is involved. DB2 on OS/390 has to be regarded as a database server for the Unix application, and translation to EBCDIC would be pointless.

! *Caution:* *ASCII and EBCDIC data cannot be used together in the same SQL statement. If joins are required between an ASCII support table and both ASCII tables and EBCDIC tables, two copies must be maintained. This will be necessary with some code, control, and reference tables.*

 ### Can I do charge-back from the DB2 accounting-records?

Yes and no. Yes, the class-3 records are called accounting records, and they contain lots of information, such as CPU consumption, time of day, and userid. The downside is that the figures can be incorrect. For example, the CICS attach has the SRB figures of all DB2 threads from that CICS system while the thread was active (there is no SRB time per thread). Also, you will find it difficult to match the DB2 records with SMF accounting records. Think twice before you start using the DB2 accounting records for charge-back.

 ### What is a good size for my active logs on OS/390?

If you archive to cartridge, you want to make sure that you fill up the cartridge (about 200MB for a normal cartridge). Also, make sure that you have enough active logs to allow for archive failure and/or large rollbacks. In order not to introduce a single point of failure, the active logs have to be dual. A minimum for a system log is $200 \times 2 \times 3 = 1200MB$. They should be sized large enough to keep archiving as low as possible, and the appropriate size will depend on the amount of system activity. Many organizations have several active logs rather than just one.

The logs should be placed on DASD devices that are on the same channel and/or controller where other busy datasets do not exist. The system logs are critical in delivering performance. The commit process will wait for a successful write to the active log, and if there is contention on the logs, performance will suffer.

 ### Can DB2 be used for 24 × 7 × 365 operation?

Yes, DB2 was designed to be a long-running database server. Several organizations run DB2 for several weeks, even months, between times it is brought down. There are two issues to keep in mind. First, the fact that DB2 is up and running doesn't always mean that your data is available. You might have to (re)load the data or do some other maintenance to your data. Second, there are still some activities that can only be done when DB2 is down (e.g., maintenance of the BSDS) or by cycling DB2 (e.g., change DSNZPARMs).

A great deal of effort was put into ensuring that DB2 system or data outages are not often required, if at all. Examples of these enhancements are the –ALTER BUFFERPOOL command that used to be maintained in the DSNZPARMs and now can be done dynamically, or the online REORG utility that has minimal impact on data availability. Future DB2 releases will address the remaining continuous availability issues.

COMPONENTS

Can I share IRLMs?

No, you should not, and in some circumstances it is not even possible. The main reason is the fact that the IRLM is crucial for DB2 operation and performance, and sharing the IRLM might give the other DB2 (or IMS) the potential to harm it. It is also not a good idea to share IRLMs from a resource point of view.

Does DB2 support DF/SMS?

Yes, for a long time now DB2 has supported DF/SMS (Data Facility/System Managed Storage) for dataset management. Great benefits can be gained by using DF/SMS. But many performance problems can also be introduced if DF/SMS is not properly set up. See Chapter 3 for more information on data storage.

When do I need DDF?

The Distributed Data Facility (DDF) is a special task that handles all requests that are not locally generated but that come from the network (clients and/or servers). DDF maintains the DRDA protocol to the party requesting services. You could view DDF as the networking component of DB2.

The DDF address space can be stopped and started independently of the other DB2 address spaces. If DB2 only services local requests, DDF is not needed. Some networking implementations do not require DDF. For example, Net.Data (Web server component) does a local attach, creates Web pages, and sends these pages to the TCP/IP network using a Web server; therefore it does not require the use of DDF.

How do I call the DSN monitor from REXX?

The problem is that the DSN monitor does not get its input from the REXX exec but has to read the input from the command stack. So, to stop the DSN monitor you have to put the input to the DSN on the stack including the END command. To be on the safe side you had best start a new stack. Here is an example:

```
NEWSTACK
QUEUE 'RUN PROGRAM(progname) PLAN(planname)
    LIB('your.load.lib')'
QUEUE 'END'
Address TSO "DSN SYSTEM("your subsystem id here")"
DELSTACK
```

What is RRSAF attach?

The Recoverable Resource Manager Services Attachment Facility (RRSAF) that was introduced in Version 5 is a new interface to DB2. Programs using this new interface can connect to and use DB2 to process SQL statements, issue commands, or issue IFI (Instrumentation Facility Interface) calls.

RRSAF uses OS/390 Transaction Management and Recoverable Resource Manager Services (OS/390 RRS). With RRSAF, you can coordinate DB2 updates with updates made by all other resource managers that also use OS/390 RRS in an OS/390 system. The RRSAF interface is the most complicated attachment and is normally used with assembler code to fully exploit its functionality. Its use is explained in detail in the IBM Application Programming and SQL Guide—SC26-8958.

What is the Instrumentation Facility Component (IFC)?

The Instrumentation Facility Component (IFC) is more commonly known as a DB2 Trace. This interface is designed to push detailed information from DB2 to the outside world. DB2 does not misuse the log to externalize this kind of information like IMS does, but allows you to choose a number of data collectors. The trace data can be flushed to SMF, GTF, an in-storage table (SRV), or a program interface (specially designed for performance monitors).

You can specify what kind of data you want to trace. For example there are the Accounting, Statistics, and Performance traces. The overhead involved with tracing can be minimal (e.g., account class 1 and 2 is about 3 percent) to very large (e.g., I/O tracing). Some (non-dangerous) traces can be turned on by default in the DSNZPARM. These are the accounting and system performance traces. Normally you want to turn both of them on because otherwise you have no idea how DB2 is behaving. To format the trace records, you need the DB2PM product from IBM or a performance monitor tool from an Independent Software Vendor (ISV).

Should I use CAF or DSN monitor for batch?

The major difference between CAF (Call Attach Facility) and DSN is that the DSN monitor doesn't start if the DB2 subsystem is not available, and your program will not get control. With DSN, all parameters to run the program are specified at runtime by keywords to the run command. This means that your program contains no logic for controlling DB2 or its environment (e.g., plan name). With CAF you have full control over DB2 and its environment, but you have to code logic in your program to do so. There is no major resource or performance difference between CAF and DSN. Alternatives to CAF and DSN are the IMS BMP environment or many solutions provided by Independent Software Vendors (ISV).

? Should I use ECSA or private memory areas for IRLM locks?

In general, ECSA is the best option to hold the IRLM locks. Because the ECSA storage can be accessed with fewer instructions, this option is the fastest. However, this is also the most dangerous option. ECSA is not protected by OS/390 and can be destroyed by other non-behaving system tasks. There is also the danger that the IRLM may take too many locks and will use all of the ECSA available in the system, destroying OS/390 in the process. Be careful when using ECSA, and make sure that the locks are limited and monitored. If IRLM put its locks in the private area, these dangers do not apply. However, if used excessively, the performance will degrade.

! **Caution:** *From Version 5 on, DBA can override the maximum locks on a tablespace, but the maximum locks per user still exist.*

Tip: *In Version 5 there are new ways to avoid locking, such as using the bind parameters CURRENT DATA(NO) and ISOLATION(UR).*

? How many bufferpools should I have, and how do I decide what to put in each one?

We will look at the OS/390 platform first.

It is highly recommended to have several bufferpools with objects separated according to the type of processing and residency characteristics. This allows for more precise tuning and sizing of each bufferpool. For example, it is ideal to keep objects that have random access in bufferpools without objects that have a lot of sequential access. Some general rules of thumb for bufferpool separation on OS/390 are listed in the following example:

BP0: Use only for the DB2 Catalog and Directory—exclusively

BP1: Use only for the DSNDB07 work tablespaces exclusively

BP2: Use for Vendor utility objects

BP3: Use for Sequential tablespaces

BP4: Use for Sequential indexes (non-matching scans)

BP5: Use for Random tablespaces

BP6: Use for Random indexes

BP7: Use for Code and reference tables

These can be broken down further, based on update and residency requirements. It might be necessary to have a separate bufferpool for highly updated tablespaces with high updated page re-reference and another for highly updated tablespaces with little or no updated page re-reference. The whole concept is based on granularity according to characteristics. The finer the granularity, the better the performance, assuming that there is enough memory to support the breakout.

For the non-OS/390 platforms, multiple bufferpool strategies depend on the amount of memory available. If the total buffer space is less than 10,000 4KB pages and specialized tuning knowledge is not available, use only one bufferpool.

If your system is not constrained by these conditions, consider separate bufferpools for the following:

● Temporary table spaces
● Data accessed repeatedly and quickly by many short update transaction applications
● Favor certain applications, data, and indexes
● Tables and indexes that are updated frequently
● Tables and indexes that are frequently queried but infrequently updated
● Data accessed by applications that are seldomly used

 Note: Watch the guideline for DSNDB07 work files as SYSPLEX query parallelism has an impact since it can use the work files on any subsystem where any part of the query runs.

 Note: Watch the guideline for DSNDB07 work files in DB2 V5 as stored procedure result sets have an impact on their size and use.

DSNZPARMS AND CONFIGURATION PARAMETERS

 ### What are hidden DSNZPARMs, and can I change them?

Hidden DSNZPARMs are those that are not accessible through the DB2 installation panels and can only be changed by directly changing the macros. Examples of hidden DSNZPARMs would be the one that sets the maximum degree of parallelism in the DB2 subsystem, the one that alters the number of read engines and write engines, and the one that turns on the hidden explain tables.

 ### Where do I find the UDB configuration parameters, and how do I change them?

The easiest way to view and change all the many configuration parameters in UDB is to use the control center, highlight the instance name, and click on it with the right mouse button as shown in Figure 5-2. From this menu, select Configure to bring up the display shown in Figure 5-3.

There are several tabs representing the categories of configuration parameters. By selecting any of the parameters on any of the tabs, an area on the bottom left of the dialog box will show the options for the parameter and allow it to be changed. The display on the bottom-right gives a description of the parameter and its allowable values. In addition, once a parameter has been changed, the column in the display titled Changed displays an indicator, as shown in Figure 5-4.

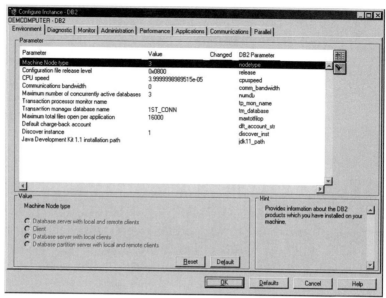

Figure 5-3 First display panel for setting UDB configuration parameters

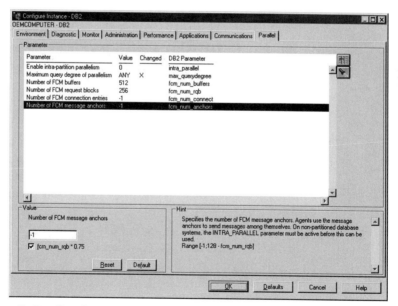

Figure 5-4 Configuration panel display showing a parameter that was changed

When I change a DSNZPARM do I have to recycle my DB2 subsystem?

Yes. In order to have a changed DSNZPARM take effect in the subsystem, you must recycle DB2 after the DSNZPARMs have been assembled. Currently, there is no mechanism for dynamic DSNZPARM changes because the infrastructure is not in place to support this. However, this is a feature that will be available in the future.

How do I control how often DB2 takes a checkpoint?

The LOGLOAD DSNZPARM determines how many active log records are written between DB2 checkpoints. The frequency will depend on the amount of update activity in the system and will help you to determine how high to set the LOGLOAD parameter. A general rule of thumb is to have your DB2 subsystem checkpoint every 15–20 minutes. Excessive checkpoint processing will result in I/O waits. You can see how often DB2 checkpoints by referring to a monitor statistics report.

How do I turn off dataset downlevel detection on OS/390?

It is possible to replace a DB2 dataset by mistake with an incorrect or outdated copy (called a downlevel copy) when using a stand-alone or non-DB2 utility, such as DSN1COPY or DFSMShsm. Also, performing a cold start of DB2 can result in a downlevel condition. There is a level ID associated with every page set or partition, and most DB2 operations detect a downlevel ID when the page set or partition is opened.

Sometimes, under extreme conditions, it is desirable to turn off downlevel detection when downlevel data is purposely going to be used. Setting the DSNZPARM DLDFREQ to 0 can turn off downlevel detection.

 Should I take the default on the NUMLKUS DSNZPARM?

Generally, defaults are never the optimal choice. The NUMLKUS DSNZPARM controls the number of locks allowed to be taken by a user. The default is 10,000. However, if you have a very high-volume environment or possibly have lock escalation turned off, this value will be exceeded, often resulting in a –904 SQL return code.

Chapter 6

Designing a Database

Answer Topics!

Designing a Database @ a Glance

Putting together a well-represented logical design is the key to being able to move into a physical design that meets your business requirements. However, the physical design of the database will determine how well the database performs and how easily it can be used and maintained. When the physical design is good, high performance is possible, which leads to doing more for the business. When the design is bad, it is either difficult or impossible to tune for performance. A good design has no potential for update anomalies; it is also a relational design with relations based on the data and not on processes.

It is important to make the correct design choices when designing physical objects such as tables, tablespaces, and indexes—once a physical structure has been defined and is being used, it is sometimes difficult and time-consuming to make changes to the underlying structure. The best way to perform logical database modeling is to use strong guidelines developed by an expert in relational data modeling, or to use one of the many relational database modeling tools supplied by vendors.

DB2 objects need to be designed for availability, ease of maintenance, and overall performance, as well as for business requirements. There are guidelines and recommendations for achieving these design goals, but how each of these are measured will depend on the business and the nature of the data.

LOGICAL DESIGN

Should I have many-to-many relationships in my logical design and use intersection tables only in the physical design?

Almost all logical designs will have tables with many-to-many relationships. For example, any book order can be for several books, and any book could be included on many orders. A database for book orders would require another table (for example, order details) containing order items that would be in one-to-many relationships with both orders and books. For example, each record in the order details table would apply to only one book and one order, but each order could be made of many order detail records, and each book could be included on many order detail records

The many-to-many relationships are sometimes handled as part of the logical design, depending on who is creating the logical design and who is creating the physical design. In other cases, these relationships are left to be implemented in the physical design process by means of an intersection table. The proper method is to resolve them in the logical model and build the physical model accordingly.

Why would I want to normalize my tables?

Normalization is a process of applying specific rules to a design that will help you avoid inconsistencies and redundancies in the data. Normalization is necessary in order to process your data with SQL. If the data is not properly designed, the power of SQL is useless. You should always go to the third normal form to get all the benefits of SQL. Many papers have been written on normal form, but there is a simple rule that applies. Every attribute (column) should be fully dependent on the whole key and nothing but the key—there can be no dependency among its attributes. If a design is not in third normal form, the design will cause update anomalies (because the same data will appear in more than one place), and these anomalies will have to be handled in the programs. This results in poor design, making it difficult to ensure data integrity.

 Is third normal form always the optimal design?

Normalization has five levels of rules for relational designing, and these five levels together are called normal form. Generally, taking a design to the third normal form will result in a good relational design. Third normal form for the majority of relational database designs is the optimal design because at this level the data is dependent solely on the key, and the redundancies, which can cause update anomalies, have been eliminated. There is a modified third normal form called the *Boyce-Codd normal form* (BCNF), which basically requires every column to be a candidate key. In certain situations, however, there are reasons to go to fourth and sometimes fifth normal form, which define how multivalued dependencies and join dependencies are handled.

It literally takes chapters in data-modeling to explain all the details of the normal forms, but in most situations, simply following the rule for third normal form, listed in the previous answer, is sufficient.

For reference, these are the problems that the five normal forms remove from a design:

● **First normal form**   Removes repeating groups

● **Second normal form**   Removes attributes (columns) that are dependent on part of a composite key

● **Third normal form**   Ensures that non-key columns are not functionally dependent on other non-key columns

● **Fourth normal form**   Removes multiple independent multivalued data

● **Fifth normal form**   Removes interdependent columns

 What is a star schema, and where is it most useful?

A star schema design is used to represent data for OLAP (online analytical processing) systems. You have a large table with data that you want to investigate. This table is called the fact table. The primary key of this table consists of foreign keys that point to dimensions of the data. Popular dimensions are time, geographic location, branch, channel, customer type, and so on. With OLAP tools, you can slice the data into

multiple dimensions, such as average sales per region by month by customer type. Once you find anomalies, you can go deeper into a dimension (for example, look at the data by month instead of by week).

Star schemas are not appropriate for all data, though. If dimensions get too large, the processing gets too heavy and produces too much resulting data. At that point, the concept doesn't work anymore. DB2 supports OLAP processing by means of CUBE and ROLLUP SQL functions.

 ## What is a snowflake schema?

A snowflake is a special form of a star schema in which the dimensions, instead of being single tables, have relations with dependent tables (hierarchical parent-child relationships). If you draw the design it looks like a snowflake. These additional hierarchies generall cause difficult table joins to be used during processing.

If the dimensions have too many relations, you might have over-normalized the model. In that case, consider denormalizing, because the SQL to be coded can get very complex.

Note: *In relational database design, the word relation is used to represent a relationship between two entiries. In simpler terms, there is a parent table which has a child table. For example, a parent table could be about your bank account, and the child table could be your checking transactions. The information in the child table would contain the account number "relating" the child to the proper account information in the parent table.*

What is a multistar schema?

A multistar is the opposite of a snowflake. The primary key has multiple relations from the same key or attributes (table columns) left that do not point to other tables. Normally this is the result of improper design or denormalizing. You should be able to recognize this kind of design; it should be redesigned to follow a more appropriate model.

Should all logical relationships map to physical referential-integrity relationships?

No, but then again this is a matter of hotly contested debate.

If data is read-only, as in data warehousing, it may not be necessary to enforce referential integrity during insert, update, and delete operations. However, there are some data warehouses that are refreshed with loaded data that is not necessarily pure—we feel this is a mistake in design, but in some of those cases declarative referential integrity is used. So with read-only systems, it can be more in the way than being a good thing. But with a system that has data updates, it is good practice to implement physical declarative referential integrity and to use triggers for the exception cases when referential integrity cannot be declared in the DDL (declarative referential integrity).

Now we need to take this one step further. Not all physical designs map to the original logical designs; additional relationships are sometimes created to make the system functional. Physical designs that map 100 percent to logical designs tend to be "performance-challenged" physical designs. There are other entities (tables) that can be defined in a logical model that never appear in the physical mode, such as code tables that might have only a few values. Rather than build a physical table to hold those values, they have be implemented through SQL DDL table check constraints. The physical conforms to the model but does not implement the model precisely.

What is metadata?

Metadata is basically data about data. It provides a description of each entity in a logical design as well as the attributes of the entity. You can think of metadata as being a series of tables that describe the data in the application's tables, such as definitions and properties for the table and each column in the table. Metadata is often found in data dictionaries that have been defined for a database application. This is a topic about which entire books have been written.

PHYSICAL DESIGN

 What are some guidelines for an optimal physical design?

The following are some general guidelines for an optimal physical design. First, design for reduced CPU overhead by considering the following points:

- **Number of SQL statements**   This is directly related to design, not to the application itself. When the design allows for navigating the data or using too many access modules, unnecessary SQL statements need to be used, driving up the resource cost of running the application. The design should be one that allows for much of the processing complexity to be encapsulated into SQL statements that do not require repetitive use. The cost of the system is directly related to how the data is stored and what SQL can be used to retrieve all the necessary data easily.

- **Number of rows/columns retrieved**   Updates are an application requirement but the number of rows retrieved is a design consideration. Retrieving unnecessary rows and columns drives up the cost of processing, generally many times that which would be required if the design were proper.

- **Sorts**   Sorting is a physical design issue related to the use and number of indexes, since some sorts would not be necessary if the proper physical indexes were defined. Sorting is also an application-design issue, since it is also dependent on the proper use of SQL, which may be able to minimize sorts.

Second, properly define and tune the following components and features in order to use the minimal amount of real I/O:

- Large buffer pools
- Multiple buffer pools

- Asynchronous write
- Sequential prefetch
- Multi-index use
- List prefetch
- No sequential prefetch
- No list prefetch

Third, all designs should minimize the locking contention so that concurrency is not an issue and so the data is fully available to applications. Keep the following points in mind during the design process to ensure data concurrency and availability.

- Design the database to minimize lock contention
- Design the database to avoid deadlocks
- Design applications taking all the concurrency issues into consideration

Can I model a given workload and its effects on my physical design?

IBM has a free product called DB2 Estimator that can forecast the resources used by a program. This product is distributed with DB2 Version 5, but it also can be downloaded from the IBM Web site; since DB2 Estimator is enhanced regularly, downloading from the Web is the best approach.

DB2 Estimator models transactions, batch programs, utilities, and so on. The tool needs a lot of input, but you can download most of this input from the DB2 Catalog (for existing applications) or you can input it all (for building new applications). Many consultants have reported that, if used correctly, the tool is good for modeling. With it, you can see that if your workload grows, the resource usage does not grow linearly.

Several independent software vendors (ISVs) have solutions for modeling bufferpools, Coupling Facilities, DASD, I/O, and other places where performance problems can occur.

What is a good method for determining whether DB2 can handle my physical design?

The DB2 Estimator tool from IBM, and other tools from ISVs, can assist in making accurate predictions. These tools have been proven to be very precise in modeling performance characteristics and in trying out different indexing structures for accessing data.

Are there any physical design considerations for a database in a data-sharing environment?

In theory, the movement to DB2 data sharing on the OS/390 servers should not have any impact on your database design or your application. However, in reality this is often not true, especially if you want your applications to perform well in the data-sharing environment. Before migrating to this environment, you should take a look at your physical objects and redesigning some of them.

For instance, you should partition tables, where possible, so that different partitions can reside on different members in the data-sharing group. Partitioning is also very helpful in exploiting parallelism. You may also want to separate the objects in the database so that read-only tables reside on one member, while read-write tables reside on another. These recommendations will help to split the workload across members.

Another table design issue that you want to eliminate is the use of row-level locking. In a data-sharing environment, row-level locking causes unnecessary overhead for the Coupling Facility, since each row accessed on a page can cause a lock to be acquired instead of just the one lock required for the page. You would want to either specify LOCKSIZE PAGE or TABLE. Row-level locking can be simulated by using MAXROWS = 1 (in Version 5) or by having a high PCTFREE to only allow one row per page, at least after a REORG. Another way to simulate row-level locking is to pad the row size so only one row fits on a page. In DB2 Version 6, there are two new page sizes of 8KB and 16KB, each of which would only require one lock.

There is much more information about data sharing in Chapter 14.

When migrating an application from IMS/DB to DB2 on OS/390, should a segment always map one-for-one to a DB2 table?

Not generally. Most, though not all, of the IMS designs are process-oriented designs, not relational designs. Process designs that are moved straight into DB2 generally cause an increase in CPU consumption between 1.5 and 2 times what was required before. In addition, if a one-for-one approach is taken, the data retrieval might be accomplished with minimal I/O in IMS compared to that required in DB2. The best way to migrate an application is to remodel the data for the relational design, map the processes to the data, and tune the physical design to support the data access.

Are there any restrictions when defining cyclical RI relationships?

A cyclical RI relationship is one in which there are two or more tables with each table being dependent on the one before it and the first is a dependent of the last. This means that every table in the cycle is a descendent of itself. You cannot create a cyclical relationship where a table has a delete rule involving the same table. Therefore, you cannot define a delete rule of CASCADE when there are only two tables in the relationship. If there are more than two tables in the cycle, at least two delete rules must not be CASCADE. However, for a self-referencing table, the delete must be CASCADE.

Caution: *Do not set all the delete rules to RESTRICT when none of the foreign keys allow nulls because you will not be able to delete any of the rows from the table.*

When do I use the data type VARCHAR when designing columns for a table?

In general, the use of the VARCHAR (variable character) datatype is only preferred to the CHAR (character) datatype if the amount of space to be saved is significant (only in the tablespace, not in indexes). The use of VARCHAR should be for columns whose values vary considerably in length. The

following are some points to keep in mind about the use of VARCHAR columns:

● Do not use VARCHAR columns unless modeling shows that it provides a benefit.

● Do not use VARCHAR columns for DASD savings:

   ● If an EDITPROC is in place for DASD compression, VARCHAR is not needed for space savings.

   ● If you are using DB2 compression (hardware only, please), VARCHAR is not needed for space savings.

● Consider putting the variable data into a separate table, linked via primary/foreign key indexes.

● Consider using multiple rows of fixed length with a sequence number instead of VARCHAR to allow textual data of any length to be handled.

● Consider using a fixed-length column instead of VARCHAR for most uses, and put the overflow in another table. This works where the data is usually near the same length.

Caution: *Do not expect the above design tactics to come from logical design. These are physical design issues.*

   • *Do not update the logical design with these physical design techniques.*

   • *Do update the data dictionary with these changes.*

Caution: *VARCHAR has a 2-byte overhead per value and will require some additional processing. It is also messy to handle in some languages.*

How do I design table row-length with minimal wasted space on a page?

When you define the length of the columns, make sure you do not define them to be just slightly longer than half a page.

(On OS/390 a full page is 4KB or 32KB through Version 5 and 4KB, 8KB, 16KB, and 32KB in Version 6. On UNIX / NT / OS/2 platforms, a page can either be 4KB or 8KB.) Doing so would allow only one row to fit on each page, leaving the rest of the page empty and unused. Defining a column length to be less than half a page will allow for more rows to fit on the page. This applies to tables that are not going to be compressed.

Tip: *When figuring out how long your row should be, do not forget to add in the DB2 overhead on each page.*

When should I use nulls?

A null value is basically a way to represent the absence of any value. A null is not the same as a zero value for arithmetic or a blank value for character data. Nulls should not be used for everything, but they do have their place. (This is a hotly debated topic that has been raging in the industry for 20 years).

For example, if a full-time employee record has a HIRE_DATE field and a RELEASE_DATE field, the value for RELEASE_DATE would not be NOT NULL (because you do not want to have to supply an employee's last day), or NOT NULL WITH DEFAULT (because defaulting to the day the employee record was entered would not make sense). Therefore, the only valid value for a RELEASE_DATE would be a NULL value (although some applications use 12/31/9999 as a default end date, which cases other problems).

DB2 will not calculate NULLS in functions, such as averages, minimums, and maximums. There is an additional byte in the table to hold the null flag for each null column.

 Caution: *The use of nulls can affect the results of queries. NULLS are not used in normal arithmetic comparisons, and you should use outer joins when joining columns that contain nulls.*

> *Note:*   *NULL should never be the default for column values. It should only be used when fully justified, and all the implications must be fully understood. For example, what should a true or false test return if a column value is null?*

How should I implement code and reference tables?

The following are some recommendations on the use of code and reference tables:

- **Small code tables**   Load these tables into memory tables or use SQL DDL table check constraints.

- **Replicate code tables**   It is possible to have multiple occurrences of these types of tables, but only for very heavily accessed code and reference tables. This is an uncommon situation and requires a data synchronization process to make sure that the tables are always updated the same way. It is also very important to never use DB2 RI for these tables, because these are not parent-child relationships. Edit validations should be accomplished by using table check constraints, insert triggers, or single functional stored procedures. In other words, do not create large RI trees just to perform simple editing.

- **Information that is not coded**   In many cases, it is possible to store unchanging data values in tables and avoid using code tables, such as for state abbreviations in Australia, provinces in Canada, or days of the week. This technique also has its place for short-lived data and where code description misspellings cannot occur.

- **Code tables combined into one code table**   One very good way to deal with code and lookup tables that have similar formats is to combine them in one table that has a code type column to differentiate the rows. When this is done, do not cluster on the primary index but on the code column, which spreads the data around through the table to permit concurrency of use. Then put the index in separate bufferpool, making it a memory-resident index, and if possible, put the entire table in a bufferpool. An example of the format of the table would be:

Table id column   Code id column   Description column   Optional nullable columns

---

> **Tip:**　*If would be optimal for performance to have all code tables and their associated indexes totally loaded into one buffer pool sized to hold all the pages. Then, since the data access is nearly always random, set the buffer pool threshold parameter VPSEQT to 0 to turn off any attempts at prefetch.*

If my business requirements include a data type that DB2 does not provide, what are my options?

In order to be able to accommodate a type of data that is not a standard data type in DB2, you can use user-defined data types (UDTs). UDTs are created based upon the existing data types in DB2, providing a more descriptive definition of the data. In the following example, a UDT has been created to support the new euro currency. We would then create a table column using the new data type.

```
CREATE DISTINCT TYPE euro
AS DECIMAL(11,2)  WITH COMPARISONS

CREATE TABLE european_sales
   (item    CHAR(10),
   quantity SMALLINT,
   cost    EURO)
```

How do I design a table to hold multimedia objects?

In order to design a table that will hold multimedia objects, such as medical x-rays or videos, you will need to create columns using special data types. In DB2 OS/390 Version 5, these datatypes are LONG VARCHAR and LONG VARGRAPHIC. In DB2 UDB on UNIX / NT / OS/2 and DB2 OS/390 Version 6, LOB (Large Object) datatypes are supported as well, but there are new data types that are a superset of the other two. These data types are BLOB (binary large object), CLOB (character large object), and DBCLOB (double-byte character large object). The following example shows how to create a table to hold an audio message.

```
CREATE TABLE voice_response
   (call_option   char(1),
    audio_response blob(10M) NOT LOGGED COMPACT);
```

The options NOT LOGGED and COMPACT tell DB2 not to log updates to the field and to decrease the amount of space required to hold the object, respectively.

The maximum size of large objects (LOBs) is 2GB per column. These could be used to support a variety of items, such as check images, audio, video (a 2GB LOB could hold up to 2 hours), or lengthy documents. When an LOB column is defined, special functions are needed to handle the processing; for text, image, audio, and video, a special set of extenders are available. These extenders are for data definition, user-defined functions (UDFs), and special processing programs such as search engines, to make dealing with these data types easier for users.

Another feature that will make using LOBs safer is the addition of user-defined data types (UDTs), also called distinct types. LOB columns of binary data (BLOBs) don't really describe the data type, since a BLOB could hold x-rays, audio, or video; it is useful to create a datatype for each of these types of data and define the column using those terms. UDTs are defined objects but they are only known within the DB2 subsystem (OS/390) or database (non-OS/390) where they are created. Even within the same subsystem or database, there could be two definitions of the same UDT with variations, since they are qualified with the schema name.

Casting functions allow operations between different data types—for example, comparing a slide from a video UDT to an expression. You must CAST the expression to a UDT type (video in this example) in order for the comparison to work. There are casting functions supplied with DB2 (CHAR, INTEGER, and so on) and there are others created automatically whenever a UDT is created with the CREATE DISTINCT TYPE statement.

What are some guidelines for the number of tablespaces per database?

There is a world of difference between the OS/390 platform and the other platforms in regards to this issue. On OS/390, a database is a naming convention, and on the other platforms, a database is primarily a single structure (like a disk subdirectory).

On the OS/390, a technique often used in support of 24×7 operations is to have one tablespace per database. This is done to remove DBD locking problems when altering data structures in a database. It also reduces the contiguous memory required for loading a single DBD structure into the EDM pool and reduces the amount of logging that occurs when changes are made to the DBD. However, it requires much more effort on the part of the administrative staff. The total number of pages from all the DBDs is larger than would be required in a single DBD, due to the DBD header pages. This also is not a problem, just a point to understand.

When designing a database in DB2 on platforms other than OS/390, it is important to choose the scope of the database carefully, because your choice will affect how it is used:

- The database will determine what objects can be used in an SQL statement, because in order to access tables you must first CONNECT to the database in which they reside. There are also several other commands that are used at a database level for monitoring and administration.

- The database sets the defaults for some parameters used to create tablespaces, such as the size of the tablespace extents (DFT_EXTENT_SZ).

- Each database will contain its own set of catalog tables to keep track of the objects in the database.

- The database can serve as a point of recovery for such operations as RESTORE and ROLLFORWARD.

- You will not be able to join tables together using normal application SQL if they exist in separate databases.

PERFORMANCE AND AVAILABILITY

 ## Why do I need to partition my tablespace?

There are several advantages to partitioning a tablespace:

- For large tables, partitioning is the only way to store large amounts of data (DB2 OS/390 Version 5 permits 254 partitions up to 4GB each, and Version 6 permits 254 partitions up to 64GB each). Nonpartitioned tablespaces are limited to 64GB of data.

- Partitioning will allow you to take advantage of query, CPU, and sysplex parallelism. Even defining a table with one partition will allow a query involving a join to enable CPU parallelism.

- You can take advantage of the ability to execute utilities on separate partitions in parallel. This also gives you the ability to access data in certain partitions while utilities are executing on others.

- In a data-sharing environment, you can spread partitions among several members to split workloads.

- You can also spread your data over multiple volumes and need not use the same storage group for each dataset belonging to the tablespace. This also allows you to place frequently accessed partitions on faster devices.

However, even with all the advantages of having partitioned tablespaces, you must keep a few disadvantages in mind when deciding about partitions. For instance, currently you cannot use the ALTER statement to add additional partitions to your table. Also, more datasets are normally opened for partitioned tablespaces, and a tablespace scan for a partitioned tablespace may be less efficient than one for a segmented tablespace (unless the SQL is coded to allow the optimizer to use page-range scans).

 ## Are there any benefits to designing a table with only one partition?

As of DB2 Version 5 on OS/390, a single-partition tablespace can participate in query parallelism, where a simple or segmented tablespace cannot. In those cases, where a single

non-partitioned table is being used in queries that use partial parallelism, it would be beneficial to partition that non-partitioned table. It is worth noting that DB2 Version 6 will allow any table to participate in query parallelism.

 What are the advantages of designing a tablespace as segmented on OS/390?

In the cases where a table is not partitioned, you should be using segmented tablespaces, and never simple tablespaces. A segmented tablespace organizes pages of the tablespace into segments, and each segment will only contain the rows of one table. Segments can be composed of 4 to 64 pages each, and each segment will have the same number of pages. The segment size will be determined at the time the tablespace is created (for guidelines on defining a segment size, see Chapter 7).

There are several advantages to using segmented tablespaces:

● Since the pages in a segment will only contain rows from one table, there will be no locking interference with other tables. In simple tablespaces, rows are intermixed on pages, and if one table page is locked, it can inadvertently lock a row of another table just because it is on the same page.

● If a table scan is performed, the segments belonging to the table being scanned are the only ones accessed; empty pages will not be scanned.

● If a mass delete or a DROP table occurs, segment pages are available for immediate reuse, and it is not necessary to run a REORG utility. Mass deletes are also much faster for segmented tablespace, and they produce less logging. Also, the COPY utility will not have to copy empty pages left by a mass delete.

● When inserting records, some read operations can be avoided by using the more comprehensive space map of the segmented tablespace.

● By being able to safely combine several tables in a tablespace, you can reduce the number of open datasets necessary.

 Note: When using a segmented tablespace to hold more than one table, make sure the tables have very similar characteristics in all categories, including backup and recovery strategies.

When should I use highly clustered indexes?

Although this might not always be possible, highly clustered secondary indexes should be constructed in certain situations.

Consider an index that has a high number of duplicates. If a scan is required for a set of like data, and the index is highly unclustered, the amount of random I/O will be high because data access, not index access, will be used. This will contribute to a slower response. Index-only access would generally not be chosen by the optimizer, even if the data required was completely contained within the index. There are often ways we can use when picking columns for this type of index that would match more closely the actual ordering of the data in the table. This ordering would allow the index to be selected by the optimizer as an access path, reducing the amount of I/O.

Do I always need an index on a foreign key?

Yes, in the majority of cases an index is necessary on a foreign key. The performance of a DELETE operation can be significantly affected when a referential constraint is involved.

For example, checking to see whether there are dependent rows when a parent row is to be deleted could cause a scan if the dependent table has no index on the foreign key with the starting columns of the index. The index can contain more columns than are defined in the foreign key and it will still be used, as long as the foreign key columns match the first columns of the index. Having this index is even more important when there is a cascading delete that could involve several tables.

By creating indexes for foreign key columns, you can reduce this impact. Although an index is not required to be created on a foreign key, it is highly recommended because many RI operations could result in multiple scans of multiple tables, and depending on the size of the tables, this could be very costly.

 Tip: *In Chapter 4, in the Catalog Information Queries section, there is a query that will help you find any existing foreign keys without indexes.*

When should I denormalize my tables for performance?

There are trade-offs to be made when normalizing tables. While the rules of normalization tells us to break tables apart in order to avoid redundancies and inconsistencies, there may be performance implications if these normalized tables are regularly being joined together. In the past, if there were tables being joined together on a regular basis, you would have considered denormalizing them (joining them together in one table) in order to avoid the overhead of the join process during each SQL execution. However, since the early 1990s, DB2 has evolved sophisticated joining methods and improved performance. Denormalization should not be needed for performance reasons today. If it appears necessary for this reason, there may be problems with the overall table design. There may also be a few rare cases where denormalization is necessary, such as in a read-only data warehouse environment.

When should I define a table using row-level locking?

All DB2 platforms support row-level locking and table locking, and the OS/390 platform supports row-, page-, table-, and tablespace-level locking. In UDB, row-level locking would normally be used.

On OS/390, row-level locking should only be used in very special cases when multiple users will simultaneously need a page of data but each user's interest in update mode is on different rows. Use row-level locking only if the increase of the cost of locking (CPU overhead) is tolerable and the need for that level of currency is real, and not a result of design problems. The more rows per page, the more users per page and the higher the resource overhead of locking. If the users' interest is on the same rows, referred to as "hot rows," row-level locking will not have any positive impact on concurrency and will only increase the CPU used for locking—in this case, with OS/390 it would be better to use page-level locking.

Chapter 7

Creating Database Objects

Answer Topics!

Creating Database Objects @ a Glance

Creating database objects is a straightforward process when using either DDL or a GUI interface. However, many questions arise about the content of the objects, and this chapter answers those questions.

When creating tablespaces, many questions arise concerning definitions for features such as compression, space allocations, concurrency, and segmentation. Tables contain column definitions, but even that raises many questions concerning referential integrity, temporary tables, column data types, and logging features. When you create indexes, you may have questions about when to reorg an index, what the foreign key requirements are, and how many indexes is too many—these questions are answered here.

In each family member of DB2, there are some differences not only in the definitions and objects but in the type of objects that exist. Questions concerning individual platform features are answered as well, especially in the area of UNIX / NT / OS/2 which has advanced enhancements, such as automatic summary tables.

TABLESPACES

What kind of DASD savings and CPU overhead can I expect when using the COMPRESS(YES) option on an OS/390 tablespace?

Using DB2 compression on a tablespace will generally reduce the data storage required. The amount of reduction is determined by the frequency of patterns in the data. Predominantly character data tables across the industry have averaged about 60 percent reduction, while heavy arithmetic data tables have average reductions in the 10 to 20 percent range. Before using COMPRESS(YES), it is possible to use a compression utility analysis tool to determine what the compression will be.

When compression is used in conjunction with the hardware assist feature, there is almost no measurable overhead for retrieval and only minimal overhead for compression. If the hardware assist feature is not used, the software emulation for compression carries significant CPU overhead, the amount varying for each table and its associated use. I/O overhead is also reduced, since more logical data is transferred per I/O. Generally, it is beneficial to try to use compression on most large tables.

Should I use MAXROWS 1 or LOCKSIZE ROW to achieve maximum benefits for row-level locking on OS/390?

DB2 on UNIX / NT / OS/2 has had row-level locking, but on OS/390 this is a relatively new feature. The CREATE TABLESPACE parameters MAXROWS 1 and LOCKSIZE ROW can essentially provide you with greater concurrency by locking on a single row only. The MAXROWS 1 can result in an over-allocation of space if you have a small row size, but it is preferable for tables in a data-sharing environment to reduce overhead for the additional locks propagated to the coupling facility when using row-level locking. The MAXROWS parameter can be altered (values 1 to 255) and will take place immediately for all newly added rows;

however, it is recommended that you reorganize the tablespace after an alteration of this nature.

Should I use LOCKSIZE PAGE or LOCKSIZE ANY on OS/390?

Although LOCKSIZE ANY is the default, which would allow DB2 to chose the size of a lock, a better choice is to choose the most suitable lock for the table, considering the application's needs. In the majority of cases, to achieve maximum concurrency with the least amount of overhead, LOCKSIZE PAGE is better.

How do I determine what to set the SEGSIZE to for a segmented tablespace?

SEGSIZE is what tells DB2 on OS/390 how large to make each segment for a segmented tablespace, and it will determine how many pages are contained in a segment. The SEGSIZE will vary, depending on the size of the tablespace. Recommendations are as follows:

Number of Pages	SEGSIZE
28 or less	4 to 28
between 28 and 128	32
128 or more	64

How do I determine FREEPAGE and PCTFREE for my tablespace or indexspace?

The FREEPAGE and PCTFREE clauses (new in DB2 Version 5.2 UNIX / NT / OS/2) are used help improve the performance of updates and inserts by allowing free space to exist on tablespaces or indexspaces. Performance improvements include improved access to the data through better clustering of data, less index page splitting, faster inserts, fewer row overflows, and a reduction in the number of REORGs required. Some trade-offs will include an increase in the number of pages (and therefore more DASD needed), fewer rows per I/O and less efficient use of bufferpools, and more pages to scan. As a result, it is important to achieve a good

balance for each individual tablespace and indexspace when deciding on free space, and that balance will depend on the processing requirements of each tablespace or indexspace. When inserts and updates are performed, DB2 will use the free space defined, and by doing this it can keep records in clustering sequence as much as possible. When the free space is used up, the records must be located elsewhere, and this is when performance can begin to suffer. Read-only tables do not require any free space.

 Note: *On UNIX / NT / OS/2 UDB, the free space for inserts and for maintaining the free space can be turned off by using the ALTER TABLE parameter of APPEND, which specifies that all new data is appended at the end of the table.*

FREEPAGE on OS/390 is the number of full pages inserted between each empty page during a LOAD or REORG of a tablespace or indexspace. The trade-off is between how often reorganization can be performed versus how much DASD can be allocated for an object. FREEPAGE should be used for tablespaces so that inserts can be kept as close to the optimal page as possible. For indexes, FREEPAGE should be used for the same reason, but improvements would be in terms of reduced index page splits. FREEPAGE is useful when inserts are sequentially clustered.

PCTFREE is the percentage of a page left free during a LOAD or REORG. PCTFREE is useful when you can assume an even distribution of inserts across the key ranges.

 ### Should I use CLOSE YES or CLOSE NO for tablespace and indexspace creation, and how is this affected by the DSMAX DSNZPARM?

DB2 defers closing and deallocating tablespaces or indexes until the number of open datasets reaches the current OS/390 limit for the number of concurrently open datasets, or until the number of open datasets reaches 99 percent of the value that you specified for DSMAX. If the DSMAX limit is reached, DB2 will close 3 percent of the datasets not in use. The CLOSE parameter identifies whether or not the tablespace should be closed if the tablespace is not being used and the limit on the number of open datasets is reached.

Using CLOSE YES allows the tablespace to be closed. CLOSE NO means that under normal circumstances the tablespace is to be left open. However, if DSMAX is reached and no CLOSE YES page sets have been defined, CLOSE NO datasets will be closed.

Tip: *The actual number of concurrently open datasets cannot exceed the OS/390 limit. This limit defaults to 10,000 but can be changed by using a listed IBM APAR.*

What is the maximum size of a DB2 tablespace (V5/V6) on OS/390?

In DB2 for OS/390 Version 5, the maximum size of the tablespace can be up to 1TB (terabyte). A tablespace can have up to 254 partitions, and each can hold up to 4GB of data. In Version 6 this is increased to a maximum of 16TB with each partition capable of holding up to 64GB of data.

What are the benefits of using segmented tablespaces on OS/390 when I only have one table per tablespace?

One major benefit to segmented tablespaces is that rows from different tables will never be intermixed on the same page; therefore, a lock on one table will not impact another table. When you only have one table per tablespace, this is not an issue; however, there are still several benefits to having a segmented tablespace for one table. The major benefit is that the tablespace will contain a segmented space map, and this will help with the speed of inserts and deletes.

How can I turn off lock escalation?

Lock escalation can be turned off by setting the LOCKMAX parameter to 0 on the CREATE TABLESPACE statement.

```
CREATE TABLESPACE tablespace-name IN database-name …
LOCKMAX 0

ALTER TABLESPACE tablespace-name.database-name …
LOCKMAX 0
```

 Note: *The object must be stopped (using STOP) and restarted (using START) for the ALTER to take effect.*

In order to use LOCKMAX effectively, the lock size must be set to either LOCKSIZE PAGE or ROW. This option can be used for user tables or for catalog tables. The one caution is to make sure that applications are committing frequently enough, or there is a chance of violating the NUMLKTS (locks per tablespace) DSNZPARM set in the DSNTIPJ installation panel. Other options for the LOCKMAX parameter that are less severe include LOCKMAX x, where you can set x to be the maximum number of page or row locks held by an application before lock escalation can occur, and LOCKMAX SYSTEM, which allows for lock escalation only when the NUMLKTS DSNZPARM is reached.

What are the benefits of using LOCKPART YES for tablespace partitions?

By using the LOCKPART YES parameter on the CREATE TABLESPACE statement for a partitioned tablespace, you enable selective partition locking (SPL). This basically moves the tablespace locks to the partition level. This will allow for only the partitions being accessed to be locked, instead of locks being taken against all the partitions in the tablespace. There are conditions that must be met in order for selective partition locking to work. For instance, partition level locking will not work if there is a Type 1 index used in the access path, if the plan is bound ACQUIRE(ALLOCATE), if the tablespace was created with LOCKSIZE TABLESPACE, or if LOCK TABLE IN EXCLUSIVE MODE is used without the PART keyword. This parameter can be altered by using the ALTER TABLESPACE parameter, and the entire tablespace must be stopped using the –STOP DATABASE command.

How can I change free space on a tablespace or indexspace after it has been created?

You can use ALTER to change the FREEPAGE and PCTFREE parameters after creation, even after data has been loaded. The command is as follows:

```
ALTER TABLESPACE PCTFREE 20
```

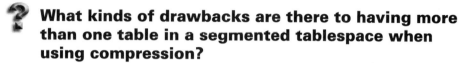

The new values will only take effect after a REORG has been performed on the altered tablespace or indexspace.

 What kinds of drawbacks are there to having more than one table in a segmented tablespace when using compression?

When compressing a tablespace with multiple tables, you will still see improvements in reducing the space required and in increasing the amount of data transferred on each I/O due to the larger number of rows per page. The one general difficulty with compressing multiple table tablespaces is that the compression dictionary is not based on a specific table's data, but on data from all the tables. Depending on the size of the tables, a single large table in the segmented tablespace may get good compression while other smaller tables will get none, due to the dictionary matching the increased frequency of occurrences in the larger table. A compression dictionary should never be built for a multiple table tablespace using a load utility, as this would create a dictionary based on the one table being loaded.

TABLES

How many tables should I have in a tablespace?

One table per tablespace is still a very good rule of thumb, because that way the individual needs of tables can be defined. Free space, locking, size, and volume placement can be addressed on a per table basis if you have one table per tablespace. However, with the industry movement toward software ERP (Enterprise Resource Planning) packages, such as SAP and Peoplesoft, we find that this is not feasible due to the large number of tables. It would not be manageable to have each table in its own tablespace, because the open dataset maximum limit would be exceeded. In cases like these it is best to group the tables together based on their usage (for example, read-only tables or static code tables in one tablespace) or on application function.

 ### Should referential integrity be placed on all related tables?

Everything is good in moderation. DB2 declarative RI (referential integrity) is no exception. RI should be used as much as possible to define the relationships that business processes depend on. It is much safer to use declarative RI than application-controlled RI, since in most programmed RI situations; ghost data (missing dependencies) gets into the database. Items like code tables and reference tables are not a good choice for RI, since using these usually requires large RI trees to be built containing many tables. Data validation by code tables should be handled through some other means than RI. Trees with many levels can also be difficult to handle, so watch for tree depth. If it is necessary for a tree to extend to many levels, there is probably an over-normalization of the data. If the depth of the multilevel tree is valid but has too many levels, then the RI tree should perhaps be broken into two, using a common program (such as a stored procedure or trigger) to maintain the relationships between the two trees.

 ### How can I recreate a dropped table on OS/390?

If a full image copy of the table is available, you will first want to create a new table exactly the same as the dropped table, and then run DSN1COPY using the image copy for input and specify the OBID, DBID translation. This will create a table from the current image copy, and then you will want to image copy this. If the table was defined using user-defined datasets (VSAM), the clusters can be used as the input for the DSN1COPY, and the data will be current up until the time of the dropping of the table.

 ### What are the benefits of creating a global temporary table vs. creating a permanent table on OS/390?

Global temporary tables can be used much like regular tables except that these tables are not logged, not recoverable, and have no indexes. One difference from a normal table is that only inserts can be performed—updates and deletes are not allowed. Global temporary tables are very useful for stored procedures. For example, they can be used as a holding area for non-relational or non-DB2 data, such as data extracted from VSAM files. The data will be held for the duration of the unit-of-work and can be referenced in SQL statements. This is particularly valuable when a LEFT or FULL OUTER JOIN is required using one DB2 table and one non-DB2 table(for example, using VSAM data). An INSERT statement can load the global temporary table with the VSAM data, and then the following SQL statement can perform the outer join:

```
SELECT * FROM T1 LEFT JOIN global-temp-name ON join predicates
```

This technique logically fits in a stored procedure, so that any other process that needs the result can simply execute it. The benefit is that the DB2 join algorithms are used to perform the outer join instead of a home-grown program.

Another major benefit of global temporary tables is to use them when a materialized set is present for a result set, a view, or a table expression, and the materialized set needs to be used more than once.

Sometimes it is necessary to use a work-around in SQL due to the 15-table limit for an SQL statement. Global temporary tables can be used to hold the results of some of the tables until a later statement combines the global temporary table with the remaining tables. This will be required until Version 6 or V5 through an APAR when the limit will be raised from 15 tables in an SQL statement to 225 tables. Also, the current limit of only 15 tables in a join is also being lifted in V6 and through an APAR in V5.

Note: *The only access path available against a global temporary table is a tablespace scan, so keep the size of the scan in mind when doing performance analysis.*

Note: *When a global temporary table is used in a join, the access path will generally be a merge-scan-join that might require sorting the global temporary table.*

Note: *A global temporary table can be held longer than a unit-of-work when it is used inside a cursor definition that is defined WITH HOLD.*

 ## How do I create a global temporary table?

A global temporary table is created in the same manner as a normal table, through DDL, except that it is not physically created in a tablespace. These tables cannot be created with default values, and they cannot have unique, referential, or check constraints defined for them. The example below shows the creation of a global temporary table that will hold rows containing an amount and a date.

EXAMPLE:

```
CREATE GLOBAL TEMPORARY TABLE SUMMARY
    (AMOUNT_SOLD DECIMAL(5,2) NOT NULL,
    SOLD_DATE DATE NOT NULL)
```

An empty instance of the table is created when the first implicit or explicit reference is made to it in an SQL statement. In normal use, an insert would be the first statement issued. The temporary table only exists until the originating application commits, does a rollback, or terminates, unless the table is used in a cursor using the WITH HOLD option.

 ## Should I give consideration to where I place my VARCHAR columns in the CREATE TABLE statement?

The placement of VARCHAR columns in a table is critical for two reasons: one is the additional CPU required for retrieving columns that occur after the VARCHAR column in the physical row, and the other is to avoid unnecessary logging overhead.

VARCHAR columns should be placed near the end of the row, before all the frequently updated columns. The reasons have to do with logging overhead and the fact that all columns accessed for selection that follow a VARCHAR column require additional instructions to determine the column mapping, because it is based on the actual length of the VARCHAR column in the particular row. For more information on the performance implications of VARCHAR columns, see Chapter 16.

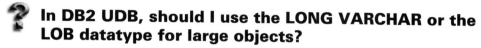

In DB2 UDB, should I use the LONG VARCHAR or the LOB datatype for large objects?

The selection of a LONG VARCHAR over a LOB (large object) column will depend on the size of the object you wish to store. The maximum size of a LONG VARCHAR field is 32KB, and the maximum size of a LOB is 2GB. LOBs are useful for storing such information as spreadsheets, photographs, faxes, audio recordings, and so on. However, there is additional overhead associated with storing LOBs (in addition to the overhead associated with both LONG VARCHARs and LOBs), because anywhere between 72 and 280 bytes are used for the descriptor of a row in a table. LONG VARCHAR only requires an additional 20 bytes for this descriptor.

What is the maximum number of columns in a table?

On OS/390, the maximum number of columns is 750 for a table that is not a dependent table in a referential integrity relationship. A dependent table can only have up to 749 columns defined.

In UDB on UNIX / NT / OS/2, 500 columns is the maximum for a 4KB page size, and 1012 columns for an 8KB page size.

Can I rename a table after I have created it?

Yes. A table can be renamed after creation by using the RENAME TABLE statement:

```
RENAME TABLE MY_TABLE TO YOUR_TABLE
```

You can change the name of the table while still preserving all privileges granted on the table and also not affecting any indexes defined. On OS/390, the OBID will remain the same, as well.

However, you cannot rename a table if it is referenced in a view, in a summary table definition, in a triggered SQL statement in existing triggers, or as the subject table of an existing trigger. In addition, the table cannot have any check constraints defined and cannot be parent or child in a

referential integrity relationship, nor can it be the scope of any existing reference column. Any plans or packages that reference the table will be invalidated and will have to be rebound.

What is the AUDIT parameter for the CREATE TABLE statement, and how do I use it?

The AUDIT parameter on the CREATE TABLE statement allows you to audit activity against a table. You can audit just changes, or you can choose to audit all activity against a table (options are NONE, CHANGES, or ALL). The audit function is only active when you start an audit trace, and it can be performed for individual IDs, if necessary. There is overhead with using the AUDIT feature, and it should only be used in exceptional cases.

When should I use the OBID parameter on the CREATE TABLE statement?

In normal circumstances, you would not need to specify the OBID when creating a DB2 table on OS/390. However, when there are specific situations in which the OBIDs are necessary (for example, restoring a table from a DSN1COPY), then this parameter should be used.

How much overhead is there when using DATA CAPTURE CHANGES?

The overhead for DATA CAPTURE CHANGES will depend on the type of processing occurring against the data, and it will have an impact on DB2 logging. For updates to data, this clause is used to capture the complete before and after images of a row on the DB2 log, whereas normal DB2 logging only records part of the row.

Inserts always get fully logged and will not contribute to any extra overhead for this option, and the same is true for deletes, except for mass deletes, which otherwise are simply marked on the space map page. Since DATA CAPTURE CHANGES needs to reference data pages changed, mass deletes are not performed on the space map but on the data page, and this will add additional overhead to the underlying process.

When a column is updated, all of the columns' before and after images are logged if you are using DATA CAPTURE CHANGES; so, unless the first and last column of a record are updated (in which case normal logging would log the entire record) this will result in additional logging. This overhead will, of course, depend on the percent of the record changed. The overhead associated with DATA CAPTURE CHANGES is generally only going to cause a performance concern when mass deletes are involved.

What is the largest table size, database size, and number of rows supported by DB2 UDB on UNIX / NT / OS/2 platforms?

The maximum number of rows is determined by partition size, and a single partition could theoretically hold 40 billion rows. The largest table size is also determined by partition, and the maximum partition size is 64GB. The current architectural limit imposes a maximum number of partitions at 1,000, so a single partitioned tablespace holding one table could be 64TB (terabytes) holding approximately 40,000 billion rows. But these are just the defined limits, and they also must be mapped into the type of storage being used, either DMS (data-managed storage) or SMS (system-managed storage). The maximum size of a long DMS tablespace is 2TB. The maximum size of an SMS tablespace is dependent on the hardware platform and operating system in use. There is probably some upper limit for the size of a database, but it is beyond a meaningful calculation and is generally just stated to be based on the maximum amount of storage that a platform can handle.

How can I influence the free space used when loading a table in DB2 UDB?

Prior to UDB Version 5.2, you could not influence free space when loading or reorganizing a table, as all inserted data was added to the end of the table. There was no concept of "free space" on the DB2 UDB platforms as there is on the DB2 OS/390 platform. That changed with the Version 5.2 enhancements, which added the PCTFREE (percent free)

parameter to the ALTER TABLE and CREATE INDEX statements. Also, an INDEXFREESPACE parameter was added to the LOAD command. These changes were made to indicate the amount of free space to be left on each page. If the previous method of adding inserts at the end of the table and not using free space is still desired, the parameter APPEND has been added to the ALTER TABLE statement to allow this.

How do I know which dependent table will be deleted first in a CASCADE delete of a parent with several children?

When using declarative referential integrity, the delete of a row in a parent table will be cascaded to the dependents in the order in which they were defined. To determine this order, you can query the SYSIBM.SYSRELS catalog table using the creation timestamp column to obtain the order of creation on OS/390; use the SYSIBM.SYSREFERENCES catalog table on the other platforms.

Should I use RI or check constraints when creating my tables?

Table check constraints provide you with the ability to better control the integrity of your data, as do to referential constraints and unique constraints. There may be situations where a business rule cannot be enforced through a referential or unique constraint because a more complex type of integrity is needed. Check integrity ensures that every row conforms to a check constraint that is defined on a table.

An example of where a check constraint may be used in place of a referential constraint is small code tables, where the RI is there simply to check code compliance (which is not a good use of RI). These codes (if relatively small in number, and static) could be more efficiently verified in a check constraint on the table.

How can I protect a table from accidentally being dropped?

In order to prevent a table from being accidentally dropped through the use of a DROP statement, use the WITH RESTRICT ON DROP clause on the CREATE TABLE statement, but only on OS/390. This will prevent not only the table from being dropped, but also the tablespace and database that store the table.

In DB2 UDB, how can I turn off logging on a table?

In order to turn off logging on a DB2 UDB table you would use the NOT LOGGED INITIALLY clause on the CREATE TABLE statement. This clause only applies to table changes made within the same transaction as the CREATE TABLE statement. The changes would not be recorded in the recovery log. This would be most useful during a load of a large table.

INDEXES

What are the benefits of using the PIECESIZE option on nonpartitioning indexes?

The DB2 OS/390 PIECESIZE option on index creation allows you to break a nonpartitioning index into several datasets (or "pieces"). A piece can be defined to be as large as 4GB; however, for practical purposes the PIECESIZE will normally be set so that a piece will fit on one DASD volume. This allows more appropriately placed datasets on different DASD volumes to relieve contention when the index is accessed. Currently, the use of the piece is limited just to physical partitioning and parallel access; however, in the future we may see the ability to reorganize or perhaps recover an individual piece.

What key indicators do I need to follow to determine if a REORG is necessary?

For any tablespace, a REORG is needed if any of the following apply (using statistics from the clustering index):

- Any dataset behind the tablespace has multiple extents
- CLUSTERRATIO < 90 percent
- (NEARINDREF + FARINDREF) / CARD > 10 percent
- FAROFFPOS / CARD > 5 percent
- NEAROFFPOS / CARD > 10 percent

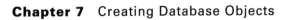

For any indexspace, a REORG is needed if any of the following apply:

- Any dataset behind the indexspace has multiple extents
- LEAFDIST > 200 if FREEPAGE is not equal to 0; LEAFDIST can be higher otherwise
- LEVELS have been increased, and LEVELS > 2

What are the benefits of Type 2 indexes on OS/390?

Type 2 indexes provide several benefits, the most important being the elimination of index locking and the reduction of lock requests, lock contentions, timeouts, and deadlocks. Others include better response time and CPU time than when using Type 1 indexes; less need to add free space for lock contention avoidance; suffix key compression in non-leaf pages; less need to add dummy columns to non-unique index keys to avoid performance problems during deletes; and CPU usage reductions averaging 15 to 50 percent for CHECK INDEX, REORG INDEX, and RUNSTATS INDEX utilities. There is an average 10 to 20 percent increase in the size of the index because of the additional 1 byte per RID and 2 bytes per key for Type 2 indexes. However, the benefits far outweigh the small increase in disk storage. As of Version 6 of DB2 for OS/390, Type 1 indexes will no longer be supported.

Should I create indexes on all my foreign keys?

It is very advisable to have indexes in place where the leading columns match the column definition of the foreign key. DB2 uses these indexes when validating constraints and enforcing referential integrity rules. Without the index to support the foreign key, DB2 would have to use a tablespace scan, adversely affecting performance.

What is the maximum number of indexes I can create on a table, and could there be any negative impact on performance?

The maximum number of indexes on a table in OS/390 is 200, and the UNIX / NT / OS/2 limit is 32,767. While indexes are key for query performance, there are performance implications for other DML functions, not to mention additional headaches in terms of maintenance. Inserts and deletes will have to be maintained in each index, as will updates if they involve index keys. Depending on the volume and sequence of inserts and updates, these will have a direct impact on the maintenance of the index and the frequency for reorganizations. The more indexes on the tables, the more REORGs are necessary. If there is no time is available for REORGs, performance for selects, updates, and inserts will suffer. Choose indexes wisely based on frequent data access, and evaluate index usage after definition. The general philosophy is to add indexes until it hurts, and then remove the last one.

Should my primary key always be defined as the clustering index?

Not necessarily. The primary key may not always be appropriate for a clustering index. The clustering index should be the index that most represents how the data is being accessed for set retrieval, and therefore how it should be stored. Normally the clustering sequence is designed to support range retrieval of data.

What happens to my data during INSERT processing or REORG processing if I do not explicitly create a clustering index?

When DB2 OS/390 processes an INSERT, it will choose the defined clustering index for insertion order. However if a clustering index has not been explicitly defined, DB2 will use the current oldest surviving index. Some call this the first index created, but contrary to popular belief, the default index chosen for insert processing is not the first index created on the table nor the index with the lowest OBID (object identifier). For example, if there were indexes A, B, C, and D on a table, and they had been defined in that order, and none was defined as the clustering index, index A would be chosen for inserts. If index A was dropped and redefined, it would become the "newest" index on the table, and index B would now be used for inserts. During the execution of the REORG utility, DB2 will choose the index to use for clustering the data in the same manner.

As of Version 5.2 of DB2 UDB, the clustering of indexes is an option; the data inserts on these platforms was handled differently before Version 5.2, and some will still want the non-clustering index method. During the execution of the REORG utility, you can specify an index to be used to order the result of the REORG if the clustering index was not defined. If no index is specified, the records are reorganized without regard to order.

VIEWS

 ## Should base table views be created?

Base table views were a common practice in the very early days of DB2. Today's recommendation is that base table views should only be used in very special situations. A base table view is a view containing all the columns in the table that the view is based on, or the primary subset of those columns. One place where base table views are used is where there are columns that need to be hidden from users and applications, such as security validation columns. In these cases, no authorizations for the base tables are granted to users or programs, only the authorizations for the views. This protects the security columns from unauthorized use.

Base table views can sometimes be more descriptive and meaningful if there are a lot of end-user ad hoc queries being used. For example, a column might be named TR_ACCT_CD, and the view name for that same column could be TRACK_ACCT_CODE. By using fully defined names, ad hoc users don't have to depend on looking up base column names that could be confusing and misleading.

 ## When should I use views rather than allowing direct table access?

Use views to simplify queries or to implement security for end-user access. Queries, such as certain joins, can be complex, but by using view definitions to handle the joins and allowing the outer referencing SQL to supply the restrictions, complex joins can be used by both end users and development staff as part of a standard development technique. This is *critically* important where a defined access path can be driven by the view, but could be missed by hard-coding the SQL in a different form.

Here is a simple example of a three-table join to define a standard business relationship:

```
CREATE VIEW ACCT_INVOICE_ITEMS
    (ACCT_NO, ACCT_NAME, INV_NO, INV_DATE, ITEM_NO, ITEM_AMT)
AS
SELECT  ACCT_NO, ACCT_NAME, INV_NO, INV_DATE, ITEM_NO, ITEM_AMT
FROM ACCTS, INVOICES, ITEMS
WHERE
    ACCTS.ACCT_NO = INVOICES.INV_ACCT_NO
    AND INVOICES.INV_NO = ITEMS.ITEM_INV_NO)
```

The SQL used by the users would be much more meaningful and easier to write, as shown here:

```
SELECT ACCT_NO, INV_NO, ITEM_NO
FROM ACCT_INVOICE_ITEMS
WHERE
    ACCT_NO BETWEEN 10 AND 100
    AND INV_DATE BETWEEN '1991-01-01' AND '1991-01-31'
```

 Can I restrict update capability though the use of a view, and how would I implement this?

There are many cases where it is preferable to restrict users and processes to only a subset of data from a table. Such a case could be where a particular user needs to work on payroll data just for departments 10 and 20. In such a case, we could create a view that filters the table to show just departments 10 and 20 and restrict updates to that same qualification. To restrict the ability to update rows through a view, use the following statement:

```
CREATE VIEW view-name AS subselect WITH CHECK OPTION
```

The WITH CHECK OPTION will check to see that the person updating with this view only affects the rows that they have access to. If the update qualifies rows outside the view, a negative SQL statement is returned.

 Can I create a view using concatenated columns?

Yes, the subselect that is supplied in the CREATE VIEW
statement (see the previous question) can include the
CONCAT keyword or | | symbol between column names for
the purpose of concatenating columns. A name should be
supplied for the expression using the AS clause.

OTHER OBJECTS

 How do I create and use a schema in DB2?

DB2 Version 6 on OS/390 will support the schema name
concept that is already implemented in UDB. A schema is a
logical group of database objects. The schema name is then
used to qualify these database objects. This could be used to
group objects by application. For example, you could create a
schema called INVENTORY using the following statement:

```
CREATE SCHEMA INVENTORY
```

You would then be able to qualify all objects used in the
inventory application by using the schema name as a
qualifier (for example, INVENTORY.PARTS). If you do not
specify a schema on an object when it is created, it will be
qualified with your authorization ID. Schemas can be used to
qualify tables, user-defined functions, user-defined datatypes,
views, triggers, and packages. Databases are not qualified by
a schema name.

 **How can I create new database objects similar to
existing objects in DB2 UDB?**

By using the DB2LOOK utility program, you can extract
DDL (Data Definition Language) from an existing DB2
database. You can not only extract the DDL for a given
database, but its statistics as well, by telling the DB2LOOK
program to build the necessary SQL UPDATE statements to
update the statistics in the DB2 catalog. This is a terrific way
to clone a database for testing purposes.

In DB2, how can I create my own specialized datatypes?

You can create custom datatypes, called distinct types, to enhance the use of DB2 built-in datatypes. This feature has been available in UDB and is now available in OS/390 DB2 Version 6. A distinct type will be based on a DB2-supplied datatype (source type) and it will have uniquely defined rules for comparisons and calculations that are applicable to your data.

For example, to create a distinct type, called CURRENCY, based on the decimal datatype, you could use the following statement:

```
CREATE DISTINCT TYPE CURRENCY
    AS DECIMAL(6,2) WITH COMPARISONS
```

The CURRENCY is based on the decimal datatype, but it will only be comparable with another occurrence of the same distinct type. By using the WITH COMPARISON clause, you are telling DB2 that this distinct type can be used in comparison operations with other occurrences of data using the same distinct type. The names of the distinct types must be unique within a schema.

Distinct types are kept in the DB2 catalog table called DATATYPES and can be given a description in this table. These datatypes can now be used by a CREATE TABLE statement or an ALTER TABLE statement.

How do I create and use automatic summary tables in DB2 UDB?

One of the enhancements in DB2 UDB 5.2 goes under the name of "aggregate aware optimization," which involves join and aggregate indexes called ASTs (automatic summary tables). In many applications, especially warehousing, there are often a large number of queries that do column aggregations like SUM. If you analyze these queries, generally you will find that these aggregations are repeated, and they perform the same aggregations over and over. Many times they may even repeat a subset of the original aggregation. In warehouses, these types of aggregations are usually performed on some of the dimension tables. Prior to UDB 5.2, there was no way to have these aggregations computed once and used over and over, and even if they were precomputed there was no way for the optimizer to select the precomputed data if a query was doing a similar type of aggregate computation. With the use of these ASTs, the aggregations are computed once and reused many times. It is even possible to retrieve data from external data sources in a warehouse, and cache the aggregations over this nonrelational data in ASTs, refreshing it as required. One of the major benefits in defining ASTs is that the optimizer can use them in satisfying preexisting queries, and no query rewrite is required.

The AST is created as are all other objects, through the use of a DDL CREATE statement. The following DDL statement shows how an AST is created using a star type join over a series of dimension tables:

```
CREATE TABLE star.my_aggregates AS (
    SELECT a.series, b.denoms, c.region, c.branch,
        SUM(d.sold) AS sold, SUM(e.redemed) as redeemed
    FROM star.a AS a, star.b AS b, star.c AS c, star.d AS d, star.e AS e
    WHERE e.something = a.something
    AND e.something = b.something
    AND b.something = c.something
    AND b.something = d.something
    GROUP BY a.series, b.denoms, c.region, c.branch
    ) DATA INITIALLY DEFERRED REFRESH DEFERRED;
```

Sometime after this particular DDL is used to create the definition, a refresh command will have to be used to populate the table, an index should be created on it, and a RUNSTATS should be used to update the catalog statistics.

Chapter 8

Utilities

Answer Topics!

Utilities @ a Glance

This chapter will answer some of the most frequently asked questions about using utilities to maintain the integrity and performance of a DB2 database. Regardless of the platform chosen for DB2, a basic set of utilities will always exist. This set will generally include utilities for data maintenance, including backups, reorganization, and recoveries. There are also platform-specific utilities used to maintain the subsystem catalog and to repair objects. Some details of the RECOVERY utility are presented here, but execution of the RECOVERY utility is covered in greater detail in Chapter 17. This chapter addresses such issues as scheduling the execution of various utilities, setting options to enhance execution for optimal performance, and using utilities to reset pending state conditions.

REORGANIZATION

 When should I reorganize my tablespaces and indexspaces?

One indicator that tablespaces should be reorganized is if the statistics in the NEARINDREF and FARINDREF fields in the SYSTABLEPART catalog table begin to increase. This increase indicates that the data is not being kept in clustering sequence either during inserts or updates requiring row relocation. A reorganization would put the data back in clustering sequence, and these values would be set back to zero. If this type of increase occurs, there may be a need to increase the PCTFREE or FREEPAGE on the tablespace to prevent these values from increasing too rapidly. Another problem could be that variable length fields are being updated causing rows to be relocated, or DB2 tablespace compression is turned on and therefore all updates may potentially cause row relocation. The consequence of having high numbers in the NEARINDREF and FARINDREF fields includes increased I/O activity and more time spent performing inserts and updates.

You can also review the NEAROFFPOS and FAROFFPOS fields in the SYSINDEXPART catalog table, for the clustering index, to determine if the data is still in clustering sequence order. Large numbers in these fields, particularly in the FAROFFPOS, can indicate that the data is not in clustering sequence. A reorganization of the tablespace would put the data back in clustering sequence.

To check whether your indexspace needs to be reorganized, review the LEAFDIST column in the SYSINDEXPART catalog table. Large numbers in the LEAFDIST column indicates that there are several pages between successive leaf pages, and using the index will result in additional overhead. In this situation, DB2 may turn off prefetch usage, as well. Reorganizing the indexspace will solve these problems.

If I reorganize a tablespace, does it automatically reorganize the corresponding indexes?

Yes. If you reorganize the entire tablespace, the indexes will be rebuilt during the BUILD phase of the REORG utility. If you reorganize only a partition of a tablespace, all of the nonpartitioning indexes are affected, but they are not rebuilt. They are simply corrected in the BUILD2 phase and these nonpartitioning indexes may require a REORG after the tablespace partition-level REORG.

How is the SORTDATA option handled in a reorganization of a multitable tablespace where some tables have explicit clustering indexes and some do not?

In a multitable tablespace, if at least one table has an explicit clustering index, then each table in the same tablespace that doesn't have an explicit clustering index will be sorted using the key of its implicit clustering index, if one exists. If none of the tables in the tablespace have an explicit clustering index, or if there is only one table in the tablespace (without an explicit clustering index), then the SORTDATA option is ignored.

How much temporary disk space is required to reorganize a table in the DB2 UDB environment?

The amount of temporary space required by REORG is about the same as required by the original table. During the reorganization, DB2 reads the original table according to the index you specify. The REORG utility reads the table into the temporary space in sorted order to avoid a subsequent sort, which would use additional space. The table is then rebuilt from the rows in the temporary space, and afterwards the index is rebuilt. Less space may be required for the

reorganization if several deletes have occurred against the original table.

What happens to my table compression during a REORG?

During the UNLOAD phase of the REORG utility, the compression dictionary is built, and it is then used during the RELOAD phase when the table is actually compressed. If you do not want the current compression ratio to change, you can use the KEEPDICTIONARY option so that the dictionary will not get rebuilt and you save the cost of doing so.

Should a REORG of an empty table complete normally?

Yes. If a REORG is performed on an empty table, DB2 will simply skip the reload phase and will reset the tablespace or indexspace.

How can I ensure that I will get the most optimal compression ratio after loading data into tablespace or a partition?

The compression dictionary built by the REORG utility is more accurate than the one built by the LOAD utility. When you use the LOAD utility on a tablespace with compression, DB2 will build the compression dictionary as the data is loaded, based upon the first x number of rows. In order to ensure an optimal compression ratio for a partition, run the REORG utility after loading the data in order to more accurately build the dictionary for compression. The REORG utility builds a more accurate compression dictionary because it uses a sampling technique for building the dictionary (using the first x number of rows) and then samples rows in the UNLOAD phase of the utility. Some DB2 users have seen a 10 percent better compression ratio when the dictionary was built by the REORG utility rather than by the LOAD utility.

What is the SORTKEYS option in the REORG utility used for?

The SORTKEYS option should be used in the REORG utility if you have more than one index to create. This option will allow for the index keys to be sorted in parallel during the RELOAD and BUILD phases of the REORG utility and will help to improve the overall performance of the execution of the utility.

COPIES/BACKUPS

Can I use the forward recovery process after I have used a DSN1COPY to restore a dropped table?

No. You cannot forward recover after using a DSN1COPY to restore a dropped table. The records in SYSLGRNX would have been deleted when the table was dropped. Even if the OBID/DBID of the newly created table were to be the same as those assigned to the old table, allowing for the records on the log to match, the RECOVER utility still would not have the necessary information for applying log changes after the DSN1COPY was applied.

How can I find out if changes have been made to a tablespace or partition to determine whether or not an image copy is required?

On OS/390, by using the CHANGELIMIT feature (DB2 V5) of the COPY utility, you can tell DB2 to look for a specified percentage of changed pages in a tablespace or partition before actually taking an image copy (full or incremental). You can specify value(s) in the CHANGELIMIT to allow for an incremental image copy or full copies to be taken only when those values are reached.

Another feature of the COPY utility that can be used to observe changes is the REPORTONLY feature, which would allow you to see if an image copy is recommended because the CHANGELIMIT values were met. This feature could help to report if any changes occurred against an object, possibly for

auditing purposes. The following example shows the use of the CHANGELIMIT and REPORTONLY features:

```
COPY TABLESPACE DBASE1.TSPACE1 CHANGELIMIT (5,30) REPORTONLY
```

This example gives a recommendation for a full image copy (but doesn't actually take the image copy because the REPORTONLY feature is also used) if the percentage of changed pages was greater than 30, or it would recommend an incremental image copy if the number of changed pages was greater than 5 percent or less than 30 percent.

When should I use full copies vs. incremental copies?

Both full and incremental copies are important for creating backups in a 24×7 environment that must always be operational, and that must be able to meet an acceptable recovery window. Full copies should be taken when:

- A table is newly loaded using LOAD
- A table is loaded with LOAD RESUME
- A table is reorganized with REORG
- Table data has been modified extensively

Incremental copies should be taken when changes have been made to the table since the last full image copy.

When making the decision whether to take a full or incremental image copy, base your decision on the percentage of pages with at least one updated row; if this number is greater than or equal to 40 percent of the entire table, it is strongly recommended that you take a full image copy.

If I use the MERGECOPY utility for merging incremental copies of a partitioned tablespace, will it delete only the copies for that individual partition from SYSCOPY?

By executing the MERGECOPY utility with the NEWCOPY option set to NO, identifying a specific partition number, old incremental copy entries in SYSCOPY will be deleted, provided they are incrementals for that particular partition.

If there are incrementals existing for the entire tablespace, they will not be deleted from SYSCOPY because they are needed by the other partitions of the tablespace.

How often should I run the MERGECOPY utility to merge multiple incremental image copies into one?

The answer to this question should be based upon the amount of exposure perceived and the amount of downtime allowed in the event of a recovery. If a recover 'to-current' is more likely, running the utility MERGECOPY more frequently would be beneficial. If point-in-time recoveries are more likely, MERGECOPY will not be beneficial.

MERGECOPY improves performance for 'to-current' recoveries because the full copy and possibly only one incremental copy would be needed to recover, instead of having to read through multiple incremental copies. However, for a point-in-time recovery (TORBA or TOCOPY), MERGECOPY may not have any benefit. Using the timeline in the following illustration, if you wanted to recover to the date of 5/20, and the MERGECOPY on 6/5 has not yet been done, the incremental from 5/20 will still be in SYSCOPY and can be used to recover to. After the MERGECOPY, the copy for 5/20 will no longer be in SYSCOPY and DB2 must then go back to the full image copy on 5/1 and do a forward log apply to 5/20 making the time for recovery longer, due to the fact that more of the log will have to be applied.

```
Full IC        Inc IC        Inc IC        Inc IC        Merge

--- |----------------- |---------------- |--------------- |----------------- |-----

 5/1           5/10          5/20          5/30           6/5
```

How can I automatically have an image copy taken after a LOAD?

A relatively new feature of the LOAD utility added in DB2 V5 on OS/390 is the ability to perform an inline copy. An inline copy is, for the most part, equivalent to a full image copy taken with SHRLEVEL REFERENCE. The only difference between an inline copy and a regular full image copy is that data pages and space map pages may be out of sequence or repeated, and if a compression dictionary was built during the LOAD, the pages will be duplicated. These differences, however, should be negligible in terms of the amount of space required for the copy data set, and the copy is still valid for recovery.

The inline copy increases the availability of your data because after the data has been loaded and the inline copy taken, the tablespace is not left in a copypending status (even if you specify LOG NO) and the data is ready to be accessed. You can take multiple image copies with this feature as well (with a maximum of two primary and two secondary image copies allowed).

RUNSTATS

 When should I run the RUNSTATS utility?

RUNSTATS should initially be executed on all columns after the data is loaded and reorganized. In addition, there are some general guidelines for RUNSTATS execution. In general, RUNSTATS should be executed whenever a tablespace or index has been reorganized and the statistics have changed significantly, after any heavy update, insert, or delete processing has occurred, before any binding/rebinding of packages or plans, and before any performance tuning that would require monitoring of the statistics in the catalog.

A RUNSTATS using SHRLEVEL CHANGE will run without any locking or interference to other processes and should be executed regularly, with the particular schedule depending on the volatility of the data in your environment. This will provide the statistics needed to determine whether or not a reorganization is necessary and whether any statistics have changed that would trigger rebinds.

RUNSTATS is a utility that is critical to a properly tuned DB2 environment. In DB2 Version 6, RUNSTATS will be imbedded in the REORG and LOAD utilities.

If I want to run a partition level RUNSTATS, do I have to first do a RUNSTATS on the entire tablespace?

Yes. You will need to initially run a RUNSTATS across the entire tablespace before you can run individual partition-level RUNSTATS. This needs to be done because there are some statistics that need to be collected at the tablespace level that will not get picked up by a partition-level RUNSTATS. The full tablespace RUNSTATS only needs to be done once, and after that the partition level RUNSTATS are fine.

Should I use sampling on RUNSTATS, and how will this affect the optimizer's use of the statistics gathered?

The RUNSTATS sampling feature, introduced in Version 5, allows you to choose the percent of nonindexed column statistics gathered and will help RUNSTATS to execute faster. The sampling technique can affect the optimizer's choice in accesspath selection because the sampling must be representative of the data; in the absence of true representation, it would assume a linear distribution of data, which would affect the filter factor and costing done by the optimizer.

Would there be a negative impact on the DB2 catalog if RUNSTATS were to fail before it finished?

If a RUNSTATS job fails before completion, all incomplete updates will be rolled back and all locks will be released. There will be no negative impact to the DB2 catalog.

LOADING

Should I load a table with ENFORCE CONSTRAINTS or run the CHECK DATA utility afterwards?

ENFORCE CONSTRAINTS is an option on the LOAD utility that will have DB2 perform checking on any referential integrity relationships and table check constraints defined on the table that is being loaded to ensure that the new data will not violate any of these relationships. The CHECK DATA utility performs the same relationship type of checking as well as structure integrity checking. Both ENFORCE CONSTRAINTS and CHECK DATA have advantages and disadvantages. We'll look at them each in turn.

ADVANTAGES OF ENFORCE CONSTRAINTS

- Automatically enforces RI/table check constraints and does not set Check Pending flag
- Will not load the rows into the dependent table if they contain a foreign key value that does not match a primary key value
- Detects and reports RI violations
- More efficient and in some cases faster (in terms of overall time for LOAD with ENFORCE CONSTRAINTS vs. ENFORCE NO with subsequent CHECK DATA)

DISADVANTAGES OF ENFORCE CONSTRAINTS

- Affects the sequence in which all related tables can be loaded (parent tables must be loaded before dependents)
- Can have a negative performance impact on the execution of the LOAD utility
- Can only delete incorrect dependent rows, which may not always be the best solution

ADVANTAGES OF USING THE CHECK DATA UTILITY

- Used after executing the LOAD utility with ENFORCE NO (does not check RI/table check constraints and sets Check Pending on all dependent tablespaces)
- The LOAD utility itself will execute faster when not using ENFORCE CONSTRAINTS
- The CHECK DATA utility detects violations and only *optionally* deletes them

- The CHECK DATA utility performs a check on the entire referential structure (LOAD only checks the row being loaded from the input file)

DISADVANTAGES OF USING THE CHECK DATA UTILITY

- Until the CHECK DATA utility can be executed, all related tables are only available for Read Only access, and the tablespace that was loaded cannot allow any DML against it
- The LOAD and CHECK DATA combination may take longer to execute than having used ENFORCE CONSTRAINTS during the LOAD

Can I put selection criteria on my input for the LOAD utility?

Yes. By using the WHEN clause on the LOAD statement you can tell DB2 which records you wish to load from the input data set. This clause provides a condition that is applied to all input records to determine whether or not they should be loaded; those not meeting the criteria can be written to a discard dataset. The following example would only load records where the first position is "H".

```
LOAD DATA
      INDDN INVENTORY
      RESUME YES
      LOG NO
      DISCARDDN SYSDISC
      INTO TABLE ADC101.INVENTORY
          WHEN (1:1) = 'H'
      (INV_NM POSITION (2:5) CHAR,
          STATUS POSITION (6:8) CHAR,
          RECVDATE POSITION (13:22) DATE EXTERNAL(10))
```

Is there any way to perform a load to a flat file from a DB2 table?

Use the DB2 unload program DSNTIAUL; it also can create control statements for use with the DB2 LOAD utility. This program can be found in your DSNSAMP dataset provided with DB2.

What are the major differences in DB2 UDB between the LOAD utility and the IMPORT utility?

While there are many differences between the IMPORT and the LOAD utility, there are a few that are that are considered major.

- The LOAD utility is generally faster on large amounts of data.

- For the LOAD, tables and indexes must exist whereas with IMPORT they can be created using the IXF format.

- IMPORT can import data into VIEWS while LOAD cannot.

- Objects are offline for LOAD and online for the duration of an import.

- IMPORT logs all rows, and with LOAD there is only minimal logging.

- IMPORT fires triggers, and LOAD ignores triggers.

- IMPORT cannot benefit from SMP parallel platforms.

- LOAD only enforces uniqueness while IMPORT enforces all constraints.

- IMPORT inserts index data row by row while LOAD sorts and builds the index after all data has been loaded.

MISCELLANEOUS

What actions cause a tablespace to be put into COPY PENDING status and how do I resolve it?

A DB2 LOAD utility or a REORG utility with LOG NO can both put a tablespace in COPY PENDING status. Also, if you run a MODIFY RECOVERY, and all the image copy entries (for a tablespace or partition) are deleted from SYSCOPY, this will cause a tablespace to be put in COPY PENDING status. The recommended way to resolve a COPY PENDING status is to complete an image copy for the tablespace.

What are the implications of doing a recovery to the current point in time vs. a recovery TOCOPY or a recovery TOLOGPOINT?

If a recover 'tocurrent' is possible, you will not have to rebuild any corresponding nonpartitioning indexes. A recovery TOCOPY or TOLOGPOINT would require index recoveries—otherwise the data and indexes have the potential for getting out of sync.

How do I get a report to determine what tablespaces need to be recovered together?

You will find that by using the REPORT utility with the option TABLESPACESET, you can obtain a report that identifies all referential relationships to a given table. From this you can determine what tablespaces need to be quiesced and image copied together. Keep in mind that this only covers the relationships defined in DB2; there may also be other application-defined relationships between tables that would have to be included in the same recovery scope.

What information about recovery does the REPORT utility provide me?

Information provided by the REPORT utility with the RECOVERY option can help you plan for recovery by providing information on:

- Recovery history from SYSCOPY
- Log ranges from SYSLGRNX
- VOL-SER numbers where archive logs and BSDS(Boot Strap Data Set) reside
- VOL-SER numbers where image copy data sets reside

What are the implications of using the REPAIR utility to reset the tablespace status?

Pending statuses are primarily set after the execution of utilities for various reasons. Copy pending, check pending and recover pending are three examples of pending status that can be set on tablespaces or indexspaces and will require an action to occur before certain operations can occur against the affected object(s). There are certain factors that should be given some consideration before using the REPAIR utility to reset any pending status on a tablespace instead of performing the recommended tasks for proper resolution. REPAIR does allow you to reset the status of a tablespace without taking other appropriate actions, but it does not provide you with the necessary fallback in the event there is a problem. For example, if you reset a copy pending status using the REPAIR utility, and you needed to recover, you would not have an image copy to recover to. If you took an image copy, which would reset the status safely, you would not be exposed to this problem. (In other words, these flags are set for a reason, and that is to protect us from potential integrity and recoverability problems.)

If you reset the copy pending status using REPAIR, the RECOVER utility cannot be successfully executed against the affected tablespace until a new full image copy is taken. It is better to take a full image copy to reset the copy pending status, if possible.

Using REPAIR to reset the check pending status can leave you with referential constraint violations. It is preferable to execute the CHECK DATA utility to reset the status.

If are going to reset the recover pending status using REPAIR (rather than executing a RECOVER or LOAD), keep in mind that there has been no consideration on the part of DB2 regarding use of image copies or log data sets and therefore the data may be inconsistent or incorrect.

How do I resolve a recover pending (RECP) state, and how do I determine what caused it?

A recover pending state can be set on tablespaces and indexspaces, and it will prevent access to the affected objects. It can be set on indexes after executing a recovery utility to TOCOPY and TORBA on a tablespace, or from utility abends or terminations of RECOVER, LOAD, or REORG. The condition can be reset by executing a RECOVER, LOAD REPLACE, or REPAIR.

What activities occur during a QUIESCE utility?

During execution, the QUIESCE utility will write changed pages to DASD when WRITE(YES) is specified.

How often should I run the MODIFY utility?

The MODIFY utility should be executed often and on a scheduled basis, depending on system activity. This will help improve performance for several different processes that access the SYSCOPY and SYSLGRNX tables as the MODIFY will delete outdated information from these tables. Due to the nature of the data in these tables, they can grow considerably and require a good deal of space. If tables are allowed to grow, the larger they become, the longer the MODIFY utility will take to run. It is recommended that if the SYSCOPY and SYSLGRNX tables are very large, that outdated information be deleted by using the MODIFY utility to delete entries by age. For example, have one run of the utility remove rows older than 20 months.

Chapter 9

Commands

Answer Topics!

Commands @ a Glance

This chapter covers how to use DB2 commands on the various DB2 platforms. Commands can be used to display information about current processes, and object settings and status. In addition to commands that display information, there are commands that perform manipulations and other types of actions. Manipulative commands include those that modify, recover, and alter objects. Other actions that can be performed by commands include the starting and stopping databases, subsystems, stored procedures, and traces.

This chapter will cover some of the most common questions regarding the use of DB2 commands. Many questions about display commands are included because they are the commands used most commonly and by the widest audience. Displays are informational only and do not perform any manipulative action; however, information obtained from the displays is often used as input for other commands. A few questions also cover the general usage of DB2 commands.

DB2 UDB comes with a very large range of executable commands. Many of the commands are quite similar to the commands available for DB2 OS/390; however, DB2 UDB also comes with several very unique and very powerful commands. Some of these unique commands will also be covered in this chapter.

INFORMATIONAL DISPLAYS

How do I find out what phase my DB2 utility is in on OS/390?

You can use the –DISPLAY UTILITY command to determine the status and the phase of a utility, as shown in Figure 9-1. The display command can also show utilities running all members in a data-sharing group, or on one particular member when the MEMBER parameter is used. You can display all utilities by using an asterisk (*), or if you know the UTILID, you can view that utility only.

How can I find out the amount of prefetch activity that is occurring against my bufferpools?

By using the –DISPLAY BUFFERPOOL (BPx) DETAIL command, shown in Figure 9-2, you can view the number of requests, the number of read I/O operations, and the number of pages read for sequential, list, and dynamic prefetch operations. You will also be able to see if any prefetch operations have been disabled due to lack of buffers, in which case you may need to increase the bufferpool size or increase the bufferpool thresholds. There is no console display command facility on the UNIX / NT / OS/2 platforms, but the same information can be seen by using the Performance Monitor facility from the Control Center. In Figure 9-3, the window shows the output of the performance monitor snapshot facility, and the statistics for the buffer pools.

```
-DISPLAY UTILITY(*)

DSNU100I - DSNUGDIS - USERID = ADC102
UTILID = TSCOPY01
PROCESSING UTILITY STATEMENT 1
UTILITY = COPY
PHASE = COPY              COUNT = 10802
STATUS = ACTIVE
DSN9022I - DSNUGC '-DISPLAY UTILITY'  NORMAL COMPLETION
```

Figure 9-1 –DISPLAY UTILITY command output

```
-DISPLAY BUFFERPOOL (BP1) DETAIL

DSNB401I  BUFFERPOOL NAME BP1, BUFFERPOOL ID 0, USE COUNT 10
DSNB021I  VIRTUAL BUFFERPOOL SIZE = 1000 BUFFERS
          ALLOCATED   =    1000  TO BE DELETED  =    0
          IN-USE/UPDATE  =    200
. . . . . . .


DSNB412I -SEQUENTIAL PREFETCH
          REQUESTS     =     32868 PREFETCH I/O = 13961
          PAGES READ   =     306528
DSNB413I -LIST PREFETCH
          REQUESTS     =     0        PREFETCH I/O = 0
          PAGES READ   =     0
DSNB414I -DYNAMIC PREFETCH
          REQUESTS     =     566      PREFETCH I/O = 42
          PAGES READ   =     629
DSNB415I -PREFETCH DISABLED
          NO BUFFER    =     0       NO READ ENGINE = 0
```

Figure 9-2 –DISPLAY BUFFERPOOL command output

OEMCOMPUTER - DB2 - RYC - Performance Details

Database   Performance variable   View   Snapshot monitor   Help

DB2 15:04:07
Path: C:\DB2\NODE0000\SQL00002\
First database connection: 01-19-1999 14:51:17
Last reset:
Last backup:

Performance variable	Category	Value	Average	Maximum	Minimum	Upper alarm	Lower alarm	D
Total Log Space Cleaners Invoked	Buffer Pool and I/O	0.00	0.00	0.00	0.00	n/a	n/a	Tc
Pages for each Cleaner	Buffer Pool and I/O	n/a	n/a	n/a	n/a	n/a	n/a	A
Page Cleans	Buffer Pool and I/O	0.00	0.00	0.00	0.00	n/a	n/a	Nc
Total Prefetch Request (4K page)	Buffer Pool and I/O	0.00	0.00	0.00	0.00	n/a	n/a	Tc
Pages for each Prefetch Request	Buffer Pool and I/O	n/a	n/a	n/a	n/a	n/a	n/a	Nc
Prefetch Requests	Buffer Pool and I/O	0.00	0.00	0.00	0.00	n/a	n/a	Nc
Buffer Pool I/Os per Second	Buffer Pool and I/O	0.00	0.01	0.24	0.00	n/a	n/a	Bu
Buffer Pool Hit Ratio, Index (%)	Buffer Pool and I/O	100.00	97.66	100.00	95.31	n/a	n/a	In
Buffer Pool Hit Ratio (%)	Buffer Pool and I/O	100.00	98.59	100.00	97.18	n/a	n/a	O-
Average Pool I/O Time (ms)	Buffer Pool and I/O	22.00	22.00	22.00	22.00	n/a	n/a	A
Average Pool Write Time (ms)	Buffer Pool and I/O	n/a	n/a	n/a	n/a	n/a	n/a	A
Average Pool Read Time (ms)	Buffer Pool and I/O	22.00	22.00	22.00	22.00	n/a	n/a	A
Average Synchronous Write (ms)	Buffer Pool and I/O	n/a	n/a	n/a	n/a	n/a	n/a	A
Average Synchronous Read (ms)	Buffer Pool and I/O	55.00	55.00	55.00	55.00	n/a	n/a	A
Total Synchronous I/O Time (ms)	Buffer Pool and I/O	110.00	35.20	110.00	0.00	n/a	n/a	Tc
Total Synchronous I/O (4K pages)	Buffer Pool and I/O	2.00	0.64	2.00	0.00	n/a	n/a	Tc
Average Synchronous I/O (ms)	Buffer Pool and I/O	55.00	55.00	55.00	55.00	n/a	n/a	A

Monitor is paused

Figure 9-3 UDB performance monitor information for bufferpool use

How can I find out what locks are being held against a table?

The –DISPLAY DATABASE(DB1) SPACENAM(*) LOCKS command will display the lock modes currently being held against a table and its associated tablespace. The first entry in the example shown in Figure 9-4 shows that there is an intent-exclusive lock (IX) on the tablespace (S), and the second entry shows an intent-exclusive lock (IX) on the table (T). Each lock is described in the left column and is represented either by name or by OBID. Additional information on these displays can be found in the DB2 version command reference manual.

When I issued the –DISPLAY DATABASE SPACENAM(*) command, I found that there were pages in LPL status. What does this mean, and how is it resolved?

LPL (logical page list) is a new page-error status that occurs when DB2 encounters a DASD error. When the object is in this status, it needs to be started with a –START command in RW or RO mode; when this happens, DB2 will try to recover the pages from the log. Running the RECOVER utility will also remove a page from LPL status. Two other possible options are to run a LOAD REPLACE on the object, or to DROP the object if feasible.

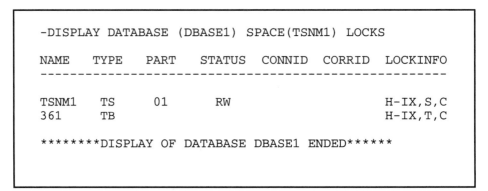

```
-DISPLAY DATABASE (DBASE1) SPACE(TSNM1) LOCKS

NAME    TYPE   PART   STATUS  CONNID  CORRID  LOCKINFO
------------------------------------------------------------

TSNM1   TS     01     RW                      H-IX,S,C
361     TB                                    H-IX,T,C

********DISPLAY OF DATABASE DBASE1 ENDED******
```

Figure 9-4 –DISPLAY DATABASE LOCKS command output

When pages that are group bufferpool dependent are placed in LPL status in a data-sharing environment, this may result from a connectivity failure involving the coupling facility, or from a structure failure. The pages would be resolved in the same manner as mentioned previously.

To explicitly find objects with pages in LPL status, you can issue the –DISPLAY DATABASE (*database*) SPACENAM(*) LPL command. The output of this command is shown in Figure 9-5.

When I issue the –DISPLAY THREAD(*) command, I see several CICS transactions hanging around, even though they are completed. What would cause this to happen?

If CICS threads are defined as high priority in the CICS RCT (resource control table) using option TWAIT=ENTRY, then they will hold on to the TCB (task control block) acquired during thread allocation and will not be released until DB2 is recycled. The way to reduce the number of inactive CICS threads (and to release the TCBs) is to define applicable threads with a low priority in the CICS RCT by using option TWAIT=POOL.

```
-DIS DATABASE(DBS0001) SPACENAM(*) LPL

DSNT360I *DB5P ***********************************
DSNT361I *DB5P *   DISPLAY DATABASE SUMMARY
               *        GLOBAL LPL
DSNT360I *DB5P ***********************************
DSNT362I *DB5P     DATABASE = DBS0001  STATUS = RW
                   DBD LENGTH = 573386
DSNT397I *DB5P
NAME            TYPE    PART   STATUS        LPL PAGES
--------------  ----    ----   ------        -------------
TBSP001         TS      RW,LPL,GRECP         000011,000013
TBSP003         TS      RW
TBSP005         TS      RW
```

Figure 9-5 –DISPLAY DATABASE LPL command output

What do the statistics produced by LSTATS on the –DISPLAY BUFFERPOOL command provide me?

By using the LSTATS option on the –DISPLAY BUFFERPOOL command, along with the LIST option, you can obtain a list of open tablespaces and indexspaces for a given bufferpool, along with detailed statistics for each open object. As shown in Figure 9-6, the statistics include information about the number of cached pages, both current and changed, and the number of synchronous and asynchronous I/O delays (average and maximum delay, and the total number of pages and total I/O count) against each object in use in the specified bufferpool.

How do I display and resolve an indoubt unit of recovery?

Indoubt threads result when a thread is involved in a two-phase commit process where the first phase has committed, but the second phase has not, due to a communication failure. When this occurs, the commit

```
-DISPLAY BUFFERPOOL(BP5) LIST LSTATS

DSNB401I *DB5P BUFFERPOOL NAME BP5, BUFFERPOOL ID 5, USE COUNT 66
DSNB402I *DB5P VIRTUAL BUFFERPOOL SIZE = 5000 BUFFERS
.........

DSNB450I *DB5P TABLESPACE = OS2D0001.OS2BCT01,USE COUNT = 1,GBP-DEP=N
DSNB452I *DB5P  STATISTICS FOR DATASET 1 -
DSNB453I *DB5P   VP CACHED PAGES -
               CURRENT    =    14   MAX          =    18
               CHANGED    =    10   MAX          =    10
DSNB455I *DB5P   SYNCHRONOUS I/O DELAYS -
               AVERAGE DELAY =    15   MAXIMUM DELAY   =    26
               TOTAL PAGES   =    18
DSNB456I *DB5P   ASYNCHRONOUS I/O DELAYS -
               AVERAGE DELAY =    27   MAXIMUM DELAY   =    82
               TOTAL PAGES   =    37   TOTAL I/O COUNT =    25
DSNB450I *DB5P TABLESPACE = OS2D0001.OS2BBK01, USE COUNT = 1,GBP-DEP=N
.........

DSN9022I *DB5P DSNB1CMD '-DISPLAY BUFFERPOOL' NORMAL COMPLETION
```

Figure 9-6   –DISPLAY BUFFERPOOL LIST LSTATS command output

coordinator, not receiving the communication about the success of the second phase, does not know how to handle the updates. It does not know whether to commit or roll back, and until some corrective action occurs, locks are held on resources that were in the process of being updated. In order to display indoubt units of recovery, you can issue the –DISPLAY THREAD command, as shown here:

```
-DISPLAY THREAD(*) TYPE(INDOUBT)
```

The output from this display will produce a list of all indoubt threads, including information about the coordinator, participant, status, and the AUTHID of the thread.

To resolve an indoubt unit of recovery, issue the –RECOVER INDOUBT command, and tell DB2 whether to commit or abort the updates in the associated unit of recovery. You can use the default connection name as input to the –RECOVER INDOUBT command (the default is the connection name from which the command was entered), or you can obtain the correlation ID, network ID, or LUWID (logical unit of work identifier) from the DISPLAY THREAD command output, and use it to recover a particular indoubt thread. If using a correlation ID or network ID, a connection name is required; for an LUWID the connection name is ignored. This command should only be used if automatic resolution is not working. In order to issue the RECOVER INDOUBT command, you will need to have SYSOPR, SYSCTRL, or SYSADM authority, or to have been given the RECOVER privilege.

The following example would recover any existing indoubt threads for the connection where the command was entered by scheduling a commit for each indoubt thread.

```
RECOVER INDOUBT ACTION(COMMIT) ID(*)
```

 How can I display only the active call-attach threads on my DB2 subsystem?

You can get information about batch, TSO, or call-attach facility processes by issuing the –DISPLAY THREAD

command for a given connection. The following illustration shows thread connections for programs using the call attachment facility.

```
-DISPLAY THREAD(DB2CALL)

DSNV401I *DB5P DISPLAY THREAD REPORT FOLLOWS -
DSNV402I *DB5P ACTIVE THREADS -
NAME     ST A   REQ ID               AUTHID   PLAN      ASID TOKEN
DB2CALL  T  *    45 ADC0001          ADC0001  PGM531XX  00D6 14734
DB2CALL  T    16243 ADC0002          ADC0002            001B     1
DISPLAY ACTIVE REPORT COMPLETE
DSN9022I *DB5P DSNVDT '-DISPLAY THREAD' NORMAL COMPLETION
```

How can I display my bufferpool threshold values?

You can display the defined bufferpool thresholds by issuing the –DISPLAY BUFFERPOOL command for all bufferpools, all active bufferpools, or a given individual bufferpool. The following illustration shows the output of the –DISPLAY BUFFERPOOL command.

```
-DISPLAY BUFFERPOOL (BP5)

DSNB401I *DB5P BUFFERPOOL NAME BP5, BUFFERPOOL ID 5, USE COUNT 66
DSNB402I *DB5P VIRTUAL BUFFERPOOL SIZE = 5000 BUFFERS
        ALLOCATED       =       5000      TO BE DELETED   =        0
        IN-USE/UPDATED  =        688
 DSNB403I *DB5P HIPERPOOL SIZE = 0 BUFFERS, CASTOUT = YES
             ALLOCATED      =          0  TO BE DELETED   =        0
             BACKED BY ES   =          0
 DSNB404I *DB5P THRESHOLDS -
        VP SEQUENTIAL       = 70  HP SEQUENTIAL         = 80
        DEFERRED WRITE      = 20  VERTICAL DEFERRED WRT =  5
        PARALLEL SEQUENTIAL = 80  ASSISTING PARALLEL SEQT=  0
```

How do I display what database I am connected to in DB2 UDB?

In order to find out what database, if any, you are currently connected to, you need to issue the GET CONNECTION STATE command. For an example of the output, see the following illustration.

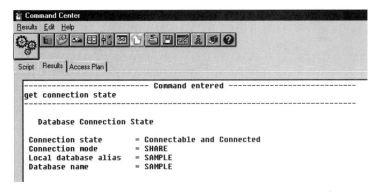

How do I display information about the database I am currently connected to in DB2 UDB?

You can display several types of information about the database you are currently connected to by using the LIST command. You can retrieve such information as a list of tables and tablespaces in the database by using the LIST TABLE or LIST TABLESPACE commands. A list of packages that you have bound, along with their state, can be displayed with the LIST PACKAGES command. You can also display node groups or nodes using the LIST NODEGROUPS or LIST NODES commands. There are several other objects that can be displayed, such as databases, applications, and indoubt threads.

The following illustration shows the output of a LIST TABLES command:

```
Command Center
Results  Edit  Help

Script   Results   Access Plan

------------------------------ Command entered ----------------------------
list tables
----------------------------------------------------------------------------

Table/View          Schema          Type        Creation time
------------------- --------------- ----------- ----------------------------
DEPARTMENT          RYEVICH         T           1998-04-18-16.10.20.800000
EMP_ACT             RYEVICH         T           1998-04-18-16.10.22.940000
EMP_PHOTO           RYEVICH         T           1998-04-18-16.10.25.300000
EMP_RESUME          RYEVICH         T           1998-04-18-16.10.28.760000
EMPLOYEE            RYEVICH         T           1998-04-18-16.10.21.460000
EXPLAIN_INSTANCE    RYEVICH         T           1998-10-12-08.11.52.290000
EXPLAIN_STATEMENT   RYEVICH         T           1998-10-12-08.11.54.040000
ORG                 RYEVICH         T           1998-04-18-16.10.18.600000
PROJECT             RYEVICH         T           1998-04-18-16.10.24.530000
SALES               RYEVICH         T           1998-04-18-16.10.30.460000
STAFF               RYEVICH         T           1998-04-18-16.10.19.700000

  11 record(s) selected.
```

How can I find out what backups are available for my database in a DB2 UDB environment?

There are two commands in DB2 UDB that will provide you with information regarding backups for a given database. You can view backups taken since a given point in time, or backups containing a particular object. The LIST BACKUP command will allow you to list restore sets for the entire database and tablespace level backups. The LIST HISTORY command will list backup entries in the recovery history file.

The first illustration shown here is a screen capture of a DB2 list backup. The second illustration contains a DB2 list history of backups made since 19980901 for a database.

```
 Command Center
Results  Edit  Help

Script | Results | Access Plan |
-------------------------- Command entered --------------------------
list backup all for sample
-------------------------------------------------------------------

                    List Recovery History File for BACKUP

Number of matching file entries = 2


Op Obj Timestamp+Sequence Type Dev Earliest Log Current Log  Backup ID
-- --- ------------------ ---- --- ------------ ------------ ----------
 B  D  19981012104337001   F    D  S0000000.LOG S0000000.LOG
-------------------------------------------------------------------
 Contains 2     tablespace(s):

 00001 SYSCATSPACE
 00002 USERSPACE1
-------------------------------------------------------------------
 Comment: DB2 BACKUP SAMPLE OFFLINE
-------------------------------------------------------------------
 00001 Location: D:\SQLLIB\bin\SAMPLE.0\DB2\NODE0000\CATN0000\19981012


Op Obj Timestamp+Sequence Type Dev Earliest Log Current Log  Backup ID
-- --- ------------------ ---- --- ------------ ------------ ----------
 B  D  19981012105844001   F    D  S0000000.LOG S0000000.LOG
-------------------------------------------------------------------
 Contains 2     tablespace(s):

 00001 SYSCATSPACE
 00002 USERSPACE1
-------------------------------------------------------------------
 Comment: DB2 BACKUP SAMPLE OFFLINE
-------------------------------------------------------------------
 00002 Location: D:\SQLLIB\bin\SAMPLE.0\DB2\NODE0000\CATN0000\19981012
```

```
 Command Center
Results  Edit  Help
  [toolbar icons]
Script  Results | Access Plan |

------------------------------- Command entered --------------------------------
list history since 19981001 for sample
--------------------------------------------------------------------------------

                         List Recovery History File for HISTORY

Number of matching file entries = 2


Op Obj Timestamp+Sequence Type Dev Earliest Log Current Log  Backup ID
-- --- ------------------ ---- --- ------------ ------------ ---------------
 B  D  19981012104337001   F    D  S0000000.LOG S0000000.LOG
--------------------------------------------------------------------------------
 Contains 2     tablespace(s):

 00001 SYSCATSPACE
 00002 USERSPACE1
--------------------------------------------------------------------------------
 Comment: DB2 BACKUP SAMPLE OFFLINE
--------------------------------------------------------------------------------
 00001 Location: D:\SQLLIB\bin\SAMPLE.0\DB2\NODE0000\CATN0000\19981012

Op Obj Timestamp+Sequence Type Dev Earliest Log Current Log  Backup ID
-- --- ------------------ ---- --- ------------ ------------ ---------------
 B  D  19981012105844001   F    D  S0000000.LOG S0000000.LOG
--------------------------------------------------------------------------------
 Contains 2     tablespace(s):

 00001 SYSCATSPACE
 00002 USERSPACE1
--------------------------------------------------------------------------------
 Comment: DB2 BACKUP SAMPLE OFFLINE
--------------------------------------------------------------------------------
 00002 Location: D:\SQLLIB\bin\SAMPLE.0\DB2\NODE0000\CATN0000\19981012
```

ACTION/MANIPULATION

How do I remove an application plan from the SYSIBM.SYSPLAN table when it is no longer in use?

By issuing the FREE PLAN command you can free an application plan and remove its entry from the catalog. The following example would remove the MYPLAN entry from the catalog:

```
FREE PLAN (MYPLAN)
```

 Can I start or stop the DDF (distributed data facility) without having to bounce the DB2 subsystem?

Yes. The DDF address space can be started or stopped without bouncing DB2, by using the –START DDF and –STOP DDF commands. When these commands are executed on a particular subsystem, they will activate/deactivate the DDF interface to VTAM and TCP/IP.

How can I cancel a thread that is not responding?

DB2 Version 4 provided the ability to cancel threads through the use of the –CANCEL THREAD command. All you have to supply this command is the token of the thread to be canceled. The token can be found in the –DISPLAY THREAD command output. Or, if you are wanting to cancel a DDF thread you will have to cancel it using its associated LUWID (logical unit of work identifier), also found in the –DISPLAY THREAD command output. Once the token or LUWID has been identified, it can be used in the –CANCEL THREAD command. You must have SYSADM, SYSOPR, or SYSCTRL authority to be able to cancel a thread.

Figure 9-7 shows the DISPLAY THREAD command, which allows you to identify the thread that needs to be canceled.

When you have the token or LUWID, the CANCEL THREAD command can then be issued for a given thread. For example, the following command will cancel the thread associated with token 15048:

```
CANCEL THREAD (15048)
```

```
- DISPLAY THREAD(*)
DSNV401I *DB5P DISPLAY THREAD REPORT FOLLOWS -
DSNV402I *DB5P ACTIVE THREADS -
 NAME      ST A   REQ ID           AUTHID    PLAN      ASID TOKEN
 T5ACIS5P  T  * 24108 AT000S52      T4CAA02   DB1ISABT  005D 15020
 T5ACIS5P  T    26536 AT000SU9      T4BAA01   DB1ISABT  005D 15048
 T5ACIS5P  N    27605 AT000SP4      T4TAA03             005D     0
 T5ACIS5P  N    23699 AT00EI00      T4TAA02             005D     0
 T5ACIS5P  N     3620 AT000SG1      T4TJJ05             005D     0

DISPLAY ACTIVE REPORT COMPLETE
DSN9022I *DB5P DSNVDT '-DISPLAY THREAD' NORMAL COMPLETION
```

Figure 9-7 –DISPLAY THREAD command output

 ## Does the ARCHIVE LOG MODE(QUIESCE) command flush the updated pages from the bufferpool?

This command does not externalize all updated pages to DASD, just the updated pages in the DB2 log buffers. The way to ensure that updated pages are written out to DASD is to either issue the –STOP DATABASE command or run the QUIESCE utility (with the WRITE(YES) option) on the tablespace(s).

The ARCHIVE LOG MODE(QUIESCE) command will stop any new update activity in order to bring all uses to a point of consistency, and at that time the current active log is truncated and the process of offloading to the archive logs begins.

 ## What can I use the –ALTER UTILITY command for?

The –ALTER UTILITY command can be used to alter values of a currently executing REORG utility that is using the SHRLEVEL REFERENCE or CHANGE parameter. There are only a few values that can be altered.

DEADLINE	Point in time in which the switch phase of the REORG utility is to start; if the switch phase does not start by this time, the utility terminates. Values are NONE (no deadline) or a given timestamp.
MAXRO	Maximum amount of time tolerated for last iteration of log processing during a REORG, when applications will only be allowed read-only access to the table. Possible values are an integer (defining the tolerable number of seconds) or DEFER (indefinite log phase).
LONGLOG	Action to be performed by DB2 if the REORG's reading of the log is not catching up with applications writing to the log. Values include CONTINUE, TERM(terminate), or DRAIN (drain the write class after a delay).
DELAY	Time delay allowed between the time the LONGLOG message is sent by the REORG utility to the console and the action specified on the LONGLOG parameter is performed.

The following example shows how the ALTER UTILITY command can be used:

```
ALTER UTILITY (TSREORG) REORG MAXRO 120
```

This would change the maximum number of seconds tolerable for last iteration of log processing to 120 seconds (2 minutes).

How do I put a tablespace in read-only mode?

You can put a tablespace or partition in read-only mode by issuing the –START DATABASE command for the given tablespace and specifying the RO (read only) ACCESS option. If you are wanting exclusive control for running utilities, you would use the UT (utility) ACCESS option so that only DB2 online utilities could access the tablespace or partition. To get the tablespace out of read-only mode or utility-only mode, stop the database and then issue the –START DATABASE command with the RW (read/write) ACCESS option.

The sequence of commands for achieving the read only mode is shown here:

```
-STOP DATABASE (DB1) SPACENAME (TS1) PART(20)
```

The preceding command stops partition 20 of tablespace TS1 in database DB1. The following command starts partition 20 in read-only mode.

```
-START DATABASE (DB1) SPACENAME (TS1) PART(20) ACCESS (RO)
```

How do I report on the organization of my table in DB2 UDB?

DB2 UDB has a unique command known as the REORGCHK command. This command will provide you with information regarding the organization of the table or set of tables. This

information will help you determine whether or not a reorganization is necessary. If you do not use the CURRENT STATISTICS parameter on the REORGCHK command, you will also update the DB2 catalog statistics for the given table being checked. The following command shows the syntax for running a REORGCHK on a specific table:

```
REORGCHK ON TABLE xxx
```

DB2 will produce a report displaying information about the table and all of its associated indexes. This information will include results from six calculations performed internally by DB2, and is represented in the output report with column designations of F1, F2, F3, F4, F5, and F6. The following list explains the column designations:

F1   The number of overflow records contained in the table

F2   The amount of free space on the table pages

F3   The number of empty pages that would potentially be retrieved during a scan of a table

F4   The clustering of the index

F5   The amount of free space on index pages

F6   The levels of the index

The two screens in Figure 9-8 show examples of the output from the REORGCHK command.

To determine if a reorganization is needed, view the results in the REORG column. This column contains three positions for values, which can either contain a hyphen (-) or asterisk (*) depending on whether or not the value calculated fell within the DB2 defined range. If an asterisk (*) appears in one of the three values, it means the calculated value was not within the DB2 defined acceptable range. Several asterisks in these fields may indicate a need for a table or index reorg.

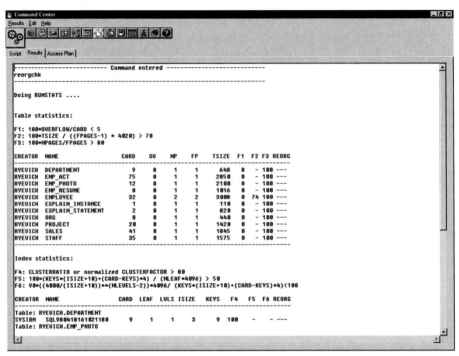

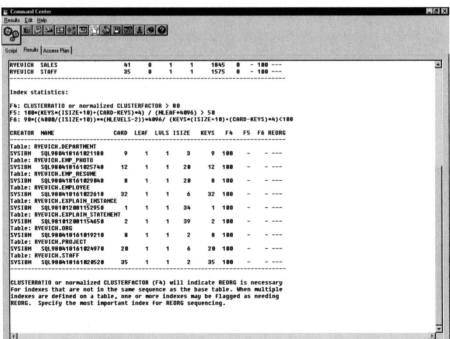

Figure 9-8 REORGCHK command output

How do I monitor the consumption of resources in a DB2 UDB environment?

There is a command in DB2 UDB that will execute a utility known as the DB2 Governor. The DB2 Governor allows you to define boundaries on the amount of resources consumed by applications or users for a given database. There is a configuration file in which rules specify limits on the elapsed time of a transaction, the number of locks held by an application or a user, and the total number of rows returned. The limits defined in this file will be used by the DB2 Governor to determine when an action should be taken against a user or an application that has exceeded the specified limits for resource consumption. As long as the Governor is running, the statistics are gathered periodically and compared to the limits.

To start the Governor, issue the following command specifying the database to be monitored, the configuration file to be used for limits, and the log file to be used for logging actions performed by the Governor:

```
DB2GOV START MYDATABS CONFIG.txt LOG.txt
```

How do I remove unnecessary entries from my recovery history file in DB2 UDB?

In order to delete entries from the recovery history file (full database backups, tablespace backups, loads, and restores) in DB2 UDB, use the PRUNE HISTORY command. This command removes entries in the recovery history file that are specified by a range. The following example would delete entries with a timestamp less than or equal to Dec. 9, 1998, from the recovery history file:

```
DB2 PRUNE HISTORY 19981209
```

How do I load a partitioned database to ensure that the data will be loaded into the appropriate partitions in DB2 UDB?

By using the DB2SPLIT command you can invoke a utility called the Splitter, which will scan all input for a table and

will prepare data for loading based upon the defined partitioning key of a partitioned database. In the following example, the "-c" parameter identifies that the filename following is a configuration file for the command. Detailed splitting information such as the name of the input file, the position and length of the partitioning key, and the name of the log file is contained in the file "splitfil.cfg".

```
DB2SPLIT -c splitfil.cfg
```

You can run in ANALYZE mode and have the data analyzed and a partitioning map prepared for later use; or you can run in PARTITION mode, where the data will actually be split into separate files for future loading by hashing the partitioning key into buckets and then mapping the buckets to partitions using the partitioning map.

MISCELLANEOUS USAGE

 ### Where can I issue DB2 commands from on OS/390?

You can issue DB2 commands from:

- The DB2I (DB2 Interactive) panel
- A DSN session
- A program using DB2 IFI (Instrumentation Facility Interface)
- An OS/390 console
- An IMS or CICS terminal

All DB2 commands can be issued from these locations except for the START DB2 command, which must be issued from an OS/390 console.

 ### How can I find out who issued a DB2 command?

This information is contained in IFCID 90 and can be obtained through a performance trace. This would give you the ability to view the text of the command issued and the ID (current user ID) by which it was issued.

 How can I route OS/390 DB2 commands to a subsystem other than that of the requester?

There are a few methods for routing commands to other DB2 subsystems. The options include:

- Use transaction routing or function shipping under the CICS or IMS attach facilities

- Use command routing in an OS/390 sysplex

- Run DB2 stored procedures that execute on the desired subsystem

- Code an application using VTAM LU 6 to send DB2 commands to the appropriate OS/390 subsystem

Chapter 10

Basic SQL

Answer Topics!

Basic SQL @ a Glance

SQL (structured query language), is the language used for queries against most relational database systems. This chapter answers questions on how the basic forms of the DB2 SQL DML (Data Manipulation Language) work, and looks at proper situations in which to use them. It lays the foundation for later chapters, in which queries are used in catalog maintenance, for example, and for the chapters on advanced SQL and performance tuning. This chapter contains some insights about SQL features that are not widely documented, together with some interesting ways DB2 internally processes SQL.

Powerful queries can be created using inner and outer joins, subselects, CASE expressions, and in-line views/table expressions, recursion, UNIONs, and other standard SELECT clauses. This strength results from the flexibility of SQL, which can be used in a variety of ways to produce the same result. SQL can be used interactively, or can be embedded in programs. The statements are written basically the same way, although there are particular constraints when embedding them in programs. The embedding of SQL will be addressed in the sections on application development and tuning.

Most of this chapter will deal with the SELECT statement; it is the most complex statement, and since it is the base of queries that retrieve data, it is the most often used.

GENERAL

 ### What is a query?

A query is a structured block of code (usually SQL) used to retrieve relational data in the following form:

```
SELECT columns
FROM table
WHERE
GROUP BY  ⎤
HAVING    ⎬ Optional clauses
ORDER BY  ⎦
```

 ### What is a subquery (a.k.a. subselects and nested selects)?

A subquery is a query enclosed in parentheses that is placed inside some outer level SQL statement. In DB2 OS/390, it is normally used within a WHERE or HAVING clause, or in a table expression in a FROM clause. There is also the concept of a scalar subquery, which is a query that returns one row of only one column. This scalar subquery can be used anywhere an expression can be used in a SQL statement. In DB2 UDB while on OS/390 there are restrictions on their use. Subqueries can be divided into two categories: correlated, and noncorrelated. In DB2 OS/390, subqueries can be nested up to the limit of 15 tables being allowed in the total SELECT statement. In DB2 UDB, there is no nesting limit, as the constraint is storage, and there is also no limit to the number of tables in a SQL statement.

 NOTE: *The table limit is being increased in DB2 on OS/390 through an APAR in V5 and enhancements in V6.*

 ### What makes a subquery correlated?

Correlation occurs when a subquery refers to a column or multiple columns of one or more tables identified in an outer-level query. Table correlation names defined in the

FROM clause help DB2 determine column-query block relationships, and are also great for documentation and readability since they show precisely what columns references belong to which table. For example, the following query is correlated because the subquery refers to A.DEPTNO which is a column from the outer level query with a table correlation name of A.

```
SELECT *
FROM SALES A ─────────────┐
WHERE BONUS  >            │
     (SELECT AVG(SALARY)  │
       FROM EMP B         │
        WHERE A.DEPTNO = B.DEPTNO)◄
```

How can I request an ORDER BY sequence on an expression?

Use the AS keyword to give a name to the expression, and then refer to the new name in the ORDER BY clause, as shown below:

```
SELECT COLA+COLB+COLC AS BONUS, COLG, COLH
FROM T1
ORDER BY BONUS
```

Although the relative position number is also allowed in the ORDER BY clause (ORDER BY 1 for the preceding example), it is recommended that the expression be renamed to maintain compliance with the SQL standards in use. Naming the expression columns also helps in dynamic SQL when viewing query results using tools such as SPUFI or QMF. More important, when a SQL statement is changed, the resulting ORDER BY clause does not have to change when the AS naming convention is used.

How can I request column name headings for a UNION statement?

When each query block has different names for the columns requested in the query blocks, resulting column heading

names default to all blanks. You can convert the blanks by renaming each column that is lined up vertically within the UNION statement to the same name. For example:

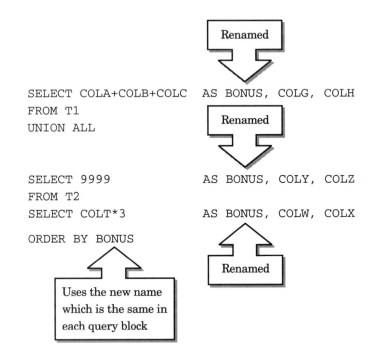

```
                                    Renamed

SELECT COLA+COLB+COLC   AS BONUS, COLG, COLH
FROM T1
UNION ALL                           Renamed


SELECT 9999             AS BONUS, COLY, COLZ
FROM T2
SELECT COLT*3           AS BONUS, COLW, COLX

ORDER BY BONUS
                                    Renamed
```

Uses the new name which is the same in each query block

How can I compute the real average of a numeric column that used zeros instead of NULL for an unknown entry?

You can use the NULLIF function to extract all the zeros. The NULLIF function compares the two items in its list, and if they are equal, a NULL is returned. The following example compares the COMMISSION column with zero, one row at a time, and returns a NULL value whenever a zero is encountered, prior to computing the AVG function on all the rows:

```
SELECT AVG(NULLIF(COMMISSION, 0)) AS AVGTOT
FROM T1
ORDER BY AVGTOT
```

 ## How do I insert rows from one table into another?

The SQL insert table statement uses either the value clause or a subquery to deliver rows to be inserted into a table. When it is required to extract rows from one table and insert them into another, perhaps with aggregations or summarizations, the subquery form of the INSERT statement can be used. In the example below, a table is built using some of the rows from another table.

```
INSERT INTO SNAPSHOTEMP41
(EMPNO, FIRSTNME, MIDINIT, LASTNME, DEPT, HIREDATE,
SEX)
SELECT  EMPNO, FIRSTNME, MIDINIT, LASTNME,
   WORKDEPT, HIREDATE, SEX
FROM  TEMPDEPT
WHERE WORKDEPT = 'D41'
```

 ## How do I delete from one table based on conditions in another table?

The SQL DELETE statement allows the use of a subquery as the predicate to set the conditions for deleting. In the example below, rows are deleted from TDEPT only if the MGRNO is found in the employee table where the DEPTNO (column name for department number) was "41". These types of subqueries can be as sophisticated as required.

```
DELETE
FROM  TDEPT
WHERE  MGRNO IN
     (SELECT EMPNO
      FROM EMP
      WHERE DEPTNO = '41')
```

MULTITABLE QUERIES

 ## What is the difference between an inner join, a left outer join, a right outer join, and a full join?

Joins are used to produce answers where there are relationships among tables. There is an inner join, usually referred to simply as a join, in which there is a list in the

FROM clause of all tables participating in the join. Normally, there are additional WHERE clauses, stating the relationships for the join. The result includes rows from all tables that match the conditions in the WHERE clauses that relate the tables to each other. These matching conditions can be any operation, such as equality, inequality, or greater than. Normally these relationship conditions work on columns that hold the same information

Sometimes the required answer needs all the data from one table, whether or not there are matching rows in other tables. To handle these conditions, outer joins are used. Outer joins always involve only two tables, which we refer to as a *left* table and a *right* table, and includes matching rows in the result as well as rows which have no matches. There are three types of outer joins:

- Left outer join
- Right outer join
- Full outer join

A left outer join produces a result that includes rows from the left table that do not match any rows in the right table, as well as rows that match in both tables. Any columns in the result from the right table where there is no matching data in the left are given the value of null.

A right outer join produces a result that includes rows from the right table that do not match any rows in the left table, as well as rows that match in both tables. Any columns in the result from the left table where there is no matching data in the right are given the value of null.

A full outer join produces a result that includes rows from both tables that do not match any rows in the other table, as well as rows that match in both tables. Any columns in the result from either table where there is no matching data in the other table are given the value of null.

How do I determine the sequence of join operations for tables in the FROM clause?

For inner joins, the join sequence is purely an optimizer decision.

```
FROM T4, T2, T3, T1
```

The optimizer calculates each join-order/join-method combination's cost. The exception occurs when using optimization class 3 or below in UDB, or when executing in OS/390. For these classes of optimization, joins beyond 9 tables and other complex operations will not have every combination calculated.

For outer joins, the determination of join sequence is related to the order in which the tables are listed in the FROM clause. The join sequence is processed left to right, unless parenthesis are used; if parentheses are used, the execution starts at the innermost parenthesis pair. The first example following will be processed from left to right; the second example will be processed from right to left, working from the innermost parentheses outward.

```
FROM T1 LEFT JOIN T2 FULL JOIN T3 RIGHT JOIN T4

FROM T1 LEFT JOIN (T2 FULL JOIN (T3 RIGHT JOIN T4))
```

Can I combine inner and outer joins?

Yes, inner joins and outer joins can be used in any combination in a SELECT statement. Either format of the inner join can be used using INNER JOIN and ON or just using a comma to separate the table names. The following illustration shows examples of the two types of formats for the inner join when used in combinations producing mixed joins:

```
SELECT COL1, COL2, COL3
FROM T1 LEFT JOIN T2
    ON T1.COL1 = T2.COL7                 INNER JOIN & ON clause format
INNER JOIN T3
    ON T1.COL1 > T3.COL3

SELECT COL1, COL2, COL3
FROM T1 LEFT JOIN T2
    ON T1.COL1 = T2.COL7                 ',' & WHERE clause format
, T3
    WHERE T1.COL1 > T3.COL3
```

 ## How do I know when I need an outer join instead of an inner join?

The easy way to detect the need for an outer join is to listen for one of these few key *condition* phrases in the request for data: "whether or not," "regardless of," "no matter what," and so on. If any of these condition phrases fit in this generic request, "get all information from this table—*condition phrase*—other information is present in the other table," a left outer join will be necessary. For example, a request for "all orders existing in one table, whether or not they have descriptions existing in another table" would require the following query:

```
SELECT ORDER_NO, COALESCE(DESC_TXT,'NO DESCRIPTION')          All orders with or
FROM ORDER O   LEFT JOIN   DESCR D                            without descriptions
ON O.ORDER_NO = D.ORDER_NO
```

If the request was to get all orders with descriptions, the following query would supply the answer:

```
SELECT ORDER_NO, DESC_TXT          Orders with
FROM ORDER   O , DESCR   D         descriptions only
WHERE O.ORDER_NO = D.ORDER_NO
```

The result sets of the two queries may or may not be different, depending on your data. If a description existed for every order, the results would be identical. If not all orders had descriptions, the second query would have fewer rows returned, and would therefore be different.

A general rule for assessing the need for outer joins is that the more optional the data relationships, the more outer joins are required. Very few outer joins are necessary for applications that require at least one dependent row for every parent row, as shown below:

```
SELECT    T1.COLA, T2.COLB, T3.COLC, T4.COLD, T5.COLE
FROM      T1, T2, T3, T4          ⎤
WHERE     T1.COL1 = T2.COL2       ⎥   Required table relationships;
    AND   T2.COL2 = T3.COL3       ⎥   rows have to be there in order to join
    AND   T3.COL3 = T4.COL4       ⎦
LEFT JOIN      T5                 ⎤   Optional table relationship T4 to T5;
ON     T5.COL5 = T4.COL4          ⎦   rows may or may not be there
```

Just the opposite is true for data relationships that are optional, as shown below:

```
SELECT      T1.COLA, T2.COLB, T3.COLC, T4.COLD, T5.COLE
FROM      T1
LEFT JOIN      T2
ON    T1.COL1 = T2.COL2
LEFT JOIN      T3
ON      T2.COL2 = T3.COL3
LEFT JOIN      T4
ON      T3.COL3 = T4.COL4
LEFT JOIN      T5
ON      T5.COL5 = T4.COL4
```

Optional table relationships T1 to T2, T2 to T3, T3 to T4, and T4 to T5; rows may or may not be there

If a query's result set seems to be missing some number of rows that you know exist in the main table, the join predicate is probably disqualifying those rows. For example, orders that do not have descriptions would be missing from the result set of an inner join. If you change the join to a left outer join, the join predicate loosens up and qualifies all orders, regardless of whether they join to a description.

 Is there a difference between in-line views (a.k.a. table expressions) and regular views?

Yes, there are distinct differences between in-line views/table expressions and views generated with a CREATE VIEW statement. An in-line view allows host variables, enabling queries using in-line views to be more flexible, as shown below:

```
SELECT T2GRP.COLX_PART, SUM(T1.COLB)
FROM T1,
     (SELECT COLZ, SUBSTR(COLX, :STRT, :LNGTH) AS COLX_PART
      FROM T2
      WHERE T2.COLY = :HV-COLY)  AS T2GRP
WHERE   T1.COLA = T2GRP.COLZ
GROUP BY   T2GRP.COLX_PART
```

Table expression; also called an in-line view

To achieve the same results with a CREATE VIEW statement, you would have to execute a statement for every unique combination of host variable values (see Figure 10-1).

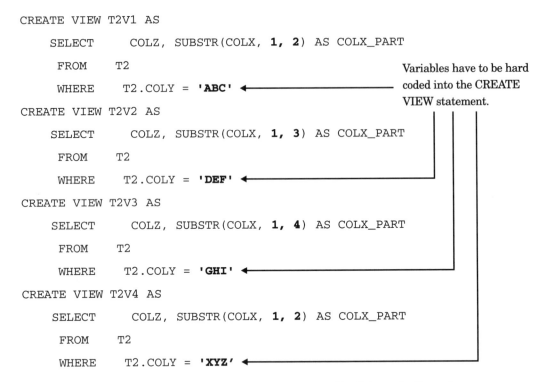

```
CREATE VIEW T2V1 AS
     SELECT      COLZ, SUBSTR(COLX, 1, 2) AS COLX_PART
     FROM      T2
     WHERE     T2.COLY = 'ABC'
CREATE VIEW T2V2 AS
     SELECT      COLZ, SUBSTR(COLX, 1, 3) AS COLX_PART
     FROM      T2
     WHERE     T2.COLY = 'DEF'
CREATE VIEW T2V3 AS
     SELECT      COLZ, SUBSTR(COLX, 1, 4) AS COLX_PART
     FROM      T2
     WHERE     T2.COLY = 'GHI'
CREATE VIEW T2V4 AS
     SELECT      COLZ, SUBSTR(COLX, 1, 2) AS COLX_PART
     FROM      T2
     WHERE     T2.COLY = 'XYZ'
```

Variables have to be hard coded into the CREATE VIEW statement.

Figure 10-1 CREATE VIEW statements are not as flexible as in-line views

Once all the CREATE VIEW combinations have been created, the views can be referenced in the following SELECT statement:

```
SELECT   T2V1.COLX_PART, SUM(T1.COLB)
FROM   T1,   T2V1
WHERE      T1.COLA = T2V1.COLZ
GROUP BY   T2V1.COLX_PART
```

View name would have to change based on which set of variables are needed

The second difference between CREATE VIEW and in-line views is that in-line views are not stored in the DB2 catalog as view definitions. At BIND time, the optimizer reads the in-line view from the SQL statement, instead of from the DB2 catalog When there is a choice of format producing the same result, the choice is normally up to site standards with specific reasons for using which format.

What is the order of execution for query blocks in which one or more blocks is a non-correlated subquery?

For non-correlated subquery query blocks, the order of execution is inside out, beginning with the innermost queries first, and continuing outward.

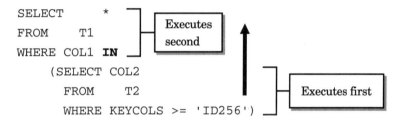

What is the order of execution for query blocks in which one or more blocks is a correlated subquery?

For correlated subquery query blocks, the order of execution is outer-inner-outer, once for each qualifying row from the outer query. The following is an example of a single correlated subquery:

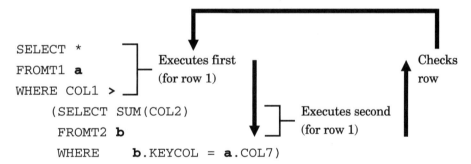

For subqueries that have more than two levels, the order of execution depends on where the correlation refers to and what operators are between the levels (IN, =, EXISTS, and so on). Typically, they execute in a top-bottom-middle-bottom-middle-bottom ... middle-top pattern. The top query executes first and prepares a list of rows that will be passed down to the correlation point, one row at a time. The middle query executes second, and prepares a list of rows that will be passed down to the correlation point, one row at a time. The

bottom query executes last and sends results up. This forms two loops, an outer loop which is top to bottom, and an inner loop which is middle to bottom. The outer loop is the driver, and the inner loop executes and continues until end of rows, once for each row in the outer loop.

For NOT EXISTS subqueries, the bottom query returns a result of true if at least one row was found to meet the condition, or false if no rows were found to meet the condition. If the result was true, the next row from the middle query is passed down to the bottom and tested again. This continues until there are no more middle query rows, or a false result is returned.

In either case, the process goes back to the middle query. If the bottom result is false, a row can be selected from the middle query, which sets the next result to true on the way up. The top query is not allowed (NOT EXISTS is true) to put the current row's information into the result set, so it instead gets the next row and starts all over again. If the bottom query result is true, a row cannot be selected from the middle query, which sets the next result to false. The top query is allowed (NOT EXISTS is false) to put the current row's information into the result set, and it then retrieves the next row and starts the process over again. Figure 10-2 is an example of a double correlated NOT EXISTS subselect with table correlation names of BLK1, BLK2, and BLK3.

This query will produce a list of suppliers that have all the same parts as supplier S2. The top list of suppliers (BLK1.S#) is the driver for the whole process. One supplier is passed from the top, all the way down to the bottom query. Next, one part (BLK2.P#) is passed from the middle, to the bottom query. Then the bottom query executes and returns an answer of true or false to the middle query. If the result of the bottom query was true (a stop condition), the middle query passes another part (BLK2.P#) down to the bottom query.

This loop continues until a false condition is met or until there are no more parts to pass. If there are no more parts, then the final answer to the bottom query is true or stop.

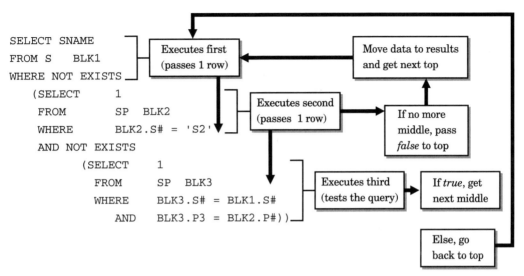

Figure 10-2 An example of a double correlated NOT EXISTS subselect

Since the middle query is not allowed to execute (on the way up), the answer is an empty set and a false is passed up to the top query. This is a go condition for the top query to move the current row's information to the final result. This moves the supplier name into the result set that has at least all the same parts as S2.

If at any time the result of the bottom query is false or a go condition, the middle query is allowed to execute and return a result of true to the top query. This is a stop condition for the top query, which then moves forward to the next supplier (BLK1.S#) and starts the whole top-bottom-middle-bottom ... middle-top process over again. This process quickly filters out any supplier that does not have at least all the same parts as S2. The sooner a false condition is detected on the bottom query, the sooner a new row from the top query is tested.

LIMITS

 How many fields can I sort by in my query?

As of DB2 for OS/390 Version 5 and UDB Version 5, the total number of columns allowed in a GROUP BY or an ORDER BY is 750 for DB2 OS/390 and 500 for DB2 UDB. The total sort row length in a GROUP BY, ORDER BY, DISTINCT, or UNION is 4,000 bytes for DB2 OS/390 and 4,005 bytes for DB2 UDB. The byte limit is based on the largest row that will fit on a page.

 How many tables can I include in a query?

A maximum of 15 tables can be included in a query in DB2 OS/390 through Version 5. In DB2 UDB, the limit is based on available storage. In DB2 OS/390 Version 6, this limit has been raised to 225 tables. This limit applies to every table reference, regardless of where it appears in a full SELECT statement. In a join, the 15-table limit is being removed in DB2 OS/390 Version 6, and this change is being delivered through an APAR to Version 5.

 NOTE: *The limit is being increased in DB2 V6 and through an APAR in DB2 V5.*

 What is the limit on UNION blocks in a query?

There is no documented limit for UNION statements, other than the limit of 32,767 bytes for one SQL statement in DB2 OS/390 and 32,765 bytes for DB2 UDB, and the limit of 15 total base tables for OS/390 through Version 5. In DB2 OS/390 Version 6, the limits of tables in a SQL statement is increased to 225.

NUANCES

 Does the order of the range variables matter when using the BETWEEN clause?

The basic syntax of a BETWEEN clause is:

```
COL BETWEEN :low AND :high
```

Reversing the sequence of the variables will not obtain consistent results. The following syntax will not return the same results as the previous query and should never be used:

```
COL BETWEEN :high AND :low
```

This also applies to the other BETWEEN clause formats:

```
:hv BETWEEN COL1 AND COL2
expression BETWEEN expression AND expression
```

How is an IN list accessed in a non-correlated subquery?

A non-correlated subquery has a unique access technique for processing IN lists. The generated IN list will be probed once for each qualifying row by the outer SELECT. Pointers to a few sparse rows in the list are placed in a small, internally created sparse index. This sparse index is dynamically created during the execution of the subquery and is deleted when the query has completed. The query in Figure 10-3 is

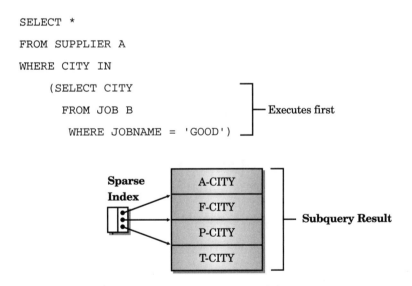

```
SELECT *
FROM SUPPLIER A
WHERE CITY IN
    (SELECT CITY
        FROM JOB B              ─┐
        WHERE JOBNAME = 'GOOD')  ─┘ ── Executes first
```

```
Sparse
Index        A-CITY      ─┐
             F-CITY       │
                          ├─ Subquery Result
             P-CITY       │
             T-CITY      ─┘
```

All cities qualified by a JOBNAME of 'GOOD' will be sorted, duplicates removed and placed in a temporary work file. A sparse index will be dynamically generated for the data in the temporary work file so the outer query can use it to probe into the list of cities in order to find a match, as the figure shows.

Figure 10-3   An example of a non-correlated subquery for IN list processing

an example of a non-correlated subquery that may cause a sparse index to be created for IN list processing.

An internal algorithm identifies which cities will be stored in the sparse index (not all city entries will be indexed). The sparse index is only generated for subqueries using the IN operator, and it is removed when the query completes.

How can I do searches on the "%" character using the LIKE predicate?

The ESCAPE phrase is used with the LIKE predicate to tell DB2 that the particular character following the ESCAPE is to be treated as a normal character in the literal string passed to the LIKE predicate. This is done to allow the wildcard characters of "%" and "_" to be used as normal matching characters in the process. The following syntax enables searching for reserved characters such as "%" and "_":

```
WHERE NAME LIKE 'C%_SON' ESCAPE %
WHERE NAME LIKE 'C%_SON' ESCAPE _
```

The first WHERE clause will look for names that begin with "C%", have any other character in the third position, and end with "SON".

The second WHERE clause will look for names that begin with "C", having any number of any other characters following the "C" and ending with "_SON".

Is there a difference in the performance of the BETWEEN predicate and the equivalent >= AND <= predicates?

No, as of the current versions of the DB2 family members, there is no difference in the performance of the execution of the following predicates:

```
WHERE COL BETWEEN :HV1 AND :HV2
WHERE COL >= :HV1 AND COL <= :HV2
```

Can I use a subquery in the SET clause of an UPDATE statement?

Yes, a special kind of subquery, called a scalar subquery, can be used in the SET clause of an UPDATE statement in DB2 UDB. A scalar subquery, by definition, can only retrieve one value as the result (one row of one column). The following query is an example of an UPDATE statement using a scalar subquery:

```
UPDATE T1
    SET COL2 = (SELECT SUM(COLX)
                    FROM T4 WHERE COL7 > 30)
        , COL3 = 90
WHERE COL1 = 'ABC'
```

How does DB2 process a singleton SELECT?

A singleton SELECT uses an internal cursor to keep track of the rows requested. The processing looks like this internally:

```
DB2 Opens A Cursor
    Fetches the first row (can be different each time
        depending on the access path)
    If row found,
        Returns the data to the host variables
        Issues second fetch
        If row found,
            SQLCODE -811
        If no additional row found
            SQLCODE +0
    Else
        SQLCODE +100
Close Cursor
```

How can I convert a NULL that is returned from a SELECT to a real value?

Use the COALESCE scalar function to convert a NULL to a real value. An example of the COALESCE function follows.

```
COALESCE('HOME PHONE ='||HOME_NO,
         'WORK PHONE =' ||WORK_NO,
         'PAGER = '||PAGE_NO,
         'CANNOT BE REACHED')
```

The function checks the values in the list from left to right. If a NULL is found, even within the expression, the check moves to the next entry. If all entries are NULL, the result of the function is NULL. However, if a constant, literal, or special register is in the final position of the list, a real value will always be returned.

Caution: *The final entry in the list must be a data type compatible with the columns that were tested. For example, if a date column was tested in the list, DATE('0001-01-01') or CURRENT DATE would be valid final entries in the COALESCE list.*

Tip: *The COALESCE function can also be used in a WHERE clause or an ON clause of a FULL OUTER JOIN.*

EXPRESSIONS

Can I test more than one column in a CASE expression?

Yes, any number of WHEN conditions can be used in the CASE expression, and each WHEN condition can reference a different column or expression. The following is an example of a CASE expression that tests multiple columns:

```
CASE (
    WHEN COL7 > 15 THEN COL7 * .0133
    WHEN COL3 = 34 THEN COL3 / .0133
    WHEN COL8 < 98 THEN 999
    ELSE NULL END)
AS MULTICALC
```

Where can I use CASE expression?

Anywhere an expression is allowed in a SQL statement, a CASE expression is also allowed. Examples include:

- SELECT clause
- WHERE clause
- HAVING clause
- Built-in function
- IN (list)
- DELETE
- UPDATE

An example of a CASE expression in an UPDATE statement follows:

```
UPDATE EMP SET BASE_SALARY  =
    CASE EMP_GRADE
        WHEN '01' THEN BASE_SALARY * :low_increase
        WHEN '02' THEN BASE_SALARY * :medium_increase
        WHEN '03' THEN BASE_SALARY * :high_increase
        WHEN '14' THEN BASE_SALARY * :no_increase
        WHEN '25' THEN
                 BASE_SALARY * :negative_increase
        WHEN '96' THEN
                 BASE_SALARY * :ridiculous_increase
    END
```

 Can I use a subquery inside a CASE expression?

In DB2 UDB, a scalar subquery can be used in a CASE expression. The following query is an example of scalar subqueries used inside a CASE expression:

```
SELECT (CASE WHEN (SELECT SUM(COLX) FROM T4
                 WHERE COL7 > 30) > 400
                 THEN 'OVER'
             WHEN (SELECT SUM(COLX) FROM T4
                 WHERE COL7 <= 30) > 400
                 THEN 'UNDER'
             ELSE 'DOES NOT REGISTER' END)
      , T2.COLY
FROM T2
WHERE T2.COL1 > :HV
```

Can I call a stored procedure in a CASE expression?

No, a stored procedure cannot be called from within a
CASE expression.

Can I use an IN list in a CASE expression?

Yes, for DB2 UDB only, you can use an IN list in the WHEN
clause of the CASE expression. In DB2 OS/390 only, the OR
can be used for multiple values through Version 5. Following
are examples showing how multiple values are used in
comparisons in a CASE expression:

```
SELECT
      SUM(CASE WHEN T1.COLX IN('X', 'Y') THEN AMOUNT END)
    , SUM(CASE WHEN T1.COLX IN('A', 'C') THEN AMOUNT END)
    , SUM(CASE WHEN T1.COLX IN('E', 'G') THEN AMOUNT END)
    , SUM(CASE WHEN T1.COLX IN('Q', 'S') THEN AMOUNT END)
    , SUM(CASE WHEN T1.COLX IN('T', 'V') THEN AMOUNT END)
FROM    T1, T2, T3, T4
WHERE   C1.T1 = C2.T2
AND     C1.T1 = C3.T3
AND     C1.T2 = C4.T4
AND      T1.COLX IN ('A', 'C','E', 'G','Q',
                    'S','T', 'V','X', 'Y')
------------------------------------------------------------
SELECT
      SUM(CASE WHEN T1.COLX ='X'
          OR T1.COLX ='Y' THEN AMOUNT END)
    , SUM(CASE WHEN T1.COLX ='A'
          OR T1.COLX ='C' THEN AMOUNT END)
    , SUM(CASE WHEN T1.COLX ='E'
          OR T1.COLX ='G' THEN AMOUNT END)
    , SUM(CASE WHEN T1.COLX ='Q'
          OR T1.COLX ='S' THEN AMOUNT END)
    , SUM(CASE WHEN T1.COLX ='T'
          OR T1.COLX ='V' THEN AMOUNT END)
FROM    T1, T2, T3, T4
WHERE   C1.T1 = C2.T2
AND     C1.T1 = C3.T3
```

```
AND     C1.T2 = C4.T4
AND     T1.COLX IN ('A', 'C','E', 'G','Q',
                     'S','T', 'V','X', 'Y')
```

How can I perform a GROUP BY on a portion of a column?

The solution is not as simple as GROUP BY SUBSTR(COL, 2,4) because this is not allowed yet in DB2. Instead, the dividing of the column needs to be done first in a table expression or a view. If you use a table expression, host variables can be used to improve the query's flexibility, as shown in the following example:

```
SELECT    T2GRP.COLX_PART, SUM(T1.COLB)
FROM      T1,
    (SELECT COLZ,
        SUBSTR(COLX, :STRT, :LNGTH) AS COLX_PART
     FROM    T2
     WHERE   T2.COLY = :HV-COLY) AS T2GRP
WHERE    T1.COLA = T2GRP.COLZ
GROUP BY    T2GRP.COLX_PART
```

What is the difference between a common table expression and an in-line view/table expression?

Common table expressions are currently only supported in DB2 UDB. The basic syntax of a common table expression is:

```
WITH  temporary_name  (column-names) AS (query)
```

Common table expressions can only be used in the following situations:

- In a top-level SELECT query
- In a SELECT nested immediately inside a CREATE VIEW statement
- In a SELECT nested immediately inside an INSERT statement

Common table expressions have two additional restrictions:

- They can not be used in a single-row SELECT statement
- They must use a cursor to FETCH rows

A common table expression is defined once, prior to the SELECT, and can be used multiple times within the same SELECT statement. In contrast, the in-line view/table expression is defined in the FROM clause of the SELECT statement and is required to be redefined each time the in-line view/table expression is needed. Figure 10-4 compares the two.

One other difference between the two is that the common table expression allows UNION statements, whereas the in-line view/table expression does not.

```
WITH sales_by_region (region_name, sales_territory, total_commission) AS
    (SELECT reg_name, territory, sum(bonus) + sum(commission)
    FROM sales_tables
    GROUP BY reg_name, territory)
SELECT region_name, sales_territory
FROM sales_by_region ◄─────────────────────────        The common table expression
WHERE total_commission =                                is defined once and used twice
    (SELECT max(total_commission)
    FROM sales_by_region) ◄──────────────────────
    ---------------------------------------------
SELECT reg_name, sales_territory
FROM (SELECT reg_name, territory as sales_territory,
        sum(bonus) + sum(commission) as total_commission        The in-line view/table
    FROM sales_tables                                            expression has to be defined
    GROUP BY reg_name, territory) AS sales_by_region            each time it is needed
WHERE total_commission =
    (SELECT max(total_commission2)
    FROM  (SELECT reg_name, territory as sales_territory2,
        sum(bonus) + sum(commission) as total_commission2
    FROM sales_tables
    GROUP BY reg_name, territory) AS sales_by_region2))
```

Figure 10-4   The difference between a common table expression and an in-line
view/table expression

Chapter 11

Advanced SQL Queries

Answer Topics!

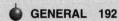

Advanced SQL Queries @ a Glance

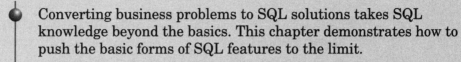

Converting business problems to SQL solutions takes SQL knowledge beyond the basics. This chapter demonstrates how to push the basic forms of SQL features to the limit.

Expand your SQL portfolio with numerous examples showcasing complex joins, recursion, CASE, correlated HAVING clauses, GROUPING SETS, ROLLUP, CUBE, and combinations of many advanced techniques.

GENERAL

 How do I retrieve detail and summary data within the same result row?

There are a few methods for merging detail row data with summary row data. The first method is an old fashioned CREATE VIEW statement. First, create a view that calculates the summary information.

```
CREATE VIEW SUMMARYVIEW AS
(SELECT REGION, SUM(SALES) AS TOTAL_SALES,
    MAX(SALES) AS MAX_SALES, AVG(SALES) AS AVERAGE_SALES
    FROM SALES
    GROUP BY REGION)
```

Next, join the summary view to the table with the detail data needed for the result as follows:

```
SELECT SALES.*, SUMMARYVIEW.*
FROM SALES, SUMMARYVIEW
WHERE SALES.REGION = SUMMARYVIEW.REGION
other conditions
```

The second method simply replaces the view with a table expression, as follows:

```
SELECT SALES.*, SUMMARY.*
FROM SALES,
    (SELECT REGION, SUM(SALES) AS TOTAL_SALES,
    MAX(SALES) AS MAX_SALES, AVG(SALES) AS AVERAGE_SALES
    FROM SALES
    GROUP BY REGION ) AS SUMMARY
WHERE SALES.REGION = SUMMARY.REGION
other conditions
```

 How do I retrieve detail and summary data within the same result set?

A few GROUP BY options, for UDB only, allow detail rows, as well as summary rows, to be returned in a single result set. These GROUP BY options include GROUPING SETS, ROLLUP, and CUBE. Each option provides a specific level of subtotaling and grand totaling.

GROUPING SETS individually specify which column or combinations of columns are to be subtotaled. Columns mentioned within parentheses are subtotaled as a set. Columns mentioned singularly will have their own subtotals. For example, GROUP BY GROUPING SETS ((A,B,C)(A,B)(A)()) will provide subtotals for A,B,C combination, A,B combination, and A alone, plus a grand total.

ROLLUP and CUBE are shortcuts to coding extensive GROUPING SETS. For example, GROUP BY ROLLUP (A,B,C) will generate GROUPING SETS ((A,B,C)(A,B)(A)()). If one of the generated subtotals is unwanted, simply code the individual GROUPING SETS.

What ROLLUP is to GROUPING SETS, CUBE is to ROLLUP. CUBE generates every combination of columns plus a grand total. For example, GROUP BY ROLLUP (A,B,C) generates GROUPING SETS ((A,B,C)(A,B)(A)(A,C)(B,C)(B)(C)()).

Figure 11-2 outlines the column subtotals and displays the results of the query in Figure 11-1 which first shows using GROUPING SETS and second, using CUBE.

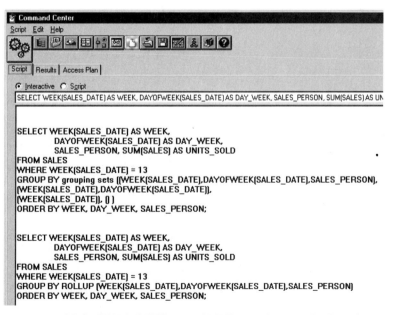

Figure 11-1 GROUPING SETS and CUBE queries producing the same results

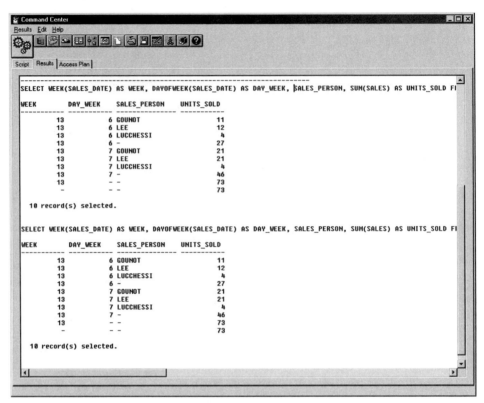

Figure 11-2 Results of the queries in Figure 11-1

How can you join more than 15 base tables together on OS/390?

When you are over the 15-table limit, it is time to create a global temporary table. Place the result of several small table joins in the GLOBAL TEMPORARY TABLE statement. Use the result in the remaining JOIN statements as follows:

```
CREATE GLOBAL TEMPORARY TABLE HOLD_DATA_TEMP
     CUSTOMER CHAR(6) NOT NULL,
     LAST_NAME CHAR(35) NOT NULL,
     AMOUNT FIXED DEC(11,2) NOT NULL)
```

```
INSERT INTO HOLD_DATA_TEMP
    SELECT T1.CUSTOMER, T2.LAST_NAME, T3.AMOUNT
    FROM T1, T2, T3
    WHERE T1.ACCOUNT = T2.ACCOUNT
      AND T2.DETAIL = T3.DETAIL

SELECT columns
FROM HOLD_DATA_TEMP, T4, ..., T17
WHERE join conditions
```

The 15-table limit per SELECT statement will be extended (DB2 UDB for OS/390 Version 6, and back leveled to Version 5) to allow more than15 tables per query block (subselect, view, table expression, union block) and in V6 up to 225 tables per SELECT statement.

How do I retrieve the top *n* rows in a stand-alone SQL statement?

To retrieve, for example, the employees with the top salaries, the value for n is placed in the host variable or is hard coded, as shown in Figure 11-3.

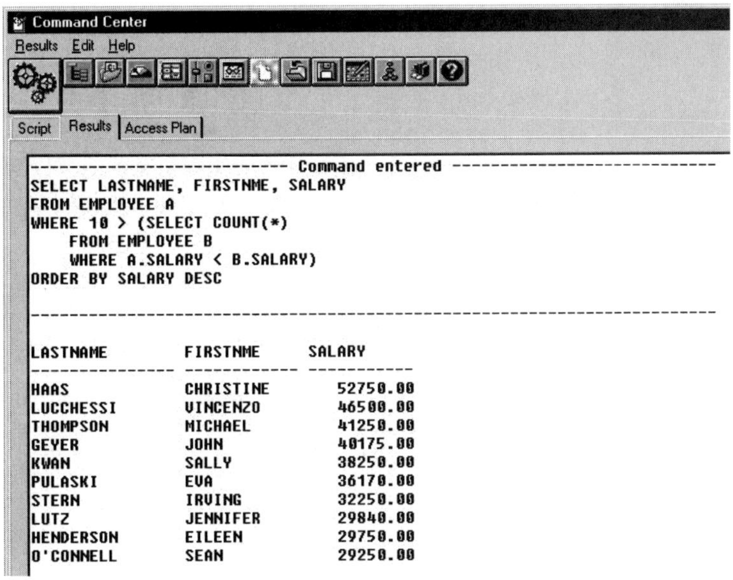

```
------------------------ Command entered ------------------------
SELECT LASTNAME, FIRSTNME, SALARY
FROM EMPLOYEE A
WHERE 10 > (SELECT COUNT(*)
    FROM EMPLOYEE B
    WHERE A.SALARY < B.SALARY)
ORDER BY SALARY DESC
-----------------------------------------------------------------


LASTNAME        FIRSTNME      SALARY
---------       --------      --------
HAAS            CHRISTINE     52750.00
LUCCHESSI       VINCENZO      46500.00
THOMPSON        MICHAEL       41250.00
GEYER           JOHN          40175.00
KWAN            SALLY         38250.00
PULASKI         EVA           36170.00
STERN           IRVING        32250.00
LUTZ            JENNIFER      29840.00
HENDERSON       EILEEN        29750.00
O'CONNELL       SEAN          29250.00
```

Figure 11-3 Query to retrieve the top 10 rows

How do I retrieve random rows?

There are several queries that can pull random rows from a table. Use the following query for retrieving random detail data on OS/390, or use the random function (RAND) on UDB.

```
SELECT columns
FROM LARGE_TABLE
WHERE
(SUBSTR(DIGITS(MICROSECOND(CURRENT TIMESTAMP))),5,1)='6'
```

Use the following query for retrieving random summary data:

```
SELECT COLA, COLB, COLC, SUM(COLX)
FROM TAB1, TAB2
WHERE TAB1.COLD = TAB2.COLZ
GROUP BY COLA, COLB, COLC
HAVING '6' =      (SELECT
   MAX(SUBSTR(DIGITS(MICROSECOND(CURRENT TIMESTAMP))),5,1)
   FROM TAB3
   WHERE TAB3.COLJ = TAB1.COLA
   AND TAB3.COLK = TAB1.COLB
   AND TAB3.COLL = TAB1.COLC)
```

How do I generate test data?

All you need is a table with a substantial number of rows and some version of the statement shown in Figure 11-4. In the example, we use the SALES table to simply define the number of rows that will be in the TESTTAB table. The query inserts one row into the test table for every row found in SALES.

How do I compare column values on different rows in the same table?

To compare column values that live on different rows, you need to join the table to itself. This enables DB2 to have two internal cursors scrolling through the table. One cursor can point to one row and the other cursor performs the comparison. These queries usually need an additional predicate, usually COL <> COL or COL > COL, that discards the unnecessary

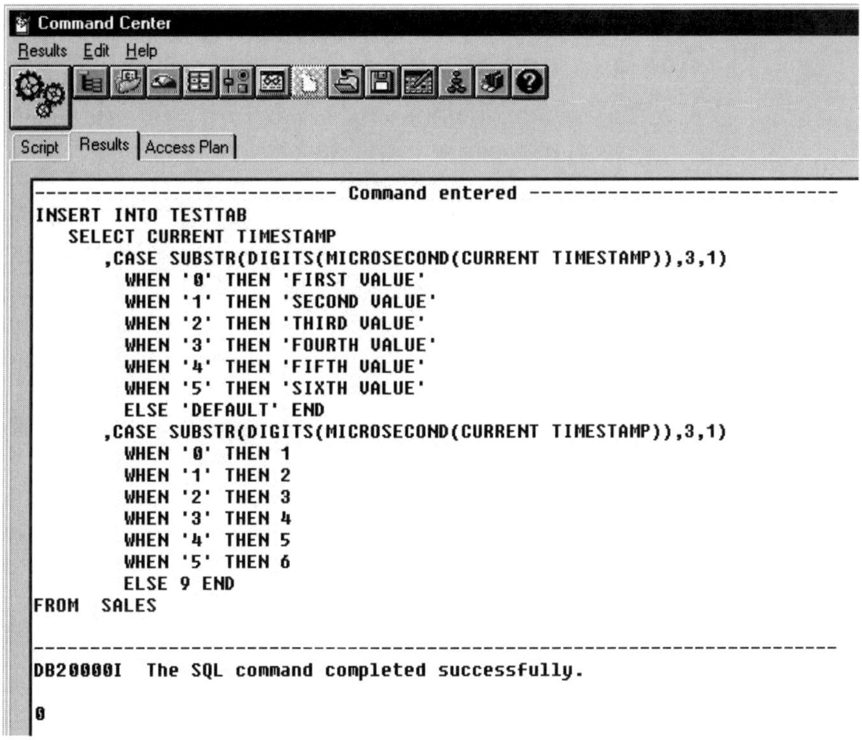

```
 Command Center
Results  Edit  Help
[toolbar icons]

 Script   Results   Access Plan

------------------------- Command entered -------------------------
INSERT INTO TESTTAB
   SELECT CURRENT TIMESTAMP
      ,CASE SUBSTR(DIGITS(MICROSECOND(CURRENT TIMESTAMP)),3,1)
         WHEN '0' THEN 'FIRST VALUE'
         WHEN '1' THEN 'SECOND VALUE'
         WHEN '2' THEN 'THIRD VALUE'
         WHEN '3' THEN 'FOURTH VALUE'
         WHEN '4' THEN 'FIFTH VALUE'
         WHEN '5' THEN 'SIXTH VALUE'
         ELSE 'DEFAULT' END
      ,CASE SUBSTR(DIGITS(MICROSECOND(CURRENT TIMESTAMP)),3,1)
         WHEN '0' THEN 1
         WHEN '1' THEN 2
         WHEN '2' THEN 3
         WHEN '3' THEN 4
         WHEN '4' THEN 5
         WHEN '5' THEN 6
         ELSE 9 END
FROM  SALES

-----------------------------------------------------------------
DB20000I  The SQL command completed successfully.

0
```

Figure 11-4   Query to insert test rows with variable test data

join relationship of a row joined to itself. The following query produces a report of all pairs of employees with the same birthdate.

```
SELECT    A.NAME, A.BDAY, B.NAME
FROM    EMP A, EMP B
WHERE   A.BDAY = B.BDAY
   AND    A.EMPNO > B.EMPNO
```

The comparison predicate is A.BDAY = B.BDAY and the discard predicate is A.EMPNO > B.EMPNO. The discard predicate never checks the comparison more than once by using the > operator instead of the <> operator. The <> predicate would have performed the comparison twice; once for A to B and once for B to A.

 How do I calculate the duration between two date fields in one table?

The most efficient way to calculate date duration within one table, especially if the dates are on two different rows, is to join the table to itself. This enables DB2 to have two internal cursors scrolling through the table. One cursor can point to one row and the other cursor can search for join criteria. Once the join relationship is found, the date duration can be calculated. These queries usually need an additional predicate that discards the unnecessary join relationship of a row joined to itself.

The following query calculates the number of days between two dates on different rows. The first date is the last check-out date and the second date is the very next check-in date (different row) for the same room. The table definition is shown in Figure 11-5. The query, shown in Figure 11-6, produces a report, shown in Figure 11-7, indicating the dates when the rooms are available and the number of consecutive days they are available.

Sample Contents - RESV_TAB

OEMCOMPUTER - DB2 - SAMPLE - RYEVICH - RESV_TAB

ROOM	CHECK_IN_DATE	CHECK_OUT_DATE
A101	1993-12-01	1993-12-02
A101	1993-12-05	1993-12-06
A101	1993-12-07	1993-12-08
A101	1993-12-10	1993-12-17
A101	1993-12-20	1993-12-22
A101	1993-12-30	1993-12-31
B302	1993-12-10	1993-12-15
B302	1993-12-31	1993-12-05
B302	1993-12-01	1993-12-05
B302	1993-12-20	1993-12-24

Figure 11-5 The reservation data table used in Figure 11-6 and Figure 11-7

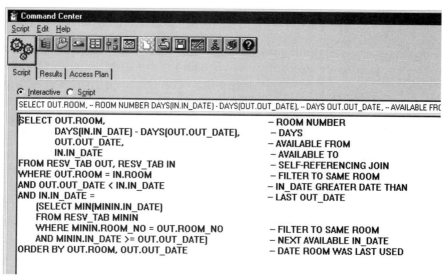

Figure 11-6 SQL query to produce a table of available rooms

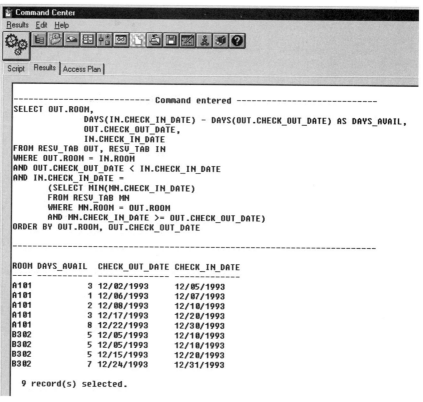

Figure 11-7 Result of the query in Figure 6

 # What makes a recursive SQL statement recursive?

The basic syntax of a recursive SQL statement contains a common table expression (not available on OS/390) with special requirements. The first requirement of the common table expression is a query that selects at least one row that is joined to another query block with a UNION ALL. The second requirement is that the bottom query of that UNION ALL has to request data from the common table expression (that is what makes it recursive). The bottom query is normally joined to the table referenced in the top query, and can also join to other tables as needed. Think of the common table expression as a to-be-built stack of rows. Every row that gets put in the result set for the common table expression will fall through to the bottom query of the UNION ALL block. Figure 11-8 demonstrates how this works.

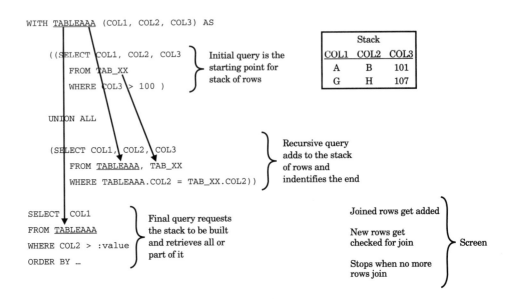

Figure 11-8   An example of a simple recursive query

Here are the rules for recursive SQL:

- Define a common table expression containing a WITH clause
- Table expression must have a UNION ALL between part 1 and part 2
- Part 1 is a normal query (also called the initial query)
- Part 2 is a query that adds more rows to the table expression based on the rows that are already there (also called the recursive query)
- Cannot contain any column functions
- Cannot contain SELECT DISTINCT
- Cannot contain GROUP BY or HAVING
- Cannot contain any lower-level subqueries that reference the common table expression
- Each column must be assignment compatible with the corresponding column of the initial query
- After the WITH clause, use the common table expression in a SELECT statement that requests the data

How does a recursive SQL statement know when to stop?

The recursive part of the query is in control of the end of the result. Either there are no more rows that will qualify in a join condition, or a simple local predicate on a generated counter will stop a recursive query, as in the example shown in Figure 11-9.

Caution: *The RAND() function will not be available for the OS/390 platform until Version 6.*

Can I put multiple starting-point queries or recursive join queries in my recursive SQL statement?

Yes, you can put multiple initialization queries prior to the UNION ALL in a recursive query. You can also put multiple recursion queries after the UNION ALL as shown in the SQL statement in Figure 11-10.

```
WITH TEMP(N) AS
        (VALUES(1)  ◄──────── Starts the stack of rows
    UNION ALL
        SELECT N+1  ◄──────── Adds to the stack of rows
        FROM TEMP
        WHERE N < 1000 )  ◄──────── Stopping point for adding to the stack of rows
    SELECT N, INTEGER(RAND() * 1000)◄
    FROM TEMP◄
```

Requests columns and calculations from the stack of rows

Requests the stack to be generated

Figure 11-9 Setting the stop conditions on a recursive SQL statement

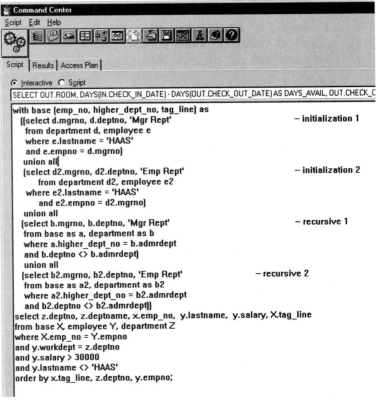

Figure 11-10 Recursive SQL queries with multiple recursions

How can I limit the number of rows coming back from a cursor?

FETCH FIRST n ROWS is a new extension to the SELECT clause. This clause, from the SQL3 standard, is available starting in DB2 UDB Version 5.2. This clause will limit the number of rows coming back from a result set; however, identifying the correct n rows will still be the job of the WHERE, GROUP BY, and HAVING clauses.

Can I combine inner and outer join syntax?

Yes, inner join syntax can be combined with outer join syntax. There are two methods for coding inner joins: INNER JOIN with an ON clause or with WHERE clauses, as shown below:

```
SELECT columns
FROM T1 INNER JOIN T2
ON    T1.COLA = T2.COLX
   AND T1.COLB = T2.COLY


SELECT columns
FROM T1,T2
WHERE T1.COLA = T2.COLX
   AND T1.COLB = T2.COLY
```

One advantage of the latter method is that it clearly separates the inner joins from the outer joins in complex queries such as the following. (Please note that this query has been greatly changed from the actual production query and the purpose is just to show how to formulate this type of query structure. The query as currently written does not allow an explanation of the data or the result, but is for demonstration only.)

```
SELECT COALESCE(MAIN.SCODE, SUB.SCODE) AS SCODE
   ,COALESCE(MAIN.SDATE, SUB.SDATE) AS SDATE
   ,COALESCE(MAIN.DCODE, SUB.DCODE) AS DCODE
   ,COALESCE(MAIN.ITEM_QT,0) AS ITEM_QT
   ,COALESCE(SUB.I_ITEM_QT,0)
      - COALESCE(SUB.DE_ITEM_QT,0) AS ITEM_QT
   ,COALESCE(SUB.I_LDGR_QT,0)
      - COALESCE(SUB.DE_LDGR_QT,0) AS LDGR_QT
```

```
            ,COALESCE(MAIN.DFC_QT,0) AS DFC_QT
            ,COALESCE(SUB.I_UNDLV_QT,0)
                - COALESCE(SUB.DE_UNDLV_QT,0) AS UNDLV_QT
            ,COALESCE(MAIN.BAL_QT,0) AS BAL_QT
        FROM
            (SELECT COALESCE(LDGR.SCODE, DF.SCODE) AS SCODE
            ,COALESCE(LDGR.SDATE, DF.SDATE) AS SDATE
            ,COALESCE(LDGR.DCODE, DF.DCODE) AS DCODE
            ,COALESCE(LDGR.BAL_QT,0) AS BAL_QT
            ,COALESCE(DF.DFC_QT,0) AS DFC_QT
            ,COALESCE(DF.ITEM_QT,0) AS ITEM_QT
            FROM
                (SELECT COALESCE(TE1.SCODE, TE2.SCODE) AS SCODE
                ,COALESCE(TE2.SDATE, '0001-01-01') AS SDATE
                ,COALESCE(TE1.DCODE, TE2.DCODE) AS DCODE
                ,COALESCE(TE1.BAL_QT, TE2.BAL_QT) AS BAL_QT
                FROM
                    (SELECT LI.SCODE AS SCODE
                    ,LI.DCODE AS DCODE
                    ,SUM(LI.BAL_QT) AS BAL_QT
                    FROM SCT_LDGR_DNM_ISS LI, SER SE
                    WHERE LI.SCT_ACCT_NR = :WS-ACCT-NR
                    AND LI.AS_OF_TRAN_DT = :WS-LDGR-TRAN-DT
                    AND LI.SCODE = SE.SCODE
                    AND LI.DCODE <> :tw
                    AND SE.BD_TYP_CD = :avalb
                    AND SE.SUB_ADD_SDATE_IN = 'N'
                    GROUP BY LI.SCODE, LI.DCODE) AS TE1
            FULL JOIN
            (SELECT LI.SCODE AS SCODE
                ,CHAR(LI.SDATE) AS SDATE
                ,LI.DCODE AS DCODE
                ,LI.BAL_QT AS BAL_QT
            FROM SS.SCT_LDGR_DNM_ISS LI, SS.SER SE
            WHERE LI.SCT_ACCT_NR = :acctnr
             AND (LI.SCODE <> :tsx
             AND LI.SDATE > :start_date)
             AND LI.AS_OF_TRAN_DT = :tran_dt
             AND LI.SCODE = SE.SCODE
             AND SE.BD_TYP_CD = :avalb
```

```
               AND LI.DCODE <> :tw
               AND SE.SUB_ADD_SDATE_IN = :ys) AS TE2
           ON   TE1.SCODE = TE2.SCODE
           AND TE1.DCODE = TE2.DCODE
           AND TE1.BAL_QT = TE2.BAL_QT) AS LDGR
       FULL JOIN
           (SELECT LD.SCODE AS SCODE
             ,CHAR(LD.SDATE) AS SDATE
             ,LD.DCODE AS DCODE
             ,LD.DFC_QT AS DFC_QT
             ,LD.ITEM_QT AS ITEM_QT
           FROM SS.SCT_LDGR_DF  LD
           WHERE LD.SCT_ACCT_NR = :acctnr
           AND (LD.SCODE <> :tsx
           AND LD.SDATE > :start_date)) AS DF
           ON LDGR.SCODE = DF.SCODE
           AND LDGR.SDATE = DF.SDATE
           AND LDGR.DCODE = DF.DCODE) AS MAIN
        FULL JOIN
         (SELECT TL.SCODE AS SCODE
         ,CHAR(TL.SDATE) AS SDATE
         ,TL.DCODE AS DCODE
         ,SUM(CASE WHEN (TL.SUB_ADD_SRC_CD = :val1
           THEN TL.SUB_ADD_QT END) AS I_UNDLV_QT
         ,SUM(CASE WHEN (TL.SUB_ADD_SRC_CD = :val2
           THEN TL.SUB_ADD_QT END) AS DE_UNDLV_QT
         ,SUM(CASE WHEN (TL.SUB_ADD_SRC_CD = :val3
           THEN TL.SUB_ADD_QT END) AS I_ITEM_QT
         ,SUM(CASE WHEN (TL.SUB_ADD_SRC_CD = :val4
           THEN TL.SUB_ADD_QT END) AS DE_ITEM_QT
         ,SUM(CASE WHEN (TL.SUB_ADD_SRC_CD = :val7
           THEN TL.SUB_ADD_QT END) AS I_LDGR_QT
         ,SUM(CASE WHEN (TL.SUB_ADD_SRC_CD = :val8
           THEN TL.SUB_ADD_QT END) AS DE_LDGR_QT
         FROM SS.TMP_ADD TL
         GROUP BY TL.SCODE, TL.SDATE, TL.DCODE) AS SUB
         ON   MAIN.SCODE = SUB.SCODE
         AND MAIN.SDATE = SUB.SDATE
         AND MAIN.DCODE = SUB.DCODE
    ORDER BY 1, 2, 3
```

ADVANCED SQL STATEMENT FUNCTIONALITY

 ## How do I remove duplicate rows?

There is always going to be an unload and a reload, whether by utility or by using SQL. If the duplicate rows are complete duplicates, then the following SQL could be used:

```
INSERT INTO NEW_TABLE
    SELECT DISTINCT *
    FROM OLD_TABLE
```

This approach does require that you build a new table exactly like the old table, and the new table should have the same indexes and especially a unique index on the key columns. It may be easier to unload the data, sort and remove duplicates, and reload (LOAD REPLACE) into the same structure.

 ## How do I compare two summary values?

There are a couple of ways to compare summary values. The first method restricts the result columns to one SELECT. Each summary value has to be calculated in separate SELECT statements. The top query requires a GROUP BY so that the comparison can be made in the HAVING clause as follows.

```
(SELECT A, B, C, D
FROM TAB1, TAB2
WHERE TAB1.D = TAB2.Z          -- join predicate
AND    TAB1.A = :hv            -- local filter
GROUP BY A, B, C, D            -- summarize
HAVING SUM(TAB1.E) <>          -- compare
    (SELECT SUM(TAB3.G)        -- summarize
    FROM TAB3
    WHERE TAB1.D = TAB3.Z))    --correlate
```

The second method allows columns from both SELECT statements in the result by using in-line views/table expressions:

```
SELECT T1T2.A, T1T2.B, T1T2.SUM_E, T3.SUM_G
FROM
    (SELECT A, B, C, D, SUM(TAB1.E) AS SUM_E
    FROM TAB1, TAB2
    WHERE TAB1.D = TAB2.Z              -- join predicate
    AND   TAB1.A = :hv                 -- local filter
    GROUP BY A, B, C, D   ) AS T1T2    -- summarize
    ,                                  -- join
    (SELECT SUM(TAB3.G) AS SUM_G       -- summarize
    FROM TAB3) AS T3
WHERE SUM_G <> = SUM_E                 -- compare
```

How do I perform join ORing (join by this or that)?

There are many options for inner join ORing and only one
option for outer join ORing. Inner joins can use a COALESCE
or a CASE expression in the join predicate to provide the OR
mechanism. The following demonstrates the two alternatives:

```
OPTION 1:
    SELECT    columns
    FROM      T1, T2
    WHERE
    COALESCE(T1.ID1, T1.ID2) = T2.COLX
OPTION 2:
    SELECT    columns
    FROM      T1, T2
    WHERE (CASE
        WHEN T1.ID1 IS NULL THEN T1.ID2 END) = T2.COLX
```

The FULL OUTER JOIN syntax is the only outer join that
provides a way to perform join ORing. Full outer join ORing
is accomplished by using a COALESCE in the ON clause as
follows:

```
SELECT COALESCE(T1.ID1, T1.ID2, ' NO ID ')
      ,COALESCE(T2.COLX, 'NO COLX')
      ,COALESCE(T2.COLY, 0)
FROM
    (SELECT COLA FROM T1 WHERE COLC > 'X')
FULL OUTER JOIN
    (SELECT COLX, COLY, FROM T2 WHERE COLX > 40)
ON
    COALESCE(T1.ID1, T1.ID2) = T2.COLX
```

 ## How do I condense multiple rows into one summary row?

Translating multiple rows into one summary row—table pivoting—is accomplished through the use of CASE statements. The table shown in Figure 11-11 contains detail data, by date, for many sales persons.

The goal is to transform the vertically stored SALES into one horizontal summary row. The CASE expressions shown in Figure 11-12 enables the transformation.

Sample Contents - SALES
OEMCOMPUTER - DB2 - SAMPLE - RYEVICH - SALES

SALES_DATE	SALES_PERSON	REGION	SALES
1995-12-31	LUCCHESSI	Ontario-South	1
1995-12-31	LEE	Ontario-South	3
1995-12-31	LEE	Quebec	1
1995-12-31	LEE	Manitoba	2
1995-12-31	GOUNOT	Quebec	1
1996-03-29	LUCCHESSI	Ontario-South	3
1996-03-29	LUCCHESSI	Quebec	1
1996-03-29	LEE	Ontario-South	2
1996-03-29	LEE	Ontario-North	2
1996-03-29	LEE	Quebec	3
1996-03-29	LEE	Manitoba	5
1996-03-29	GOUNOT	Ontario-South	3
1996-03-29	GOUNOT	Quebec	1
1996-03-29	GOUNOT	Manitoba	7
1996-03-30	LUCCHESSI	Ontario-South	1
1996-03-30	LUCCHESSI	Quebec	2
1996-03-30	LUCCHESSI	Manitoba	1
1996-03-30	LEE	Ontario-South	7
1996-03-30	LEE	Ontario-North	3
1996-03-30	LEE	Quebec	7
1996-03-30	LEE	Manitoba	4
1996-03-30	GOUNOT	Ontario-South	2
1996-03-30	GOUNOT	Quebec	18
1996-03-30	GOUNOT	Manitoba	1
1996-03-31	LUCCHESSI	Manitoba	1
1996-03-31	LEE	Ontario-South	14
1996-03-31	LEE	Ontario-North	3
1996-03-31	LEE	Quebec	7
1996-03-31	LEE	Manitoba	3
1996-03-31	GOUNOT	Ontario-South	2
1996-03-31	GOUNOT	Quebec	1
1996-04-01	LUCCHESSI	Ontario-South	3
1996-04-01	LUCCHESSI	Manitoba	1
1996-04-01	LEE	Ontario-South	8
1996-04-01	LEE	Ontario-North	
1996-04-01	LEE	Quebec	8

Close   Help

Figure 11-11 SALES table used in the query in Figure 11-12

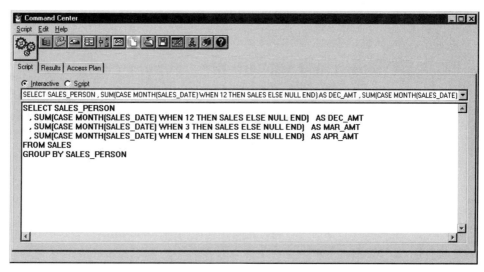

Figure 11-12 CASE expressions showing table pivoting

For example, using sales person LEE prior to the GROUP BY operation, the intermediate result rows consist of:

```
LEE        6    null    null
LEE     null      60    null
LEE     null    null      25
```

The result of the GROUP BY and SUM calculation completes the transformation, as shown in Figure 11-13.

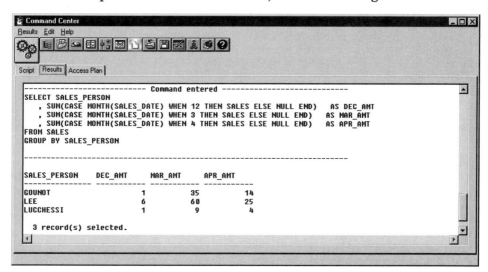

Figure 11-13 Output of using the table-pivoting CASE expression

The SELECT statement can be extended to handle any number of row transformations.

 ## How can I GROUP BY a generated value?

Any calculation or derivation you can dream up within an in-line view/table expression can be used in the outer SELECT statement's GROUP BY clause, as follows:

```
SELECT    T2GRP.QUARTER, SUM(T1.COLB)
FROM      T1,
    (SELECT COLZ AS NEWZ, (CASE MONTH
            WHEN BETWEEN 1 AND 3   THEN '1Q'
            WHEN BETWEEN 4 AND 6   THEN '2Q'
            WHEN BETWEEN 7 AND 9   THEN '3Q'
            WHEN BETWEEN 10 AND 12 THEN '4Q'
        ELSE NULL END) AS QUARTER
    FROM    T2)   AS T2GRP
WHERE   T1.COLA = T2GRP.NEWZ
GROUP BY    T2GRP.QUARTER
```

How can I perform a join using generated values?

Any calculation or derivation you create within an in-line view/table expression can be used in a join predicate, as follows:

```
SELECT PROJNO, MATCHPROJNO, MATCHPROJNAME, PROJNAME, NUMDAYS
FROM
    (SELECT PROJNO, PROJNAME,
        DAYS(PRENDATE) - DAYS(PRSTDATE) AS NUMDAYS
    FROM PROJ) AS FIRST
LEFT OUTER JOIN
    (SELECT PROJNO AS MATCHPROJNO,
        PROJNAME AS MATCHPROJNAME,
        DAYS(PRENDATE) - DAYS(PRSTDATE) AS JOINDAYS
    FROM PROJ) AS SECOND
ON NUMDAYS = JOINDAYS
    AND PROJNO <> MATCHPROJNO
```

Summary Rows with Detail for Large Answer Set Queries

When a GROUP BY query returns thousands of rows, it may not be feasible to join it to detail data for a report or other processing. The join will force the summary information to be scanned once for each detail row. A solution is required that eliminates all the passes against the summary data.

The following example is a very "data specific" solution for retrieving detail and summary information in one pass of the data. The sample data is listed first and then the query is listed that processes this data to formulate the result that follows the query. SQL comments starting with two hyphens follow each line for documentation purposes. They should be on the end of the preceding line, but had to be separated here for reasons of spacing.

THE DATA

CUST_ZONE	CUST_ID	NAME	SALES_QTY	PRIORITY
AA	369.00	SMITH	4,000	Z
AA	368.00	SMITH	10,000	A
AA	367.00	ADAMS	2,000	Q
AA	366.00	ADAMS	200	Y
AA	365.00	ADAMS	700	Z
BB	864.00	BIGGS	88	Y
BB	869.00	BIGGS	4,000	Z
BB	868.00	JONES	10,000	A
BB	867.00	JONES	2,000	Q
CC	266.00	CLARK	200	Y
CC	265.00	CLARK	700	Z
CC	264.00	CLARK	88	C
DD	999.00	LARSEN	2,200	A
.....				

THE QUERY

```
SELECT S.CUST_ZONE
    ,SUBSTR(MIN((S.PRIORITY
-- pulls out the lowest PRIORITY detail row
    CONCAT DIGITS(S.CUST_ID)
-- appends tag and converted key
    CONCAT S.NAME)),11,30) AS NAME
-- SUBSTR past PRIORITY &
-- CUST_ID and display NAME in the result
    ,DECIMAL(SUBSTR(MIN(S.PRIORITY
-- pulls out the lowest PRIORITY
    CONCAT DIGITS(S.CUST_ID)
-- appends key and converted decimal
    CONCAT DIGITS(S.CUST_ID)),11,9),9,0)  AS CUST_ID
-- SUBSTR past PRIORITY & CUST_ID, and
-- converts CHAR back to DECIMAL for display
    ,SUM(S.SALES_QTY)
-- the summary information requested
FROM
    (SELECT
    CUST_ZONE   -- GROUP BY column
    ,CUST_ID    -- Key
    ,NAME       -- Detail needed with summary
    ,SALES_QTY -- Summary calculation needed
    ,(CASE      --Tags the detail rows
        WHEN P_IND IS NULL THEN 'Z'
-- Translation of bad values
        WHEN P_IND = 'O' THEN 'Y'
- - raises unwanted priorities
        ELSE P_IND
-- all other indicators will be lower than Z & Y
      ND) AS PRIORITY
-- the lower the character, the higher the priority
    FROM SALES ) AS S
GROUP BY S.CUST_ZONE
FOR FETCH ONLY WITH UR
```

THE RESULT

CUST_ZONE	CUST_ID	NAME	SUM (SALES_QTY)	MIN (PRIORITY)
AA	368.00	SMITH	16,988	A
BB	868.00	JONES	16,088	A
CC	264.00	CLARK	988	C
DD	999.00	LARSEN	2,200	A

Chapter 12

Application Development

Answer Topics!

Application Programming @ a Glance

This chapter covers application development in DB2. There are subtle differences in each of the platforms, but most of the processes and methods have a basic similarity.

Questions regarding program design, preparation, and SQL use are covered.

The first section of this chapter, The Basics, covers questions on the techniques of program preparation, binding packages and plans, and the many issues surrounding SQL cursor use and the different styles of cursors.

The section on program functionality discusses the many issues concerning the proper use of SQL, both dynamic and static. Common methods of handling error conditions in programs, both transactional and batch programs, are covered.

In the final section on performance, some general performance details are discussed, including specific considerations for program design.

THE BASICS

 ### Can I use Java with DB2?

Yes, everywhere. Java is a supported language for all versions of DB2. Java can be used for application systems, applets for Web interaction with DB2, and DB2 stored procedures (even on OS/390). There are also many special features that enable Java to work with DB2 as well as all other languages do.

There is JDBC, which is a SQL interface for Java that uses dynamic SQL. This allows Java from any platform to use dynamic SQL through the JDBC interface and be run on any other platform.

There is also SQLJ which is a SQL interface for Java that uses static SQL. This performs at a higher throughput level than JDBC because the SQL is precompiled and the access paths have been determined before the Java program is run.

In addition, on OS/390, IBM is providing a high-performance Java compiler to translate the Java byte code into machine language. There are application development environments which support the use of Java and the DB2 interface, such as VisualAge for Java.

 ### What is DCLGEN?

On the OS/390 platform, the DCLGEN (Declaration Generator) is how DB2 turns table definitions in the DB2 catalog into structures usable by the host language; it produces a DECLARE statement to be included in the application program. The DCLGEN output, shown in Figure 12-1, is put into a PDS (partitioned dataset) and then copied into the program at compile time. The DCLGEN can be done though the ISPF DB2I panel, from TSO through a DSN command, from a clist that issues the DSN command, or JCL. On the other platforms, all declaration of host variables is left up to direct coding or to proprietary utilities.

The DCLGEN is then included in the program using the following SQL statement:

```
Exec SQL
      INCLUDE member-name
End-Exec;
```

```
*********************************************************************
* DCLGEN TABLE(DSN8510.DEPT)
*     LIBRARY(TEST01.DCLGEN.LIB(DEPT))
*     LANGUAGE(COBOL)
*     APOST
* ... IS THE DCLGEN COMMAND THAT MADE THE FOLLOWING STATEMENTS
*********************************************************************
    EXEC SQL DECLARE DSN8510.DEPT TABLE
    ( DEPTNO              CHAR(3) NOT NULL,
      DEPTNAME            VARCHAR(36) NOT NULL,
      MGRNO               CHAR(6),
      ADMRDEPT            CHAR(3) NOT NULL,
      LOCATION            CHAR(16)
    ) END-EXEC.
*********************************************************************
* COBOL DECLARATION FOR TABLE DSN8510.DEPT
*********************************************************************
01  DCLDEPT.
    10 DEPTNO           PIC X(3).
    10 DEPTNAME.
       49 DEPTNAME-LEN     PIC S9(4) USAGE COMP.
       49 DEPTNAME-TEXT    PIC X(36).
    10 MGRNO            PIC X(6).
    10 ADMRDEPT         PIC X(3).
    10 LOCATION         PIC X(16).
*********************************************************************
* THE NUMBER OF COLUMNS DESCRIBED BY THIS DECLARATION IS 5
*********************************************************************
*
```

Figure 12-1   DCLGEN Output

 Tip: *It is always advisable to create a DCLGEN for each table and include it in the DB2 program so that you are certain the host structure fields will exactly match the columns in the DB2 tables.*

 ## What is performed at precompile time?

For OS/390, DB2 does not have to be operational during the precompile process. During the precompile process, each INCLUDE is expanded, each EXEC SQL block is commented out and replaced with a call to the DB2 runtime interface module with appropriate parameters, and each SQL statement is placed in one database request module (DBRM). If all the previous steps are successful, both the DBRM and modified program source are marked with the same timestamp token.

For UNIX / NT / OS/2, the precompile process is invoked by issuing either the PREP or PRECOMPILE command using the command-line processor (CLP). This will result in either creating a bind file (using the precompiler option of BINDFILE, deferred binding) or in creating an application package (non-deferred binding). The BINDFILE option produces output that will have to be bound in another step, but is the most common method of binding applications on these platforms.

What is performed at bind time?

DB2 does have to be operational to bind a plan or a package. During the BIND process, the syntax of each SQL statement in either the database request module (DBRM) on OS/390 or the BINDFILE on UNIX / NT / OS/2 is validated for table and column definitions, and optionally, authorizations. If all of the previous checks are successful, the optimal access path of each SQL statement is determined by the optimizer and placed in the database. Each package (or plan on OS/390) will have an entry in the database that contains segments with individual access paths for every executable SQL statement within that plan or package.

The optimizer determines the optimal access path. The access path is based on DB2 catalog statistics gathered on indexes, data organization, and table size, as well as buffer pool specifications, number of processors, and other pertinent information specific to the individual platform.

What is the difference between the program isolation levels?

There are 4 levels of program isolation. They are as follows:

● **Cursor Stability (CS)**   This level of program isolation will only hold a lock on the row or page (depending on the lock size defined) if the cursor is actually positioned on that row or page. The lock will be released when the cursor moves to a new row or page, except the lock will be held until a commit is issued if changes are being made to the data. This option allows for the maximum concurrency for applications that are accessing the same data that cannot allow for uncommitted reads.

- **Repeatable Read (RR)** This option will hold a lock on all rows or pages touched by an application program since the last commit was issued, whether or not all those rows or pages satisfied the query. It will hold these locks until the next commit point, which ensures that if the application needs to read the data again, the values will be the same (no other process could update the locked data). In terms of concurrency of applications, this option is the most restrictive.

- **Read Stability (RS)** This option will hold locks on all rows or pages qualified by stage 1 predicates for the application until the commit is issued. Non-qualified rows or pages, even though touched, are not locked as with the RR option. Uncommitted changes of other applications cannot be read, but if an application issues the same query again, any data changed or inserted by other applications will be read, since RS allows other applications to insert new rows or update rows that could fall within the range of the query. This option is less restrictive but similar in function to repeatable read.

- **Uncommitted Read (UR)** This option will allow for the maximum concurrency between applications and it is highly recommended for applications that do not need to have absolutely current information. It will increase performance because applications will not have to wait for locks to be released and deadlocks will not occur. UR allows you to read though a lock in order to see the data, even if it is not committed.

When should I use a cursor?

A cursor should be used when more than one row will be manipulated from a multirow result set when using a SELECT statement. The exception is when no data is required; however, a test for 0, 1, or more rows is needed for proper existence checking. The following is an example of a singleton SELECT used for existence checking:

```
SELECT 1
INTO     :hv1
FROM TABLE
```

```
WHERE COLX = :inputx
IF SQLCODE = 0
      1 row found
IF SQLCODE = 100
      0 rows found
IF SQLCODE =-811
      more than 1 row was found
```

 Note: More often than not, a cursor with OPTIMIZE for one row works faster.

 What is an ambiguous cursor?

When DB2 does not know whether or not you will use the cursor for updating or deleting, it will prepare for a worst-case scenario (that you do perform an update). When DB2 is in doubt about this, the cursor is called ambiguous and the access path chosen by the optimizer will not necessarily be the best for the function being performed. The way to avoid ambiguous cursors is to code a FOR UPDATE OF clause when the cursor will be used in an UPDATE WHERE CURRENT OF statement, or to code a FOR FETCH ONLY or FOR READ ONLY on the cursor when it is only going to be used to retrieve data.

 What is a singleton select?

A singleton select is a SQL SELECT statement that expects only one row to be returned (for example, retrieving by the primary key). You can avoid the overhead of declaring a cursor by coding the INTO section in the SELECT statement.

A singleton SELECT should be used in a program whenever exactly one row is returned. There are two ways to ensure that exactly one row is returned. The first way is to request the result of a built-in function, as in the following:

```
SELECT SUM(SALARY), AVG(SALARY)
FROM EMP
INTO :totalsal, :avgsal
WHERE WORKDEPT = :workdept
```

The second way is to provide a WHERE clause that uniquely identifies a row, as in the following:

```
SELECT LASTNAME, ADDRESS, BIRTHDAY
FROM EMP
INTO :lastname, :address, :birthday
WHERE EMPNO = :EMPNO
```

> **!** *Caution:* *If you code a singleton select and DB2 has more then one row after execution of the statement, a SQLCODE of –811 will be set.*

Should I fetch using fields or structures?

From a performance point of view, fetching into a structure is better than fetching into a field. Every field that DB2 has to service involves a separate movement from DB2 to the program, as DB2 moves one column at a time from the DB2 address space to the program storage using a cross-memory process. When fetching into a structure, only one data transfer is required since the data in the structure matches the column order in the row. This is also the reason that you should limit yourself to only selecting the columns needed by the application program. However, from a coding point of view, fetching into fields makes your programs more readable and maintainable. SELECTS in programs that are frequently executed should always be reviewed and optimized by using structures.

Should I use application-enforced referential integrity or DB2-defined referential integrity?

DB2-defined referential integrity (correctly called declarative referential integrity because it is declared using DDL definition) is always the preferred method over using and maintaining application-enforced referential integrity for several reasons:

- Application-enforced relationships must be documented and accounted for when running utilities that require related tables be included in the tablespace set for integrity purposes.

- Each program has to account for the same relationships between related tables in their application program logic. This becomes difficult to ensure and maintain. When

programs are modified or enhanced, the application-enforced referential integrity is often overlooked, thus causing unrelated data to be allowed in the system, which can potentially cause serious data integrity problems.

● DB2-defined referential integrity is kept in the DB2 catalog, can be easily reported on with an SQL query, and would be accounted for in the DB2 Report utility.

● Declarative referential integrity also has a performance benefit in most cases, because the access path used to check on the existence of relationships is done by DB2 with less overhead than that which is incurred when application-enforced referential integrity is used.

What is the difference between a plan and a package?

When a program is preprocessed for DB2, there are normally two outputs: a modified source program to be passed to a compiler where the original SQL statements have been replaced by statements to invoke the appropriate DB2 interface functions, and another output containing information on how those SQL statements will be used by DB2. This second output, called a DBRM (database request module) must be bound so that all the DB2 functions used in the program can be checked for validity and authorization, and so a proper access path can be determined.

On OS/390, a DBRM can be bound in a package or directly into a plan. In addition, packages can be bound into logical groups called collections. These packages or collections can then be bound into a plan. A package can be bound for only a single SQL statement, for a subset of the program, or for an entire program, and it will contain information representing optimized SQL, which may just be an access path for the SQL to use to process the data required, or it could be information representing an SQL statement that was first rewritten by the optimizer.

A plan can be bound for multiple packages, collections, and/or DBRMs. Each package can be bound independently of a plan. If a DBRM is bound to a plan and then is rebound, all DBRMs are rebound as well. On UNIX / NT / OS/2, the result of all binds is just a package and there is no concept of a plan, but all the processing is basically the same, with the output containing the access path information for each SQL statement.

Should I only use one plan containing all packages?

It is extremely difficult to justify the use of one plan containing all the packages for an installation or even for just all CICS transactions or batch jobs. There was a misrepresentation of this strategy made in the past that has lead to the continuing myth of putting all packages into one plan. Plans need to be granular, the same as all other definitions. Large, cumbersome plans cause performance degradation, buffer pool problems, and EDM pool problems that are discussed in detail in Chapter 16. The number of packages put into a single plan needs to be based on functionality, such as all the packages supporting a particular function of an on-line application. Generally, each batch job should have a separate plan, which could be comprised of certain collections, but should be as specific as possible.

How can restart be done when sequential files are used in DB2 batch?

If you program your DB2 application into discrete units of work, you will have commits (EXEC SQL COMMIT) in the program. When SQL COMMITs are used, if your program fails and not all work is finished, you will want to restart processing from your last commit point—the last point at which database integrity is guaranteed. There are many ISV solutions to restarting, but you can also program restart points yourself. Rather than rolling back everything (EXEC SQL ROLLBACK) after the last commit, DB2 offers you some help. There are two solutions: one is for use when the connection to DB2 is through IMS, and the second is for all other cases.

First, if you are an IMS user, you can run your program as a BMP and define your sequential files as GSAM files.

Second, if you are not using IMS or do not want to use the IMS BMP interface, you can create your own DB2 restart logic. First you need to design a running-job control table. The trick to this is identifying the key. If you never have two or more jobs with the same name running concurrently, you can use the job name as the key, or even perhaps the program name or a combination of both. Otherwise, the best solution is to generate a key and print it when the batch program starts.

Once you have this key, you can create a control structure (a row) in the DB2 control table representing your running job. Make sure that you don't hold the update locks for too long and cause locking problems in this table. The best thing to do is use a large character block that will fill the page if you are using page-level locking, or to use row-level locking. In the programs, you map this to your structure where you keep track of things, such as current values for cursors, positions in non-DB2 files, and so on. This may not seem like the tidiest solution to the problem, but it accommodates the varying needs of different programs; The SYSUTILX structure in DB2 works similarly. For all sequential input files, you must keep track of the count in the control structure in your program. Before you issue the commit for your unit of work, you can update your row in the running-job control table. If the commit is successful you can commit your updates to the running-job control table.

Every time a job starts, it must check the running-job control table for its name or for the unique name passed via JCL to the program, which is used as the key to the row in the table. If the program finds the row in the running-job control table, this is a restart condition. In that case, you can reposition the input files using the record count in the structure, and then continue at the restart point in the program, making any adjustments that are necessary. Make sure that you have a program that is able to remove the rows from the running-job control table or that your program knows to ignore the record in the table (for example, by passing "no restart" from the JCL). Also, remember that your sequential output files might be incomplete and cannot be easily repositioned. In your program control structure, be sure to record what might have been written by code and then rolled back during the failure recovery process. The same applies to spooled output of your program, which cannot be repositioned. Another solution for output print files is to use DB2 tables for print output of sequential output files. A separate unload program could print or create the output file.

There are ISV solutions that deal with these problems and that are generally easier to use, since they are normally invoked by a simple programmatic call statement.

What are triggers?

Triggers have been in existence in the UNIX / NT / OS/2 platforms for DB2 for quite some time, and recently DB2 Version 6 for OS/390 announced support for triggers. A trigger is a set of SQL statements that will be executed (triggered) when a particular event occurs on a table (INSERT, UPDATE, DELETE). These triggers can be both *before*-triggers and *after*-triggers, meaning that the SQL can be executed before the update process occurs on the target table, or after. Normally before-triggers are used for application-enforced referential integrity, to edit check values in the columns or to add additional information to the data being updated. After-triggers are generally used for maintaining auditing tables, cross-reference tables, or summary tables. More information about triggers can be found in Chapter 13.

What information is contained in the SQLCA?

The SQLCA (SQL communications area) is used to pass information from DB2 to the application program after completion of any SQL statement. The most commonly used information contained in this area includes SQL return codes, such as SQLCODE (the error code or 0 if the statement was processed successfully) and SQLSTATE (cross-platform error code defined by the SQL92 standard). Other information passed in this area includes error messages, the number of rows affected by INSERT, UPDATE, and DELETE

statements, seven different warning indicators, and other status information. Every program that has uses SQL needs to include an SQLCA.

```
Exec SQL
    Include SQLCA
End-Exec.
```

 ### Should I use CLI or embedded SQL?

The major difference between embedded SQL and the CLI (Call Level Interface) based on both the Microsoft ODBC specification and the ISO CLI standard is that embedded SQL is static and CLI is dynamic.

To compile a program that uses static SQL takes more steps, such as precompiling and binding, whereas CLI does not need to be precompiled or bound because it uses common access packages (normally called APIs) provided with DB2. The advantage with static SQL is that the optimization is done once and is reused again and again. Because of this, static SQL might provide better performance when used often (as in OLTP) or if the SQL statement is often repeated. CLI is beneficial when a single program needs to be run on different platforms and portability is an issue.

✳ ***Note:*** *From Version 5 on, DB2 on OS/390 has special facilities to better serve dynamic SQL (dynamic statement caching).*

 ### What is the difference between SQLCODE, SQLSTATE, and reason codes?

SQLCODE is a proprietary code from DB2 that signals the success or failure of an SQL request. Negative codes are failures, positive codes are warnings, and a SQLCODE of 0 means a successful request.

The SQLSTATE comes from the ODBC/CLI environment and is a cross-platform industry standard. The same codes are used for all relational DBMS systems by all vendors. There are more SQLSTATEs than SQLCODEs, but there is a one-to-one mapping from SQLSTATE back to SQLCODE.

The SQLCODE and SQLSTATE are normally both parts of the SQL communications area (SQLCA), so your program can use both. On some platforms and DBMS systems, the SQLCODE and SQLSTATE have to be declared separately. After an interaction with DB2, the SQLCA contains feedback on the success or failure of the interaction.

Whenever a process is aborted due to a error situation on OS/390, DB2 will provide a special code showing that the process was aborted. These reason codes and abend codes (which are different from the statement SQL codes), are described in the IBM Messages and Codes manual and can be used to determine the severity of the error and provide useful detailed information about the type of error and component involved. Some codes describe minor failures (such as a stopped tablespace), and some describe a complete subsystem failure that will stop DB2.

 ## When can I justify using dynamic SQL?

Dynamic SQL is a very powerful way of coding highly flexible applications. A flexible application is one that allows "zero to many" input variables for a particular query. The more input variables, the easier it is to justify using dynamic SQL.

There are several ways to code an application that would provide the desired result set when using variable input. One option would create one SQL statement that contains all the possible predicate combinations joined together with ORs. For example, the following pattern would be used to retrieve a fixed set of columns from one or more fixed tables:

```
SELECT     A.COL1, A.COL2, A.COL6, A.COL7
FROM       TAB1   A
WHERE      (Predicate for variable 1)
   OR      (Predicate for variable 1 AND Predicate for variable 2)
   OR      (Predicate for variable 1 AND Predicate for variable 2 AND
            Predicate for variable 3)
   OR      (Predicate for variable 1 AND Predicate for variable 3)
   OR      (Predicate for variable 2 AND Predicate for variable 3)
```

There are two problems with the statement above. First, the statement expands greatly with each variable. Second, the performance of the SELECT is usually poor because index screening is minimal due to the OR conditions.

A second way of approaching this task can take care of the poor performance by creating one better-performing SELECT statement for each unique variable combination. The following five SELECT statements would be required to handle the same unique requests:

```
SELECT        A.COL1, A.COL2, A.COL6, A.COL7
FROM      TAB1   A
WHERE      (Predicate for variable 1)
SELECT        A.COL1, A.COL2, A.COL6, A.COL7
FROM      TAB1   A
WHERE      (Predicate for variable 1
   AND Predicate for variable 2)
SELECT        A.COL1, A.COL2, A.COL6, A.COL7
FROM      TAB1   A
WHERE      (Predicate for variable 1 AND Predicate for variable 2
   AND Predicate for variable 3)
SELECT      A.COL1, A.COL2, A.COL6, A.COL7
FROM      TAB1   A
WHERE      (Predicate for variable 1
   AND Predicate for variable 3)
SELECT        A.COL1, A.COL2, A.COL6, A.COL7
FROM        TAB1   A
WHERE        (Predicate for variable 2
 AND Predicate for variable 3)
```

Program logic would be required to detect which input variables have been entered in order to execute the correct SELECT statement. This takes care of the performance problem; however, it leaves a maintenance nightmare when more than five variables are involved.

A third option solves the maintenance nightmare: a fixed-list dynamic SELECT statement that contains two parts. The first part is the fixed portion of the statement, usually the SELECT and the FROM clause. This is stored separately in a work area of the program. The second part is built using program logic to concatenate the correct predicates together based on the detected input variables. The following is the format of the dynamic statement:

```
SELECT    A.COL1, A.COL2, A.COL6, A.COL7
FROM    TAB1   A
WHERE    Build the where clause in the program
        to match the input options (parameter
        markers ,'?', can be used).
```

The steps you need to follow to build and execute a dynamic SELECT statement are as follows:

1. Build the statement using program logic and save it in a work-area variable. Parameter markers can increase the flexibility of the statement. The following statement is stored in a program variable:

```
DYNSTRING:
    SELECT COL1, COL2
    FROM TABLEX
    WHERE    COL6 = ?
       AND COL7 > ?
       AND COL8 LIKE 'ABC%'
```

2. Create a link between a cursor name and a BIND name to be created in the next step using the following syntax:

```
DECLARE C1 CURSOR FOR DYNAMPLAN
```

3. BIND the stored statement and give the access plan a name using the following statement:

```
PREPARE DYNAMPLAN FROM :DYNSTRING
```

4. Fill in the parameter variables if used and process the cursor as you would any other cursor using the following statement:

```
OPEN C1 USING :PARM1, :PARM2
```

This cursor can be closed and re-opened as many times as you like without having to re-PREPARE the statement. Parameter variables can be changed between each opening.

5. Retrieve rows from the cursor, just as you would any other cursor, using the following statement:

```
FETCH C1 INTO :VAR1, :VAR2
```

6. Close the cursor, just as you would any other cursor, using the following statement:

```
CLOSE C1
```

 Is there any need to have more than one varying-list dynamic SQL program per site?

The difference between a fixed-list dynamic SQL statement, as shown above, and a varying-list dynamic SQL statement is

that the columns and the tables can change for each execution. This means that a varying-list dynamic SQL program can accept any SELECT statement with each execution. Since any statement can be accepted, there is no need to have more than one varying-list dynamic SQL program. IBM's Query Management Facility (QMF) is an example of a varying-list program.

 ### How do I get a return code or abend code in OS/390 DB2 batch?

If you execute your programs under the normal TSO batch procedures, you never will see, external of your program, failed (for example, abended) or ended SQL statements with a return code other than zero. This is because the TSO batch monitor (IKJEFT01) does an OS/390 attach and will print the results of the execution, but does not notify the outside world of these events. IKJEFT01 always ends with return code of zero.

To see the true results you need to look at the output. There is, however, an official back door that will show the results to the outside world. Instead of IKJEFT01, execute IKJEFT1A or IKJEFT1B. The difference between the two is that IKJEFT1A will still intercept abends and IKJEFT1B will not catch abends. With IKJEFT1B, if your program abends, the step will abend.

Tip: *You can read more about this in the IBM manual SC28-1872 TSO/E Customization Guide.*

 ### Why can't I update my DB2 table from ODBC?

The main reason people run into trouble updating tables from an ODBC environment is because the ODBC interfaces require a primary key to update the data. Because the interfaces need to be at a compliant ODBC level, they allow for a scrollable cursor in both directions. To implement this, the interface reads the complete result set from an SQL query into storage. Therefore, there is no current cursor positioning to do the update. In order to make sure that the correct row will be updated from the program, the ODBC interfaces make sure that the primary key is in the result set, and when an update is done they add a WHERE clause to the

update mentioning the key. These ODBC implementations restrict a result set to browse only when the table has no primary key.

What is SQLJ?

SQLJ is an implementation of static SQL to be used with the Java programming language. It was designed by IBM, Oracle, and Sun to eliminate the weaknesses of JDBC, which is dynamic SQL. SQLJ is implemented in DB2 Version 6 for OS/390 and is available for DB2 Version 5. UDB Version 5.2 also has support for SQLJ.

PROGRAM FUNCTIONALITY

Should I code retry logic for –911, –912, –913 SQL return codes?

A –911 SQL return code means that a deadlock or a timeout occurred and DB2 has issued a successful ROLLBACK to the last commit point. If the ROLLBACK was not successful, the application will receive a –913 SQL return code signifying that a ROLLBACK was not performed. There is also a –912 SQL return code, which occurs when the maximum number of lock requests has been reached for the database (because insufficient memory was allocated to the lock list). With a –912 or a –913 return code, the application needs to issue a COMMIT or ROLLBACK statement before proceeding with any other SQL.

When a –911 occurs, the choice of whether or not to use retry logic depends on the individual application. If a large amount of work has been rolled back, and if there are other non-DB2 files present, it may be difficult to reposition everything and retry the unit of work. With most –911 situations, a restart process (vendor supplied or user-written) is generally easier than a programmatic reposition and retry. If a small amount of work was lost, then a simple retry could be performed up to some fixed number of times. It is important not to retry with a breakpoint since the source of the problem that caused the negative codes might still exist.

With the –913 SQL return code, the single statement could be retried, and if successful the program could simply

continue on. However, if repeated attempts at retry logic fail, then the application probably needs to be rolled back.

 ### Should I use retry logic for other codes besides –911 through –913?

There are situations for which a –904 SQL return code could best be handled by using retry logic. While a –904 means some required resource is unavailable, there are many condition codes that further describe the type of resource. Some of the resource types become unavailable only for short periods, such as in data sharing where a component has currently failed but is in a fail-over state that might only last for a few seconds. In cases such as this, it would be better to wait for a period and retry the failing SQL statement rather than abort the entire process, which potentially could cause worse problems.

 ### What are heuristic control tables and how are they used?

Heuristic control tables are used to allow great flexibility in controlling concurrency and restartability. Simply put, these are tables that have rows unique to each application process to assist in controlling commit scope (number of database updates or time between commits). They can also have an indicator in the table to tell an application that it is time to stop. Each application or batch job would have its own unique entries.

These tables are accessed each time an application commits. The normal process is for an application to read from the table at the very beginning of the process to get the dynamic parameters and commit time to be used. The table stores information about the frequency of commits as well as any other dynamic information that is pertinent to the application process, such as the unavailability of some particular resource for a period of time. Once the program is running, it both updates and reads from the control table at commit time. Information about the status of all processing at the time of the commit is generally stored in the table so that a restart can occur at that point if required.

If I have to follow an SQL statement with a lot of IF statements, does it mean that I should be putting more functionality into the SQL statement?

The more IF logic you perform following an SQL statement, the more tests you are missing in your SQL statement. Move the program-functionality work into the SQL. For example, the following program tests:

```
IF RCODE = 'B'
THEN AMOUNT + B-AMOUNT
ELSE IF RCODE = 'C'
THEN AMOUNT + -AMOUNT
ELSE IF RCODE = 'D'
THEN AMOUNT + D-AMOUNT
```

can be transferred to the following SELECT clause:

```
SELECT SUM(CASE WHEN RCODE = 'B' THEN AMOUNT)
     , SUM(CASE WHEN RCODE = 'C' THEN AMOUNT)
     , SUM(CASE WHEN RCODE = 'D' THEN AMOUNT)
FROM TABLE
INTO :b-amount, :c-amount, d-amount
```

Should I be making extensive use of I/O modules?

No, extensive use of I/O modules in relational database applications usually causes performance degradation. This is because an I/O module that performs a simple "get next row from table" function will contain a simple SELECT statement. This SELECT is not part of any relational join or any other complex function that can be performed by the relational engine.

Specific SELECT statements should be formed to push as much work as possible into the relational engine. These more complicated statements can also be combined with program logic to perform logical business functions, such as "enroll new employee." This type of module is the preferred I/O module in today's relational database application—logical functions are re-used instead of logical database reads being issued.

❓ How do I get the complete DB2 error message in my application?

If you are running in a local (static SQL) environment on OS/390, you can call the DSNTIAR routine to format your messages using the SQLCA as input. Refer to the IBM DB2 Application Programming and SQL Guide—SC26-8958 for examples. In a CICS environment, you should use the DSNTIAC routine. If running in a CLI, Unix, or Win/NT environment you should call the SQLAINTP routine to retrieve your messages after an unsuccessful call to DB2.

❓ When do I need to reposition and access rows from a cursor result set?

When you scroll through screens of data, you need an efficient browsing technique—a way to search tables with only partial search criteria. Also, a batch application that cannot use CURSOR WITH HOLD, must also use a browsing technique to navigate a DB2 table when frequent commits are required or for restartability.

❓ How do I reposition and access rows from a cursor result set (for scrolling and restart)?

Although the ORDER BY clause is critical for browsing, you should focus on the WHERE clause, which will use an index to browse DB2 tables.

There are two types of cursor statements used for browsing tables. One is based on a single-column index; the other is based on a multiple-column index. The single-column index browsing technique is quite simple. Using the table BRWZUM, (Table 12-1) which is listed below, assume COL1 is a unique index for the table. Also assume a sample online screen can hold a total of five rows of data. The first time the cursor is opened, you would like to start fetching at the beginning of the table. To do this, set the host variable for COL1, :COL1-LAST, to low-values, zero, or a default data

BRWZUM TABLE

COL1	COL2	COL3	COL4	COL5
A	1	TT	99	data
A	1	UU	77	data
A	4	SS	66	data
B	2	RR	66	data
B	3	RR	77	data
B	3	RR	88	data
B	3	SS	66	data
B	4	SS	99	data
B	4	UU	88	data
C	1	SS	66	data
C	1	SS	77	

Table 12-1   BRWZUM TABLE

('0001-01-01'), depending on the data type, and then open the following cursor:

```
DECLARE    C_BRWZUM1 CURSOR FOR
SELECT    COL1, COL2, COL3, COL4, COL5
FROM    BRWZUM
WHERE    COL1> :COL1-LAST
ORDER BY COL1
```

The screen is filled with the first five rows fetched, and the cursor is closed.

The second time the cursor is opened, you want to start fetching at the sixth row. The value of COL1 from the last line on the screen, saved in a protected work area, is placed in the host variable :COL1-LAST. When the cursor is opened for the second screen, you'll start fetching at the sixth row.

This process continues until SQLCODE = 100, which means there is no more data to be returned. It is recommended that you fetch one more row than you need for each screen in order to detect when the end of the results corresponds to the

last line on the screen. This also saves an additional OPEN, FETCH, and CLOSE execution. Beware that fetching from a perfectly clustered, read-only table does not guarantee the sequence in which rows are retrieved. The ORDER BY clause is what guarantees that this browsing process is accurate.

The following cursor allows an inclusive range for COL1, which changes the WHERE clause only slightly:

```
DECLARE    C_BRWZUM1 CURSOR FOR
SELECT     COL1, COL2, COL3, COL4, COL5
FROM       BRWZUM
WHERE      COL1 BETWEEN :COL1-LOW AND :COL1-HI
ORDER BY   COL1
```

Now you have two values to store: the initial COL1-HI value and the last COL1 value on the screen, which is placed in :COL1-LOW prior to each OPEN CURSOR. To scroll backward with either cursor, all you need to do is store the last value of COL1 from two pages previous. This will be the :COL1-LAST value of the C-BRWZUM1 cursor, or the :COL1-LOW value of the C-BRWZUM1 cursor, used by the OPEN CURSOR statements for scrolling forward (no descending index required). The only drawback to this method of scrolling backward is that inserted rows will change the screen contents as you scroll forward again. If you have heavy insert activity, you may want to restrict the number of screens the user can scroll backward.

A second type of cursor statement used for browsing is much more complex because it is based on a multiple-column index. The added complexity is due to the fact that data in the high-order column, COL1, may not change between screens, so you cannot just open WHERE COL1 > :COL1-LAST.

You could get around this by using C-BRWZUM1 and always open and close the cursor when COL1 does change. This works for a few batch programs that have a consistent number of COL1 values and where the total number of common values (the number of rows between COMMITs) closely reflects the commit scope required (the time between COMMITs). Since many batch programs have changing COMMIT scopes, this work-around is probably not an option.

Instead, you need a cursor that works without special knowledge of the data. There are two common techniques for accomplishing multi-column index browsing. The first technique uses Boolean logic to browse. Assume the unique index on the BRWZUM table is now a composite of COL1, COL2, COL3, and COL4. The following cursor has four logical sections (one for each column in the index), a fixed pattern of operators and parentheses, and is easily memorable:

```
DECLARE   C_BRWZUM3 CURSOR FOR
SELECT    COL1, COL2, COL3, COL4, COL5
FROM    BRWZUM
WHERE    ((COL1 = :COL1-LAST
    AND    COL2 = :COL2-LAST
    AND    COL3 = :COL3-LAST
    AND    COL4 > :COL4-LAST )
OR
      (COL1 = :COL1-LAST
    AND    COL2 = :COL2-LAST
    AND    COL3 > :COL3-LAST )
    OR
      (COL1 = :COL1-LAST
    AND    COL2 > :COL2-LAST )
    OR
      (COL1 > :COL1-LAST))
ORDER BY COL1,COL2,COL3,COL4
```

The host variable values are initially set to low-values, zero, or a default date, just like C-BRWZUM. Upon first OPEN, the first five rows are fetched and the last values of COL1 through COL4 are stored. The second OPEN is where the repositioning begins. The first three lines of the following WHERE statement look for the same values for COL1, COL2, and COL3, and the comparison for COL4 has to be a greater-than comparison in order to start at the next value above 77.

```
WHERE    ((COL1 = 'B'
    AND    COL2 = 3
    AND    COL3 = 'RR'
    AND    COL4 > 77 )
```

The rows that qualify by matching the first three comparison are concatenated with all the remaining section's results. The second section, following, is looking for the same values for COL1 and COL2; however, COL3 has to be greater than its previous value. (COL4 can be any value because it is not mentioned.)

```
OR
       (COL1 = 'B'
AND     COL2 = 3
    AND     COL3 > 'RR' )
```

The third section, following, looks for the same value of COL1, a greater value for COL2, and COL3 and COL4 can be any value).

```
OR
            (COL1 = 'B'
     AND     COL2 > 3  )
```

The fourth section only looks for a greater value for COL1.

```
OR
      (COL1 > 'B'))
```

The combination of the results qualifies rows that have not previously been retrieved from the C-BRWZUM3 cursor. Like the single-column cursor, this cursor can also be used to browse backwards by saving the bottom values from two previous screens; use the hidden index values from the two screens previous to scroll back one screen, the values from three screens previous to scroll back two screens, and so on. Once you memorize the pattern of the AND, OR, >, and = elements, you can create a browsing cursor for a ten-column index in minutes. Like the single-column index cursor, an ORDER BY statement is required to guarantee the results.

Another cursor technique that retrieves rows based on a multi-column index uses negative logic to browse. Assume the same unique index on the BRWZUM table of COL1, COL2, COL3, and COL4. The following cursor has four logical sections (one for each column in the index), a fixed pattern of operators and parentheses, and is not as easily memorable as the first one:

```
DECLARE     C_BRWZUM4 CURSOR FOR
    SELECT    COL1, COL2, COL3, COL4, COL5
    FROM      BRWZUM
    WHERE     COL1 >= :COL1-LAST
              AND NOT
       (COL1 = :COL1-LAST
        AND    COL2 < :COL2-LAST )
              AND NOT
        (COL1 = :COL1-LAST
        AND    COL2  = :COL2-LAST
        AND    COL3  < :COL3-LAST )
              AND NOT
          (COL1 = :COL1-LAST
        AND    COL2 = :COL2-LAST
        AND COL3 = :COL3-LAST
        AND    COL4 <= :COL4-LAST)
    ORDER BY COL1,COL2,COL3,COL4
```

Upon the first OPEN, the first five rows are fetched and the last values of COL1 through COL4 are stored. The second OPEN is where the repositioning begins. The first section of the WHERE is looking for every row that has a COL1 value greater than or equal to the last COL1 value. The rest of the sections exclude rows from this long list by using AND NOT, which is why this is sometimes called the exclusion cursor.

```
WHERE    COL1 >= 'B'
```

The second section excludes rows (using NOT) that have the same value for COL1 and a smaller value for COL2.

```
AND NOT
          (COL1 = 'B'
    AND    COL2 < 3 )
```

The third section excludes rows that have the same value for COL1 and COL2 and a smaller value for COL3.

```
AND NOT
          (COL1 = 'B'
    AND    COL2  = 3
    AND    COL3  < 'RR' )
```

The fourth section excludes rows that have the same value for COL1, COL2, and COL3, and an equal or smaller value for COL4.

```
AND NOT
        COL1 = 'B'
    AND COL2 = 3
    AND COL3 = 'RR'
    AND COL4 <= 77)
```

The rows left after all the exclusions are the remaining combinations of COL2, COL3, and COL4, together with rows that have a greater value for COL1. This cursor also requires an ORDER BY clause to guarantee results.

While the options for browsing a table seem diverse, the real solution is consistency. Choose one of the multi-column index browsing techniques for each site and publish it in an application-coding standards document. Each technique can be extended to handle ranges (using BETWEEN or LIKE) for any of the columns in the index.

An improvement for the browsing cursors is a new extension to the SELECT clause: FETCH FIRST 20 ROWS. This clause from the SQL3 standard is available for DB2 UDB Version 5.2 only. This clause will limit the number of rows coming back from a result set; however, to point the cursor to the correct 20 rows, you will still need to use one of the above-mentioned browsing techniques.

What is the difference in the access paths of the common scrolling techniques?

All the techniques shown in the preceding question use a one-matching column index scan, regardless of how many columns are included in the index. This is because the optimizer has knowledge of the first column in the index. The rest of the index columns (for a multi-column index) are involved in Boolean logic, which excludes the matching condition.

When do I use null indicator variables?

A null indicator is used in programming languages either to flag a column that has received a NULL value or suffered a

conversion error, or to set a column to nulls. Use of the null indicator variable is never forbidden, even when the column you retrieve is defined as NOT NULL. The null indicator can receive three values: 0 means a value was set, –1 means the column is NULL or the value of the hostvariable is invalid, and –2 means the column suffered a conversion error (for example, the result of a sum function did not fit into the host variable). A null indicator is a program variable. When you retrieve a column, you can specify :Hostvar:indicator for the INTO part of the SELECT—by putting the fields together without a space, you indicate to the precompiler that this is a null indicator.

The obvious place to use them is for retrieving columns that are defined to allow NULLs. The not so obvious places are outer joins and built-in functions. FULL and LEFT outer joins return NULL for columns that have missing join relationships. Every built-in function except for COUNT returns NULL when no rows qualify for the SELECT statement. In all these cases, the COALESCE scalar function can be used in the SELECT clause to convert the NULLs to precise values in order to avoid having to code indicator variables, as follows:

```
SELECT COALESCE(SUM(SALARY), 0)
FROM EMP
WHERE WORKDEPT = :workdept
```

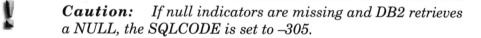 **Caution:** *If null indicators are missing and DB2 retrieves a NULL, the SQLCODE is set to –305.*

 **Tip:** *The use of the COALESCE function can prevent a column from becoming NULL.*

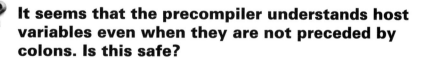 **It seems that the precompiler understands host variables even when they are not preceded by colons. Is this safe?**

No, it is not. You should always declare your variables in an EXEC SQL BEGIN/END DECLARE SECTION and refer to them with colon prefixes in your SQL statements. The latest versions of DB2 enforce it, and you might run into trouble if

you coded your batch programs incorrectly, specifying host variables without the colon.

❓ Why do I get strange abends if the first access is to DB2 and not to IMS in an IMS/DB2 program?

The problem is in the linkedit—you get the wrong language interface. When you linkedit an IMS program, force the inclusion of module DFSLI000 (or one of the more popular entry points like COBTODLI). This module can execute DB2 and IMS. If you don't do this and the first call is to DB2, you will include the DB2 interface that will execute the DB2 call, but all IMS calls will abend because the IMS interface is not properly set up.

❓ How do I find the timestamp in the DB2 load module that matches the timestamp in the DBRM?

On OS/390, in order to find the timestamp (consistency token) in the DB2 load module that matches the timestamp in the DBRMLIB, you can use the following steps:

- Go to the DBRMLIB and view the DBRM member in hex.
- Make note of the first eight characters after the DBRM name.
- Go to the DB2 Load Module and locate the hex number from the DBRM (it will be reversed, such that the last four characters will be first, and the first four characters will be last). Search on the first four in hex (F X'xxxxxxxx').
- This number should match the value in SYSSIBM.SYSPACKAGES, which you can find by viewing HEX(CONTOKEN) for the package.

On UNIX / NT / OS/2, there is a tool called "db2bfd" that will produce an output listing which includes both the encoded and decoded timestamp from the bind file. Then an SQL query can be used to retrieve information from SYSCAT.PACKAGES that will show the encoded timestamp. These two can be compared to see if the bind file has been bound to the database and if it is consistent. The command and the SQL required are listed here:

Command:
```
    db2bfd -b program.bnd
```
SQL:
```
    SELECT PKGSCHEMA, PKGNAME, UNIQUE_ID
    FROM SYSCAT.PACKAGES
    WHERE PKGNAME = 'program'
```
Compare UNIQUE_ID from SQL to timestamp output from db2bfd

 How can OS/390 global temporary tables be used?

Global temporary tables (GTTs) can help improve performance in many different ways. Any time there is repetitive SQL being used to return a result set, producing exactly the same result each time, a GTT might provide benefit. A subquery that is used more than once is a prime example. It would be better to issue the subquery once, storing the result set rows in the GTT and use the GTT in subsequent subqueries. Another use would be to retrieve and hold data from non-DB2 sources, and then join or otherwise use this data in SQL statements.

The biggest advantage of global temporary tables is that no logging is done since no recovery is possible. However, no indexing is done either, so a tablespace scan will always be used as the access path. Also, no modifications can be made to the data in the GTT by either an SQL UPDATE or DELETE. Only INSERTs are allowed. The GTT will exist for the duration of the unit of work, being automatically deleted when a commit is issued unless the table is used in a cursor definition using CURSOR WITH HOLD.

 Note: *IBM is currently working on adding temporary tables to DB2 that would be used like any other table, but be temporary in nature.*

 How can I use a column function on a column function?

There are many times when it is necessary to perform a column function on the results produced by a previous column function, such as getting the maximum value from a set of sub-totals. While it is impossible to use MAX(SUM(column)), it is possible to use the first or inner column function in a

table expression, and use the second or outer function in the outer SQL over the result of the inner table expression. This is shown in the following example, where the maximum, minimum, and average commission is used over the total of commissions for each employee.

```
SELECT  T1.state,  T1.region,
   MAX(TX.total),  AVG(TX.total),  MIN(TX.total)
FROM  TOUTER  AS  T1,
       (SELECT  empno,  SUM(commissions)  AS  total
       FROM    TINNER
       GROUP  BY  empno)  AS  T2
WHERE  T1.empno  =  T2.empno
GROUP  BY  T1.state,  T1.region
```

PERFORMANCE

 ## When should I rebind my packages?

Packages should be rebound when any of the following are true, based on current statistics from the catalog:

Changes > 20% (NLEAF, NPAGES, NACTIVE)
Clusterratio < 80%, NLEVELS increases > 2
HIGH2KEY and LOW2KEY ranges change > 10%
Cardinality and Row Count change > 20%

What are the benefits of dynamic SQL caching, and when should I use it?

On OS/390, when using dynamic SQL, a prepare must be reissued after every commit. As of Version 5, DB2 can save the cost of having to issue the prepare again by caching the dynamic statement that has already been prepared. When a dynamic statement is prepared, it is automatically stored in the cache. The cache is a separate memory area and the result of the prepare is maintained in the EDM pool. In order to be reused, the statement must be identical and have the same authorization ID and the same bind options.

> *Caution:* Turning on dynamic SQL caching is done on a subsystem basis. Therefore, all dynamic statements, even those from query tools such as QMF, are cached. Many queries may never be reused but will take up space in the cache and make it difficult for dynamic statements with a lot of reuse to remain in the cache.

Should I use RELEASE(COMMIT) or RELEASE(DEALLOCATE) on my package bind?

Using the RELEASE(COMMIT) option on the bind package statement will release table and tablespace intent locks (IS, IX) at each commit point. Use of this parameter will destroy information required to help reduce some labor-intensive processes as well as information needed to help performance. One area in which this can occur is in programs doing multiple inserts and updates against the same table. DB2 will monitor the inserts and then after every third insert, it internally builds an executable procedure to perform this process so that it does not have to continually build the code necessary to perform subsequent inserts. This procedure is referred to as an IPROC (insert procedure). After the fifth insert occurs, use of the established IPROC will help to reduce CPU overhead, and improve insert performance.

There is a similar concept used for updates called a UPROC (update procedure). If you use the RELEASE(COMMIT) parameter in conjunction with a frequently committing program, the IPROCs/UPROCs are built and then destroyed before they provide very much benefit, but after the overhead to build them was incurred. Also, the cache used for sequential detection to determine when to turn on dynamic prefetch is also erased, as well as the cache used for index lookaside operations to help DB2 avoid index probes. Losing the special code created by using RELEASE(COMMIT) can cause performance degradation in programs with heavy insert/update operations.

Binding a program with the RELEASE(DEALLOCATE) option will solve this problem; this option should be used for the majority of batch programs and for some online programs. This will allow for the UPROCs/IPROCs and caches to

remain until the end of the program despite the commits. The DEALLOCATE option will hold intent lock through to the end of program; however, this will not cause any concurrency problems because page locks and row locks are still released when a commit is performed.

Since RELEASE(COMMIT) is the default, several organizations have the majority of their programs bound with this option. When choosing to bind programs with RELEASE(DEALLOCATE), be careful and approach this wisely. If CICS thread reuse is used and you rebind the heavily used transactions with RELEASE(DEALLOCATE), you will begin to require more memory in the EDM pool, so this resource needs to be monitored. Do not just perform a mass rebind using RELEASE(DEALLOCATE); bring into play maybe an 80/20 rule for program rebinds (80% of the processing is normally consumed by only 20% of the programs or transactions).

! *Caution:*   *Using RELEASE(DEALLOCATE) does not release any locks acquired by the LOCK TABLE statement.*

What does the bind parameter CURRENTDATA have to do with lock avoidance?

Lock avoidance was introduced in DB2 to reduce the overhead of always locking everything. DB2 will check to be sure that a lock is probably necessary for data integrity before acquiring a lock. In order to achieve lock avoidance, you need to have your programs bound with CURRENTDATA(NO).

When should I use uncommitted read (UR)?

The isolation level uncommitted read (UR) has many uses in the application development lifecycle. The first and most practical use of UR is retrieving read-only data, and the more the better. Any table that is read-only *at the time* the data is selected, should have WITH UR included in the SELECT. Up to 30 percent of CPU time can be saved from long-running queries.

Although UR is nicknamed the "dirty read," a more appropriate name is the "high-performing read." This speed is the reason why there are more practical uses than just selecting read-only data. Another use for UR is estimating. This occurs when summary information is needed, but the answer does not have to be exact. An example of estimating is running a query to calculate an average over a large amount of rows that are constantly being updated, inserted, and/or deleted.

Browsing rows of data is another good use of UR; for example, an online application that is displaying a list of rows with all last names beginning with "LAR%". It usually is not necessary to have the precise, up-to-the-second names listed for selection. This is especially true when the list can change within a matter of seconds. After the estimated list is displayed and one of the names is selected, a second screen can retrieve the detail using a stricter isolation to enforce proper locking.

 What is the best locking option if I need to read or update an entire table?

You can save the overhead of multiple lock acquisitions needed for locking table data by using the LOCK TABLE statement. This statement will allow you to lock an entire table in either share mode or exclusive mode. This lock will be held until the end of the transaction. While using the exclusive mode will not allow concurrent transactions to either read/update the table, the transaction that issued the lock-table statement may finish more quickly because it will not have to wait on locks or find that data is unavailable due to locks held by other transactions.

 What is a persistent prepare?

By using the new KEEPDYNAMIC bind option in Version 5, DB2 will preserve dynamic statements past commits. In order to use this option effectively, you will need to re-code the application to eliminate unnecessary prepare requests that follow a commit, make sure that distributed applications are bound DEFER(PREPARE), and make sure prepare statement caching is active. Prepares can be moved out of loops and executed once.

> ! **Caution:** *The DBD lock acquired on the initial prepare will be held until a commit. However, this should not be a concern.*

How often should I commit?

There are two good reasons to commit: to improve concurrency and to prevent massive, long-running rollbacks when abnormal terminations occur. Even programs that have no concurrency problems should at least do a commit every 10 minutes as a general rule.

If you design a good batch program, commit processing is part of it. If you do commit processing, you have to identify the unit of work in your program and also design the batch program such that it is restartable. This is why several programmers claim that this will complicate their logic and was never included as part of the original design. Many of these programs must be redesigned when they begin to cause concurrency problems. The best thing is to do design the program properly the first time.

When concurrency is an issue, you probably want a commit frequency somewhere between 2 seconds and 20 seconds. A very good practice is to make sure the commit frequency can be influenced from the outside. Identify a logical unit of work in your program and execute this x number of times before doing a commit. The magic number x could come from a control card to your program or from an heuristic control table. This way, programs that cause concurrency problems can be tuned, and you could also have separate settings depending on the time of day.

> ✛ **Tip:** *It is a good idea to have the same design in all of your programs. There are software solutions available from the Independent Software Vendors (ISVs) that take care of all commit/restart problems.*

Should online transactions commit?

No, it is not good practice to do intermittent committing in online transactions rather than commit at the end of the transaction. When you have a long-running (background)

transaction (printing, for example) you should design your transaction such that it will reschedule itself and then terminate (doing an implicit commit). This way all resources are released and the transaction server can shut down in an orderly way when needed.

 ## Is there a way to prevent lock escalation caused by programs?

If you need to lock and cannot frequently commit, consider the use of SQL LOCK TABLE statements. After successful execution, your batch will have an S or X lock on the table, so you will not have the problem of page or row locks escalating to table locks automatically, potentially causing unforeseen problems with lock contention. This solves the problem of failing batches caused by the lock not being granted, and you also save a lot of resources.

When should I use row-level locking for concurrency?

DB2 UNIX / NT / OS/2 only supports row-level locking, but it is an option on the OS/390 platform, which supports both row- and page-level locking. Row-level locking should be used when a page of data is simultaneously needed by other users, and each user's interest is on different rows. Use row-level locking only if the increase of the cost (concurrency and wait-time overhead) of locking is tolerable. The more rows per page, the higher the cost.

If the users' interest is on the same rows, also referred to as "hot rows," row-level locking will not have any positive impact on concurrency and will only increase the cost of locking.

Chapter 13

Stored Procedures, Triggers, and UDFs

Answer Topics!

Stored Procedures, Triggers, and UDFs @ a Glance

- There are three main ways to extend the power of the DB2 engine when using SQL. *Stored procedures* offer a way to have a process or program invoked directly by an SQL call. *Triggers* allow SQL processes to be automatically invoked when any kind of update action is taken against a table, and those SQL processes can then can invoke stored procedures and UDFs. *UDFs* (user-defined functions) extend SQL statements by directly invoking a process or program as a function. Through the use of any of these extensions, DB2 and SQL can be used to perform a variety of new and interesting actions limited mainly by a developer's imagination.

- Stored Procedures are compiled programs that are stored either on a local DB2 server or a remote DB2 server developed to execute several SQL statements. Stored procedures are called from a client with all of the database processing occurring on the database server. This returns only a result set to the client application, thereby reducing network traffic between the client application and the database server by a considerable amount. Stored procedures can be coded in several languages and DB2 stored procedures in particular are very portable among various platforms. They are not without their complexities, however, and often a rethinking of application logic and process is in order.

- Triggers are actions that are automatically invoked by predetermined events or actions against a table. These actions consist of a series of SQL statements to be executed when the trigger is invoked. Triggers are very flexible and can be very powerful and can be used to perform actions even outside of the database. However, their powerfulness can also lead to confusion or misunderstandings about how they operate.

- User Defined Functions (UDFs) are defined to allow for SQL statements to be extended by invoking a user-defined program that was defined as part of the function. There are limitations to what kind of functions can be defined. For instance, user-defined functions can only be defined as 'scalar' functions, not column functions. Despite any limitations present, UDFs can become very complex and useful in creating functions that can replace several lines of application code.

 The variety of options gives rise to many questions about creating and testing these functions and procedures: when and how to use them, and how they interact and affect other processes. That is what this chapter addresses.

STORED PROCEDURES

 When should I use stored procedures?

Stored procedures can be local or remote—they can be called by programs running on the same server or by programs running remotely. There are many different reasons for using stored procedures.

One situation in which stored procedures are useful is when a client/server application must issue several remote SQL statements. The network overhead involved in sending multiple SQL commands and receiving result sets is quite significant. Using stored procedures will lessen the traffic across the network and reduce the application overhead.

You can also use stored procedures to access information on the host server that is required to be secure. This information will remain more secure due to the fact that you can use result sets to return the required data to the client, and the client will only need to have authority to execute the stored procedure, not the DB2 tables.

Stored procedures should also be used to encapsulate business functions that can be programmed once and executed by any and all processes—OLTP, local, remote, warehouse, ad hoc, or others. Such a functional process might add a purchase order or update a purchase order. In both of these examples, the transactions are long and involve accessing and updating many tables. They are processes that are invoked both in OLTP and batch environments. Therefore, writing the process as a stored procedure allows the function to exist in only one place, and yet to be used anywhere in the system, as any type of process. If, for some reason, the business needs to change the way this function is implemented, then only this one program needs to be changed. Similarly, if the database structure changes, only that one program needs to be updated.

Another possibility is to code complex processes in a stored procedure that can then be invoked by any process in the network. This can be especially useful when applications require the use of non-DB2 data. For instance, when data needs to be retrieved from a VSAM or IMS data store and used by a DB2 client, a stored procedure can retrieve the data into a global temporary table and then the application can use SQL and result set logic for row retrieval of this data, alone or combined through joins with other DB2 data.

Why are column names from my DB2 stored procedure result sets not coming back to my client application?

The default in DB2 is to not return column names for stored procedures. However, updating a DSNZPARM parameter can change this default. If the SELECT statements inside the stored procedure are static, you must set the DESCSTAT parameter to YES on the host DB2 where the procedure was compiled in order to retrieve column names from your stored procedure result sets. Then you will need to rebind the stored procedures application packages. If the SELECT statements inside of the stored procedure are dynamic, the result-set column names should be returned automatically.

What is the difference between a WLM-established address space and a DB2-established address space for executing stored procedures in a DB2 OS/390 environment?

WLM (Workload Manager)-established address spaces provide multiple isolated environments for stored procedures so that failures do not affect other stored procedures. WLM-established address spaces also reduce demand for storage below the 16MB line, removing the limitation on the number of stored procedures that can run concurrently. These also inherit the dispatching priority of the DB2 thread that issues the CALL statement. Inheriting the dispatching priority of the thread allows high priority work to have its stored procedures execute ahead of lower priority work and their stored procedures. In a DB2-established address space

you cannot prioritize stored procedures, and you are limited by storage in the address space. There is no separation of the work by dispatching priorities and high priority work gets penalized.

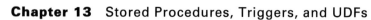 How do I pass parameters in stored procedures?

A stored procedure must declare each parameter passed to it (though it is possible to have a stored procedure that has no parameters). Through Version 5 on OS/390, the PARMLIST column of the catalog table SYSPROCEDURES must contain a compatible SQL data type declaration for each parameter.

In Version 6 and UDB, however, parameters are defined through the CREATE PROCEDURE statement. Each parameter is defined as IN, OUT, or INOUT to specify the mode, name, and data type of each parameter. One entry in the list must be specified for each parameter that the procedure will expect. The parameters are then passed in the EXEC SQL CALL statement.

What languages can a stored procedure be written in?

A stored procedure for DB2 OS/390 through the initial release of Version 5 can be written in COBOL, Assembler, C, C++, or PL/I. Stored procedures for UDB can be written in any language that conforms to the parameter passing and linkage conventions defined by either the C language or by the Java language. The C calling and linkage convention is defined by the standard ANSI C prototype. To conform to the Java language convention, the database manager must call the stored procedure as a method in a Java class.

The capability to write stored procedures in Java using SQLJ or JDBC, PSM, and REXX will be added to DB2 for OS/390 V5, UDB and beyond. The Java stored procedures will be able to use SQLJ (static SQL for Java) and JDBC (dynamic SQL for Java). Java stored procedures would be written the same way as the other languages and also have the benefit on OS/390 of a high performance Java compiler.

REXX is also being enhanced as a DB2 stored procedure language, but it will still be interpreted, not compiled. It will be able to contain SQL but will be limited to only one output

parameter. In addition, all parameters passed to REXX have to be strings.

To achieve a higher level of portability and assist in migrations to DB2, PSM (SQL3 syntax standard) will be made available as well. PSM would be used to define the stored procedure process in the CREATE PROCEDURE definition, rather than have the process written in a compiled or interpreted language. An example of a PSM stored procedure follows:

```
CREATE PROCEDURE YLASSOC (IN x_acct CHAR(5),
            OUT x_name CHAR(20),
            OUT x_address CHAR(80),
            OUT x_code INT)
        LANGUAGE(SQL)
    BEGIN;
        SET x_code = 0;
        SELECT x_name, x_address
            FROM YLASSOC_ACCTS
            WHERE ACCT = x_acct;
        IF SQLCODE < 0 THEN
            x_code = SQLCODE;
    END;
```

This would actually get prepared as a procedure by a DB2 supplied REXX stored procedure.

Why should a stored procedure be coded as reentrant?

Stored procedures should be coded as reentrant for performance reasons. First, if the stored procedure is coded as reentrant, it will not have to be loaded into storage each time it is called. Second, a reentrant stored procedure will have a single copy shared by several threads, thus allowing for less virtual storage to be used.

Does a stored procedure require a plan to execute?

No. You do not need a plan in order to execute a stored procedure because it executes under the thread of the calling application and uses the plan from the client program. It is simply bound as a package.

Can I invoke a stored procedure from a Java application?

Yes. Any language, tool, or application that supports the appropriate parameter passing and linkage conventions can issue the SQL commands necessary to invoke a stored procedure. Java can invoke a stored procedure using either JDBC (Dynamic SQL) or SQLJ (static SQL).

The following extracts show the differences in calling a stored procedure from Java using SQLJ and JDBC.

```
SQLJ:
#sql (con) {CALL SP1 (:IN parm1, :OUT parm2)};


JDBC:
CallableStatement yevsql=con.prepareCall("CALL SP1(?,?)");
yevsql.setString(1,parm1);
yevsql.registerOutParameter(2,java.sql.types.VARCHAR);
yevsql.executeUpdate();
parm2=yevsql.getString(2);
```

What is LE/370?

LE/370 (Language Environment 370) is a run-time library used by DB2 on OS/390 to establish a run-time environment for stored procedures. It provides run-time services, such as storage management and exception condition handling, and can be used regardless of the application programming language. You will have to specify the LE/370 run-time library to the link-edit step as well as any language-specific libraries. LE/370 also has a feature to help you in debugging your stored procedures.

Can I issue a DB2 command from a stored procedure?

Yes, you can issue a DB2 command from a stored procedure by using IFI (Instrumentation Facility Interface) calls on DB2 OS/390.

How can I improve the performance of my stored procedures?

On UNIX, Windows, and OS/2, there are a few options for improving the performance of stored procedures. First you can set the KEEPDARI option to YES to keep the process required for stored procedure execution active after the stored procedure is finished so the db2dari process does not have to rebuild it for each stored procedure execution. Second, for the most frequently used stored procedures, use the SQLZ_HOLD_PROC parameter to keep the stored procedure in main memory after the first execution. Last, by using compound SQL, you can improve stored procedure performance because compound SQL reduces the overhead involved in the inter-process communication and it also helps to code the stored procedure using embedded static SQL.

On OS/390, there are numerous options available for improving the performance of stored procedures when the procedures are defined or created. Procedures can be coded as MAIN or SUB—main programs or subroutines. SUB allows a shorter code path for entry and exit logic but makes it much more difficult to write the program since all initializations, entry and exit logic, and other environmental issues have to be handled. This option is only for very knowledgeable programmers and is to be used only in very special situations where that last bit of code length reduction is required. Other performance techniques that can be used for improvement include using the residency feature to keep the program in memory once it is loaded, and making the code reentrant to handle multiple requests. Using the WLM-established address space option of OS/390 is another way to improve performance—it will establish additional address spaces when the need arises due to increased workload.

Can I start and stop a DB2 stored procedure without recycling DB2?

Yes, you can start or stop a stored procedure without recycling the DB2 subsystem. This can be performed by issuing the following DB2 commands.

```
-stop procedure(procedure name) or (*)
-start procedure(procedure name) or (*)
```

What is the difference between a fenced and a nonfenced stored procedure?

A fenced stored procedure executes in a separate process from the database agent. Nonfenced stored procedures will

execute in the same process as the database agent and can increase application performance because less overhead is needed for communication between the application and the DB2 coordinating agent. However, nonfenced stored procedures can overwrite the DB2 control blocks. A stored procedure that is not fenced is generally one that is considered "safe" to be run in the database manager operating environment's process or address.

On OS/390, all stored procedures are fenced. On the other platforms, the procedure can be defined as fenced or non-fenced.

What are the benefits of COMMIT ON RETURN option?

The COMMIT ON RETURN option for stored procedures reduces network traffic and allows locking in a stored procedure to be performed on a predictable basis. Without COMMIT ON RETURN, the locks would be held until the connected application issued the commit. This interchange is made up of many more network messages, and the locks are held during this conversation. With the COMMIT ON RETURN option, the locks are freed as soon as the stored procedure ends.

What are the benefits of using result sets in stored procedures and how do I code for them?

With DB2 Version 5, stored procedures can return result sets to the client, allowing data to be retrieved more efficiently and improving application security by only requiring a client to have execution authority on a stored procedure, not access to the referenced tables. Result sets from DB2 or nonrelational sources can be returned from either base tables or temporary tables to clients on any DB2 server. In order for a stored procedure to return multiple result sets to clients, the following must be present:

- Cursors must be opened using the WITH RETURN clause
- Rows in the SYSIBM.SYSPROCEDURES catalog table must contain a value greater that 0 in the RESULT_SET column.
- DRDA client needs to support Level 3 result sets

In order to prepare a distributed application to receive result sets, you will need to be using a CLI application or an ODBC or CLI application tool able to receive result sets such as Visual Age, PowerBuilder, or Visual Basic. If the application code is running on the same OS/390 server as the stored procedure, there are new additions to the SQL language to support this. The following is a skeleton example of coding to receive a stored procedure result set when the application program is running on the same OS/390 server running the stored procedure.

```
exec sql
    BEGIN DECLARE SECTION;
exec sql
    RESULT_SET_LOCATOR VARYING locater1;
exec sql
    END DECLARE SECTION;

exec sql
    CALL SP1(:parm1, :parm2, …);

exec sql
    ASSOCIATE LOCATOR (:locater1) WITH PROCEDURE SP1;
exec sql
    ALLOCATE CSR1 CURSOR FOR RESULT SET :locater1;
exec sql
    FETCH CSR1 INTO :acctno, ;billingno;
```

To allow for result sets to be returned from the stored procedure from the server, the WITH RETURN clause must be used in the cursor definition in the stored procedure and the cursors cannot be closed before the program ends. DB2 will return the rows in the result set from the opened cursors to the application program when the stored procedure ends. The following example shows the stored procedure code necessary to return the result set to the application code shown in the previous example.

```
EXEC SQL
    DECLARE SP_CSR1 CURSOR
        WITH RETURN FOR
            SELECT ACCT_NO, BILLING_NO
            FROM  ORDER_TABLE
            WHERE ITEM = :parm1;
```

```
EXEC SQL
    OPEN SP_CSR1;

return;
```

TRIGGERS

 If I add a trigger to a table that already contains rows, will rows that violate the trigger be rejected?

No, rows that are in violation of a newly added trigger will not be rejected. When a trigger is added to a table that already has existing rows, it will not cause any triggered actions to be activated. If the trigger is designed to enforce some type of integrity constraint on the data rows in the table, those constraints may not be enforced by rules defined in the trigger (or held true) for the rows that existed in the table before the trigger was added.

 When will a trigger cause a package to become invalid?

A trigger will cause a package to become invalid under the following circumstances:

- If an update trigger without an explicit column list is created, packages with an update usage on the target table are invalidated.

- If an update trigger with a column list is created, packages with update usage on the target table are only invalidated if the package also has an update usage on at least one column in the *column-name* list of the CREATE TRIGGER statement.

- If an insert trigger is created, packages that have an insert usage on the target table are invalidated.

- If a delete trigger is created, packages that have a delete usage on the target table are invalidated.

When should I use a trigger vs. a table check constraint?

If a trigger and a table check constraint can enforce the same rule, it is better to use a table check constraint. While triggers are more powerful than table check constraints and can be more extensive in terms of rule enforcement, constraints can be better optimized by DB2.

Table check constraints are enforced for all existing data at the time of creation, and are enforced for all statements affecting the data.

Can I use a CASE expression in a trigger?

Yes, a CASE expression can be used in a trigger, but it needs to be nested inside a VALUES statement, as shown here:

```
BEGIN ATOMIC
    VALUES CASE
        WHEN condition
            THEN something
        WHEN other condition
            THEN something else
    END
END;
```

What is MODE DB2SQL?

The phrase MODE DB2SQL is the execution mode of the trigger. This phase is required for each trigger to ensure that an existing application will not be negatively impacted if alternative execution modes for triggers are added to DB2 in the future.

How do I force a rollback inside of a trigger?

If you use the SIGNAL statement to raise an error condition, a rollback will also be performed to back out the changes made by an SQL statement as well as any changes caused by the trigger, such as cascading effects resulting from a referential

relationship. SIGNAL can be used either before or after triggers. Other statements in the program can either be committed or rolled back.

What is the difference between the SIGNAL and RAISE_ERROR?

SIGNAL SQLSTATE is a statement that is used to cause an error to be returned with a specified SQLSTATE code and a specific message. This statement can only be used as a triggered SQL statement within a trigger.

RAISE_ERROR is not a statement but a function that causes the statement that includes it to return an error with a specific SQLSTATE, SQLCODE -438 and *a message*. The RAISE_ERROR function always returns NULL with an undefined data type. RAISE_ERROR is most useful in CASE expressions, especially when the CASE expression is used in a stored procedure. The following example shows a CASE expression with the RAISE_ERROR function.

```
BEGIN ATOMIC
    VALUES CASE
        WHEN condition
            THEN something
        WHEN other condition
            THEN something else
ELSE RAISE_ERROR('50001',
            'No matches in Triggered CASE')
END
END;
```

Can I use a user-defined function in a trigger?

Yes, you can use a user-defined function in a trigger, and these types of functions can help to centralize rules to ensure that they are enforced in the same manner in current and future applications. To just invoke a UDF in a trigger, the VALUES clause has to be used. In the example below, PAGE_DBA is a user-written program, perhaps in C or Java, that formulates a message and triggers a process that sends a message to a pager. By using these kinds of UDFs as triggers, it is possible for a trigger to perform any kind of task and not just be limited to SQL.

```
BEGIN ATOMIC
  VALUES(PAGE_DBA('Tablespaces:' CONCAT TS.NAME,
    'needs to be reorged NOW!'));
END
```

Can I have a trigger invoke other triggers and stored procedures, and if so, what are the benefits and drawbacks?

Triggers can cause other triggers to be invoked, and through SQL, can call stored procedures. These stored procedures could issue SQL updates which invoked other triggers. This allows great flexibility—we can use triggers to enforce business rules, create new column values or edit column values, validate all input data, or maintain summary tables or cross reference tables. The trigger is just a way of getting control whenever a table's data is modified.

A single trigger invoked by an update on a financial table, could, for example, fire off a user-defined function and/or a stored procedure to invoke an external action that triggers an e-mail to a pager notifying the DBA of a serious condition. There is currently a safe limit to the cascading of triggers, stored procedures, and user-defined functions—a runtime nesting depth of 16.

How can I use triggers to perform actions outside of a database?

Triggers can only contain SQL, but through SQL, stored procedures and user-defined functions can be invoked. Since stored procedures and user-defined functions are user-written code, almost any activity can be performed from a triggered event. The action causing the trigger may need a message sent to a special place via email. The trigger might be a before trigger written to handle complex referential integrity checks which could involve checking if data exists in another non-DB2 storage container. Through the use of stored procedures and user-defined functions, the power of a trigger is almost unlimited.

USER-DEFINED FUNCTIONS

 What are user-defined functions?

User-defined functions (UDFs) are functions that are created by the user though DDL using the CREATE FUNCTION statement. This statement can be issued in an interactive query interface or in an application program. There are three types of UDFs.

- **Sourced functions** mimic other functions. These functions can be column functions, scalar functions, or operator functions.

- **External scalar functions** are written in a programming language, such as C, C++, or Java, and return a scalar value. External scalar functions cannot contain SQL, cannot be column functions, cannot access or modify the database, and can only perform calculations on parameters.

- **External table functions** can return a table and can be written in C or Java.

 What is a table function?

A table function is a particular type of user-defined function that takes individual scalar values as parameters and returns a table to the SQL statement. This type of function can only be specified within the FROM clause of a SELECT statement. Table functions are external functions and can be used to retrieve data from a non-DB2 source, passing it to a SQL statement with the output of the table function participating in a join. This is a way to build a table from non-DB2 data, by using an INSERT into SELECT FROM statement where the FROM is really a table function or a table function joined with other DB2 data.

❓ Can I use user-defined functions for column functions?

There are no user-defined "column" functions, only user-defined "scalar" functions in any version of DB2. For example, suppose a UDF is used on the SELECT line of a SQL statement. The UDF would get control when each result set row is being "constructed." It does not have knowledge of the previous result set row or the next result set row. Even if it tried to get smart and store each result set row column data in another medium, there is no mechanism to fire off that UDF at EOJ (end of result set) to do something with all that column data.

❓ How can I updating UDF statistics for the optimizer?

The optimizer will use statistics, if available, for estimating the costs for access paths where UDFs are used. The statistics that the optimizer needs can be updated by using the SYSSTAT.FUNCTIONS catalog view.

Chapter 14

Data Sharing

Answers Topics!

Data Sharing @ a Glance

DB2 has been operating in organizations for over 15 years now, and just when you thought you had a handle on DB2 operations and performance, along came a new feature with Version 4 known as Data Sharing. This section is going to cover the most common data-sharing topics: application selection, migration, problem diagnosing, and tuning for overall system performance. It will include questions on how to migrate effectively to the data-sharing environment, tuning the current DB2 environment in preparation for data-sharing migration, and troubleshooting after the migration. There will also be several corresponding examples of reporting, to demonstrate how to monitor and diagnose problems in this new environment.

DB2 performance is critical in a data-sharing environment. Data sharing presents new complications for DB2 performance and tuning, and there are several new places to look for problems—from application selection to post-implementation troubleshooting. Old performance problems that were acceptable or tolerable in the past are magnified in the data-sharing environment. Several questions regarding performance tuning will be covered to help answer questions most often associated with the added complexity of tuning a data-sharing environment and its applications.

What makes data sharing so complex is the introduction of new hardware and new rules. Contrary to popular belief, data sharing is not just an install option! The introduction of the coupling facility in the parallel sysplex data-sharing architecture accounts for a whole new set of performance factors to be concerned with. This is due to the number of accesses DB2 must issue to the coupling facility: LOCK/UNLOCK requests, physical directory reads, cache updates, and reads of buffer invalidated data.

Recovery questions will also be covered in this chapter, because data sharing introduces new logging methods and recovery techniques for DB2 subsystems. There are also additional considerations for off-site recovery, such as the use of ICMF, or possibly, the new technology provided by the GDPS.

ENVIRONMENT AND IMPLEMENTATION

 What factors determine processing costs involved in migrating to a data-sharing environment?

Processing costs for data sharing will vary as a result of the following:

- the degree of data sharing
- hardware and software configurations
- workload characteristics
- locking factors
- application design/options
- physical design

The processing costs can be controlled to some degree by application and system tuning. Data-sharing costs are a function of the processing required for sharing, in addition to the normal processing required to provide concurrency control for inter-DB2 interest and data coherency. The amount of actual data sharing required (the amount of read/write interest in the same pages by multiple DB2 users), will directly affect the cost associated with operating in a data-sharing environment.

Hardware and software costs can include the speed of CPs and the level of CF (coupling facility) code, CF structure sizes, CF link configurations, the level of the hardware, the level of software maintenance, and the number of members in the data-sharing group.

Workload characteristics can include real, false, and XES (Cross System Extended Services; a set of OS/390 services allowing multiple instances of an application or subsystem to utilize data-sharing features through the use of the coupling facility) contention, DASD contention, workload dynamics, thread reuse, and an application's use of lock avoidance.

Physical design and affinity processing can dramatically alter the costs of data sharing. The physical design of tablespaces, use of different partitioning strategies, changes to partition level locking, and index design are only some of

the many factors. In certain situations, using affinity processing (separating functions to individual data-sharing members) can reduce processing associated with the CF.

Should I start with a new DB2 subsystem or use an existing subsystem to create a new data-sharing group?

Whether you start with a new DB2 subsystem or use an existing one will depend on the size and complexity of the subsystems that are to be involved in the data-sharing group. When you migrate subsystems to the new data-sharing group, all of the objects need to be moved to the new consolidated catalog. If there is a subsystem with several thousand objects, you could make this subsystem the originating member and migrate all other subsystem objects to its catalog. If you do this, you then wouldn't have to move all of the objects in that large subsystem, since it becomes the originating member.

If you are enabling data sharing from an existing DB2 subsystem, you may need to derive a naming standard from the existing names in the originating subsystem member. In this way, you will reduce the impact to the existing application. However, you will be limited by having to retrofit all migrated DB2 objects to a naming standard that may or may not be appropriate for the data group. If you are starting a new data-sharing group, and not using an existing DB2 subsystem as the originating member, then you can begin with a new naming standard to be propagated throughout all your data-sharing environment objects. This will provide you with the ability to develop a naming standard that is flexible and meaningful for all data-sharing objects.

How do I rename a subsystem in an existing data-sharing group?

DB2 does not give you the flexibility to change the group or subsystem name after data sharing has been enabled. If you had the ability to change a group or subsystem name after enabling data sharing, you would also have to make additional changes to the BSDS, SYSLGRNX, SYSCOPY,

work files, and the coupling facility. The processes involved in performing such tasks are risky, as they leave open many opportunities for mistakes that could lead to the failure the entire data-sharing group.

Choosing appropriate naming standards is key to having a flexible convention for the data-sharing group. Names should be chosen wisely for the data-sharing group, its members, data sets such as the BSDS, active/archive logs, IRLM, and coupling facility structures. The individual subsystem name, or member name, is the most limited (four characters) by DB2.

Once you've established an individual system name, it can be used as a basis for all of the other names. For example, if your subsystem (or member) name is DBxD, where x represents the individual member number, then the BSDS and log data sets could follow a convention such as DSN01.DB1D.BSDS01, and DSN01.DB1D.LOG1.

What types of applications are suitable for a data-sharing environment?

Not all applications belong in a data-sharing environment, and some applications will still benefit from isolation. Application analysis, or selection, is the process of evaluating which applications will benefit from data sharing and belong in a data-sharing environment.

You will need to determine the application objectives for data sharing in order to set performance objectives. Questions, such as the following, need to be asked and answered:

- What is our overall goal in implementing data sharing?
- Are we looking to offload CPU cycles?
- Will we benefit from transaction-routing capabilities?
- Is 24 × 7 the driving requirement?

These are just a few of several questions that should be addressed in order to appropriately implement data sharing with maximum benefit.

 How can I determine the status of a member in a data-sharing group?

In order to dynamically determine the status of a data-sharing group member you can issue the –DISPLAY GROUP command from any member. The output from this command, issued from the DB2P member, is shown in the following illustration. This output shows you the results of the DISPLAY GROUP command with the status of each member and whether it is active, quiesced, or failed.

```
-DB2P  DISPLAY GROUP DETAIL

DB2                  SYSTEM      IRLM
MEMBER   ID   SUBSYS  CMDPREF  STATUS  NAME   LVL SUBSYS   IRLMPROC
------------------------------------------------------------------

DB2P     1    DB2P    -DB2P    ACTIVE  MVSA   510  ZRLM     ZRLMPROC
------------------------------------------------------------------
SCA    STRUCTURE SIZE:      1024 KB, STATUS= AC, SCA IN USE:   11%
LOCK1 STRUCTURE SIZE:      1536 KB,            LOCK1 IN USE:  < 1%
NUMBER LOCK ENTRIES:      262144, LOCK ENTRIES    IN USE:   33
NUMBER LIST ENTRIES:        7353, LIST ENTRIES    IN USE:    0
```

PERFORMANCE AND LOCKING

 Should I use PC = YES or PC = NO in the IRLMPROC in a data-sharing environment?

The use of the PC = YES or PC = NO option, as defined in the subsystem IRLMPROC, is going to depend on whether you are memory-constrained or experiencing performance

problems. PC = YES will not use ECSA memory for locks, thereby eliminating storage creep problems caused by the use of this area in memory. However, PC = YES will come with some amount of CPU overhead and will vary by CPU model.

Are there any items I need to evaluate in DB2, and are there applications to ensure that data sharing will perform well?

Yes. To ensure optimal performance, there are several items that need to be evaluated before you move to data sharing. The following list includes a few of the most important items.

- Using Type 2 indexes, regardless of whether or not you are in a data-sharing environment or not. Type 2 indexes have reduced expected locking rates by an average of 50 percent. The reduction is as low as 25 percent for environments with Version 4 or 5 in general and in data-sharing environments with low read/write activity, and as high as 75 percent in some data-sharing environments with high read/write activity. It should also be noted that support for Type 1 indexes has been dropped in Version 6.

- Reducing row-level locking is very important, because a page level P-lock will be taken for every row lock. Consider using MAXROWS=1 or traditional "padding" methods. Uncommitted reads should be evaluated for programs and statements that do not require absolutely current data for processing. This will help reduce the number of locks propagated to the coupling facility.

- Reducing the level of data sharing will result in less concurrent access between members on particular DB2 objects. This may appear to somewhat defeat the purpose of being able to share objects and route workload, but it is all a matter of appropriate application selection and tuning.

- Using the CURRENTDATA(NO) option on the bind is a recommendation even in cases where you are not data

sharing; however in the data-sharing environment lock avoidance can help reduce global locking.

- Using RELEASE(DEALLOCATE) on your package binds and defining appropriate CICS protected threads can help to reduce XES contention, and can also help to reduce global and false lock contention.

- Using the bind parameter of UR (uncommitted read) , as much as possible, helps to reduce the number of locks acquired, and prevents additional locks from being propagated to the coupling facility when they are not required.

Should I use the RELEASE(DEALLOCATE) parameter on my packages in a data-sharing environment?

Using the RELEASE(DEALLOCATE) parameter in conjunction with CICS protected threads can help to reduce XES contention, and it can also help to reduce global and false lock contention. The number of locks taken will decrease, because the transactions will now only hold onto the parent locks. The number of locks propagated to XES will also decline as parent locks are maintained.

You should see a decrease in the class 2 CPU time as well. However, do not go overboard with using RELEASE(DEALLOCATE). Use the 80-20 rule for deciding which transaction threads would be the most beneficial, and change a few packages at a time and measure the results. By observing the thread deallocations per commit in the Accounting Detail reports, you can get an idea of the amount of thread reuse currently being achieved. Overdoing the usage of this parameter could cause your EDM pool to grow enormously if the transactions are heavily accessed, and this would in turn require more memory to support the EDM pool.

For instance, a 4-way data-sharing customer with each EDM pool at 35MB experienced an increase in each EDM pool up to 70MB when 3 heavily used CICS threads were defined in the RCT as protected and the plans/packages were bound RELEASE(DEALLOCATE). The EDM pool is affected

by the use of RELEASE(DEALLOCATE) and protected threads, because plan/packages are held for a longer period of time in the EDM pool. However, since the EDM pool is in virtual memory, expansion has less impact than you might expect.

What causes false contention?

False contention occurs when two or more incompatible lock requests from two or more DB2 members for two or more resources are hashing to the same lock table slot and there is no real contention.

False contention, as a percent of total contention, is the number of unlock requests divided by the total number of requests multiplied by 100, and this number needs to be kept under 50 percent of the total global contention to avoid the overhead of extra processing for false contention resolution.

The calculation shown in Figure 14-1 is an example from a long statistics monitor report of how to find out if there is false contention.

```
             False contention calculation:

    1894 / (19454 + 18629 + 1894) × 100 = 4.74

DATA SHARING LOCKING              QUANTITY
------------------------------    --------
SYNCH.XES - LOCK REQUESTS         19454
SYNCH.XES - CHANGE REQUESTS       18629
SYNCH.XES - UNLOCK REQUESTS       1894
ASYNCH.XES - RESOURCES            ..

SUSPENDS - IRLM GLOBAL CONT       646022
SUSPENDS - XES GLOBAL CONT        101182
SUSPENDS - FALSE CONTENTION       656118
INCOMPATIBLE RETAINED LOCK        ..
```

Figure 14-1 False contention calculation from a statistics monitor report

 How do I reduce or eliminate false contention?

To eliminate or reduce false contention, a lock requester could be suspended until the determination of whether or not the contention is false is made. As false contention increases, transactions can terminate and response time increases.

The lock structure, which contains the lock table, is one of the three structures in the CF. The lock structure needs to be sized appropriately for optimal performance, since it is used by the IRLM for lock control. The lock structure should always be kept separate from the GBP (group bufferpool) structure. The lock table controls locks, and the other item in the lock structure, the record list, contains the modify and retained locks Decreasing the granularity of locks can help to ease false contention but has its own implications, such as applicability to processing needs and, of course, increasing the possibility of real contention. The number of users connected to the lock structure can also be decreased so that more lock entries can fit on the structure; however, this is usually not a feasible option.

 What is global contention, and how can I resolve it?

The global contention is the total number of suspends caused by contention. Global contention can be real or false. Real contention occurs when two processes (on the same or different subsystems) try to obtain the same lock. This results from the workload characteristics, and it is tuned the same way as in a single subsystem environment (commits, concurrency of processes, and so on). The goal is to keep the total global lock contention under 2 percent so that the total number of combined lock, change, and unlock requests should not exceed 98 percent.

Global contention can be limited by reducing the amount of locks, especially the number of P-locks, propagated to the coupling facility, or through the use of lock avoidance by performing application tuning. The example in Figure 14-2 calculates global contention from the same monitor report used in Figure 14-1.

Global contention calculation:

$$\frac{\text{sync. XES}}{(\text{IRLM global cont.}) + (\text{XES global cont.}) + (\text{false cont.})} \times 100 =$$

$$\frac{(\text{lock requests} + \text{change requests} + \text{unlock requests})}{(\text{IRLM global cont.}) + (\text{XES global cont.}) + (\text{false cont.})} \times 100 =$$

$$\frac{19454 + 18629 + 1894}{646022 + 101182 + 656118} \times 100 = 2.85$$

Figure 14-2 Global contention calculation

What is the difference between L-locks and P-locks?

L-locks (logical locks) are used for controlling concurrency of access to objects, while P-locks (physical locks) are used to maintain data coherency, and allow multiple subsystems to be concurrently updating the same database object. This allows a member to determine page-set interest by another member, and tells the member whether or not a page set is group-bufferpool dependent. P-locks are also used to maintain EDM pool consistency among members in data sharing. L-locks exist in both data-sharing and non-data-sharing systems, while P-locks are exclusive to data sharing. L-locks are transaction locks owned by programs, and can be local or global in scope, while P-locks are owned by a member and are only global.

Why do L-locks get propagated to the coupling facility when P-locks are actually being used to do the actual resource locking?

In a data-sharing environment, many members may be active, and in certain situations it becomes necessary to propagate L-locks to the coupling facility, making them global. All parent L-locks get propagated to the CF, with only minor exceptions, while most child L-locks do not get propagated to the lock structure in the CF. Propagation only

occurs when there is inter-member conflict at the parent-lock level (for example, one member has an IX lock on a tablespace, and another member has an IS lock on the tablespace).

What are retained locks?

Retained locks are locks that are held by a failed DB2 member, and result from existing modify locks being held when the member's subsystem failed (that is, active locks that were being used to control updates to data). These locks will prevent access by other DB2 members in the data-sharing group from getting to the data, because the locks are held in the coupling facility until a restart is completed and they are released. The reasoning behind retained locks is that there needs to be a mechanism for protecting uncommitted data from being accessed by other DB2 members in the data-sharing group.

How do I resolve retained locks?

Retained locks can only be resolved by the DB2 member that acquired the locks; therefore, the failed DB2 member must be restarted, and the locks must be resolved by either converting them to active locks by reacquiring the lock, or by purging the lock entirely.

What trace classes and IFCIDs should I use to diagnose locking problems in a data-sharing environment?

To diagnose locking problems in a data-sharing environment, you use many of the same traces and IFCIDs (Instrumentation Facility Component Identifiers) as you would in a single subsystem. A class 3 Statistics Trace contains deadlock and lock timeout information in IFCIDs 172, 196, 250, 261, 262, and 213. A class 6 Performance Trace contains summary lock information in IFCIDs 20, 44-45, 105, 106, 107, 172, 192, 213-214, and 218. A class 7 Performance Trace contains

```
DSNT375I - PLAN p1  WITH CORRELATION-ID id1 CONNECTION-ID
LUW-ID id3 ID DEADLOCKED WITH PLAN p2 WITH CORRELATION-ID
id4 CONNECTION-ID id5 LUW-ID id6 ON MEMBER id7

DSNT376I - PLAN p1 WITH CORRELATION-ID id1 CONNECTION-ID id2
LUW-ID id3 IS TIMED OUT. ONE HOLDER OF THE RESOURCE IS PLAN
p2 WITH CORRELATION-ID id4 CONNECTION-ID id5 LUW-ID id6 ON
MEMBER id7
```

Figure 14-3   Deadlock detection return codes for data-sharing members

detail lock information in IFCIDs 21, 105, 106, 107, and 223. Page P-locking activity can be found in both statistics and accounting trace classes, and additional detail can be found in performance trace class 20 (IFCID 251) and in class 21 (IFCID 259).

There are a few new DB2 return codes that help to diagnose deadlocks and timeouts in data sharing. These messages identify the member where the deadlock or timeout occurred, as shown in Figure 14-3.

 Should I use the GBPCACHE ALL option for all pages of a table that is constantly referenced?

The GBPCACHE ALL option on the CREATE/ALTER TABLESPACE clause will allow you to cache all read pages of a table or index in the group bufferpool as they are read in from DASD, regardless of whether there is any inter-DB2 read/write interest in the page. The benefit of using the GBPCACHE ALL feature is to avoid reads of the same page from DASD from different DB2 members of the data-sharing group. Applications that have a high amount of inter-DB2 interest would benefit; access would be faster, because frequently used pages would stay resident in the group bufferpool.

However, using the GBPCACHE ALL feature does not come without tradeoffs; there will be an increase in the resources used in the coupling facility while this feature is enabled.

What are some of the causes of a hang or delay in the data-sharing environment?

Data-sharing environment hangs can occur for a variety of reasons. Here are some potential scenarios:

- **Global locking contention** Global locking—depending on whether it is real or false contention—can cause delays. Real contention hangs (911's) are dealt with much as in a single-system environment, except the resource could be held by another subsystem.

- **P-lock negotiation** P-lock negotiation occurs through XES and may or may not cause a delay in the application process, depending on whether false or real contention is detected. Structures (LOCK, SCA, GBP) can become unavailable for various reasons; this will cause a failure in the data-sharing group and they will need to be rebuilt.

- **Unavailability of a CF structure** If an entire CF is unavailable, the structures will rebuild in another CF if the policies are defined so that this happens.

- **Thread hangs (DB2, CICS)** Thread hangs can be caused by a number of different factors. It is important to identify the thread (–DISPLAY THREAD), the holder, and the implications caused by canceling the thread.

- **IRLM notification messaging** DB2 uses IRLM notification to send notify messages among members in a DB2 data-sharing group. A hang could also result if a sender is held up waiting for a response (IRLM notification messaging is used by other service components as well).

What is XES contention, and how can it be controlled?

XES (Cross System Extended Services) is a set of OS/390 services allowing multiple instances of an application or subsystem to utilize data-sharing features via the coupling

facility. XES activity occurs for both L-locks and P-locks when a lock/unlock/change request is made against an object with inter-DB2 interest, and contention occurs when truly compatible locks are viewed by XES as being in contention for the same resource. This occurs because XES only views locks as S or X, whereas the IRLM is actually issuing IS or IX locks. XES is used to determine whether contention for a resource is real or not. A lock requester may or may not be suspended until this determination is made, depending on whether it can run a process in parallel with this activity.

XES activity can be monitored through a monitor statistics long report (Figure 14-4), through which you can observe the number of requests and amount of contention. A reduction in tablespace locking will help to reduce the amount of XES-detected lock contention.

```
DATA SHARING LOCKING                QUANTITY
------------------------------      --------
LOCK REQUESTS (P-LOCKS)
UNLOCK REQUESTS (P-LOCKS)
CHANGE REQUESTS (P-LOCKS)

SYNCH.XES - LOCK REQUESTS           19454
SYNCH.XES - CHANGE REQUESTS         18629
SYNCH.XES - UNLOCK REQUESTS         1894
ASYNCH.XES - RESOURCES

SUSPENDS - IRLM GLOBAL CONT         646022
SUSPENDS - XES GLOBAL CONT          101182
SUSPENDS - FALSE CONTENTION         656118
INCOMPATIBLE RETAINED LOCK

NOTIFY MESSAGES SENT
NOTIFY MESSAGES RECEIVED
```

Figure 14-4   XES Requests report example

COUPLING FACILITY STRUCTURES

 How do I determine the size and placement of my coupling facility structures?

There are some general rules of thumb for sizing and placement of the coupling facility structures: SCA (Shared Communication Area), and Lock Structure and GBP (Group Bufferpools). Structure placement should include the Lock Structure and the SCA in one coupling facility, and the Group Bufferpool in another. When there is a coupling facility failure, the lost structures will be rebuilt in the surviving coupling facility. For sizing, we need to discuss each structure individually.

Group Bufferpools

The sizing of the group bufferpools is a complex issue. There are many thresholds and parameters that have to be adjusted in sizing local and group bufferpools, including:

- number of members
- degree of data sharing
- transaction access patterns
- frequency of updates
- use of the GBPCACHE option
- castout thresholds

The size of the GBP will depend on the change activity and data access. If GBPCACHE (CHANGED) is set, this number will vary between 5 and 50 percent of the sum of local bufferpools (and hiperpools). If GBPCACHE (ALL) is set, this could vary between 50 and 100 percent of the sum of the local bufferpools. Local bufferpools should be sized at a minimum, and objects should be placed in separate bufferpools accordingly. Oversizing local bufferpools will not be of any benefit in a data-sharing environment, and can be a detriment affecting the size of the GBP directory ratio.

There are some general formulas in the IBM documentation, but they only apply if there is a good basis of underlying information from the current systems to start

with. Ratios of pages read to pages updated at an object level need to be known, as well as residency of pages that might be referenced after being updated. When the following items are known for all members, the basic formulas can be used for sizing.

- Total number of virtual pool buffers pages
- Total number of pages in all hiperpool buffers
- Total number of all pages using all types of prefetch at any average point in time
- Total number of synchronous group bufferpool read requests with read hits
- Total number of synchronous group bufferpool read requests without read hits
- Total number of GETPAGE requests
- Total number of all pages written to DASD each second
- Page residency time
- Estimate of the degree of data sharing

Lock Structure and SCA

Sizing for both the SCA and the Lock Structure should be determined by the formulas and tables listed in the IBM documentation. The basic rule is to set the SCA at 32MB and the Lock Structure at either 16, 32, 64, or 128MB, depending on the monitored locking activity in the originating system, or estimates made on a new system. The size can be set so it starts at 16MB, and if locking problems occur, use of the SETXCF operator command can be made to adjust the size upward to the next power of 2. Increasing the size is important if there is a high occurrence of false contention.

How do I determine what the correct setting for the RATIO parameter on the GROUP BUFFERPOOL should be?

The RATIO parameter represents the ratio of the number of directory entries to the total number of data pages for all group bufferpools. The default is 5 directory entries per data page. This and other GBP parameters can be changed using the –ALTER GROUPBUFFERPOOL command and will take effect during the next allocation of the group bufferpool.

To determine a more appropriate value for your group bufferpool, you need to consider the read/write ratio of your processing. More directory entries will be required if this ratio is very high. If there are a large number of distinct pages being cached, you will need to have more directory entries, because a directory entry will be needed for each distinct page. However, if there are many pages being re-referenced, this value can be lowered. A good starting value for the number of directory entries would be the total number of group bufferpool pages, plus the result of the total number of pages allocated in each virtual pool and hiperpool, multiplied by the factor used for the degree of data sharing.

How do I monitor the group bufferpools?

Group bufferpools need to be monitored for reclaims due to directory entries, cross invalidations, appropriate size, write failures due to lack of storage, and overhead associated with pseudo-close. These items can be monitored in a monitor statistics long report. In addition to using statistics reports, the –DISPLAY GROUPBUFFERPOOL command, the output of which is shown in Figure 14-5, can also quickly assist with monitoring these items.

Tuning for reduction of reclaims will often require an increase to the group bufferpool and an increase to the RATIO parameter. This tuning can be done using the ALTER GROUPBUFFERPOOL command. Cross invalidations occur when a changed page is written out to the GBP. If a copy of the changed page exists in a local bufferpool, it is marked as invalid. When tuning to decrease the number of "directory reclaims due to cross invalidations," there is a certain amount of balancing that must be performed to increase the ratio enough, but not so high that it will interfere with the castout process. The individual bufferpools should be kept to a minimum size to hold only what is required by the system processing.

```
 DB2P   DISPLAY FOR GROUP BUFFER POOL GBP0 FOLLOWS
-DB2P   DB2 GROUP BUFFER POOL STATUS

        CONNECTED                                       =YES

        CURRENT DIRECTORY TO DATA RATIO                 =5
        PENDING DIRECTORTY TO DATA RATIO                =5
-DB2P   CLASS CASTOUT THRESHOLD                         =10%
        GROUP BUFFER POOL CASTOUT THRESHOLD             =50%
        GROUP BUFFER POOL CHECKPOINT INTERVAL           =8 MINUTES
        RECOVERY STATUS                                 =NORMAL
-DB2P   MVS CFRM POLICY STATUS FOR DSNDB2P_GBP0         =NORMAL
        MAX SIZE INDICATED IN POLICY                    =17920
        ALLOCATED                                       =YES
-DB2P   ALLOCATED SIZE                                  =16128 KB
        VOLATILITY STATUS                               =VOLATILE
-DB2P   NUMBER OF DIRECTORY ENTRIES                     =16103
        NUMBER OF DATA PAGES                            =3220
        NUMBER OF CONNECTIONS                           =4
 DB2P INCREMENTAL GROUP DETAIL STATISTICS SINCE 14:20:44
-DB2P   GROUP DETAIL STATISTICS
        READS
        DATA RETURNED                                   =6618
-DB2P   DATA NOT RETURNED
        DIRECTORY ENTRY EXISTED                         =511
        DIRECTORY ENTRY CREATED                         =413
        DIRECTORY ENTRY NOT CREATED                     101,0
-DB2P   WRITES
        CHANGED PAGES                                   =14256
        CLEAN PAGES=0
        FAILED DUE TO LACK OF STORAGE                   =0
        CHANGED PAGES SNAPSHOT VALUE                    =26
-DB2P   RECLAIMS
        FOR DIRECTORY ENTRIES                           =0
        FOR DATA ENTRIES                                =2950
        CASTOUTS
-DB2P   CROSS INVALIDATIONS
        DUE TO DIRECTORY ENTIRES                        =0
        DUE TO WRITES                                   =7195
```

Figure 14-5   DISPLAY GROUPBUFFERPOOL command output

 How does DB2 know where to build the coupling facility structures in the event of a failure?

The structures are defined in the CFRM (Coupling Facility Resource Management) policy, and an alternate coupling facility is assigned in the preference list of each of the structures to define where the structures are to be rebuilt in the event that a coupling facility is lost. If the Lock Structure or SCA cannot be rebuilt, DB2 will abnormally terminate.

How do I monitor the activity occurring against the coupling facility structures?

In order to monitor and tune coupling facility structure activity, you can use RMF (Resource Measurement Facility) reports. Figure 14-6 shows an example of the RMF coupling facility report for the structure activity, and shows the asynchronous/synchronous requests for each structure.

How do I resolve a "failed persistent" state in the coupling facility?

A "failed persistent" state in the coupling facility can occur when connectivity to the lock structure occurs and there is no active SFM (System Failure Management) policy defined, or the weighted loss is less than the REBUILDPERCENT in the SFM. In a failed persistent state, DB2 comes down and the

```
STRUCTURE NAME = DB2PGP1_LOCK1   TYPE=LOCK
         #REQ -------------REQUESTS----------- -------DELAYED REQUESTS------
SYSTEM   TOTAL        #   %OF  -SERV TIME(MIC)-   REASON #  %OF --AVG TIME(MIC)
NAME     AVG/SEC   REQ ALL   AVG STD_DEV                REQ REQ  /DEL  STD_DEV

MVS1     0000 SYNC    00 00%   000.0    000.0
         0000 ASYNC   00 00%   0.0      0.0     NO SCH 0 0.0%  0.0   0.0
         0000 CHANGED 00 00%   INCLUDED IN ASYNC

STRUCTURE NAME = DB2PGP1_GBP1   TYPE=CACHE
         #REQ -------------REQUESTS----------- -------DELAYED REQUESTS------
SYSTEM   TOTAL        #   %OF  -SERV TIME(MIC)-   REASON #  %OF --AVG TIME(MIC)
NAME     AVG/SEC   REQ ALL   AVG STD_DEV                REQ REQ  /DEL  STD_DEV

MVS1     0000 SYNC    00 00%   000.0    000.0
         0000 ASYNC   00 00%   0.0      0.0     NO SCH 0 0.0%  0.0   0.0
         0000 CHANGED 00 00%   INCLUDED IN ASYNC

STRUCTURE NAME = DB2PGP1_SCA   TYPE=SCA
         #REQ -------------REQUESTS----------- -------DELAYED REQUESTS------
SYSTEM   TOTAL        #   %OF  -SERV TIME(MIC)-   REASON #  %OF --AVG TIME(MIC)
NAME     AVG/SEC   REQ ALL   AVG STD_DEV                REQ REQ  /DEL  STD_DEV

MVS1     0000 SYNC    00 00%   000.0    000.0
         0000 ASYNC   00 00%   0.0      0.0     NO SCH 0 0.0%  0.0   0.0
         0000 CHANGED 00 00%   INCLUDED IN ASYNC
```

Figure 14-6   An example of an RMF coupling facility report

structure remains allocated. To resolve this failed persistent state, you will first need to fix the problem that caused the loss of connectivity, and then restart the failed member on a system that is already connected to a coupling facility or manually rebuild an alternative coupling facility.

A failed persistent state can also occur when a member loses connectivity to one or more group bufferpool structures and there is no active SFM policy or the weighted loss is less than the REBUILDPERCENT. Applications using the group bufferpools are then quiesced, and pages may be added to the LPL list (Logical Page List, list of pages that are logically in error), and then the GBP is disconnected.

To resolve the scenario in which a member loses connectivity to one or more group bufferpool structures, the initial problem must be resolved, the structure must be manually rebuilt in an alternate coupling facility, and then the DB2 needs to be restarted on a system with a coupling facility connection.

 ### How do I determine if a DB2 member has any page sets opened that are group-bufferpool dependent?

The −DISPLAY BUFFERPOOL(BPx) LIST(*) command will provide you with information regarding GBP dependency, as shown in Figure 14-7. This information may be useful when it is necessary to bring a DB2 member down or have a member disconnected from the group bufferpool.

```
-DB2P BUFFERPOOL NAME BPO, BUFFERPOOL ID 0, USE COUNT 2
-DB2P VIRTUAL BUFFERPOOL SIZE = 1000 BUFFERS
ALLOCATED           =        1000 TO BE DELETED    =      0
IN-USE/UPDATED =     15
-DB2P HIPERPOOL SIZE      = 10000 BUFFERS, CASTOUT = YES
ALLOCATED           =        0       TO BE DELETED =     0
BACKED BY ED   = 0
-DB2P THREASHOLDS
VP SEQUENTIAL        = 80    HP SEQUENTIAL                = 75
DEFERRED WRITE       = 85    VERTICAL DEFERRED WRT  = 80
PARALLEL SEQUENTIAL = 50    ASSISTING PARALLEL SEQT       = 50
-DB2P TABLESPACE = DSNDB01.DBD01, USE COUNT = 1, GBP-DEP = Y
-DB2P TABLESPACE = DSNDB06.SYSDBASE, USE COUNT = 1, GBP-DEP =Y
```

Figure 14-7 Sample output from the DISPLAY BUFFERPOOL command

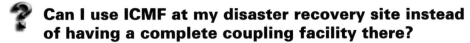

RECOVERY

Can I use ICMF at my disaster recovery site instead of having a complete coupling facility there?

Yes, Integrated Coupling Migration Facility (ICMF), LPAR can be used to emulate a parallel sysplex at a disaster recovery site without actually requiring a coupling facility to be present. It is not recommended to use an ICMF in a normal data-sharing environment with a heavy amount of coupling facility traffic, and even using ICMF at a recovery site has a few caveats. An ICMF adds some additional overhead, and the emulator channels do not have the same speed as normal coupling facility channels. Also, if the CPC you are running the ICMF on should fail, you would not only use the DB2 on the CPC but the entire coupling facility as well.

Can I recover a single subsystem in a non-data-sharing mode at a disaster site if the member was defined as data sharing before?

No. If a DB2 subsystem was in data-sharing mode before the need for disaster recovery, it must be brought up in data-sharing mode at the recovery site. The recovery site must be identical to the local site in terms of the data-sharing group. This includes the group name, number of members, member names, and CFRM policy names. The number of OS/390 systems and hardware configurations can differ.

How are the DB2 logs processed in a data-sharing environment during recovery?

In a data-sharing environment, each DB2 has its own logs. During a recovery, each DB2 can access the logs on the other DB2 subsystems in the data-sharing group and then merge them together in the appropriate sequence. The Log Record Sequence Number (LRSN) is used to perform this merge process because it has a unique identifier that provides coordination of the logs in the group. When a recovery is

performed, the LRSN on the data page header is compared with the LRSN on the log record header, and this comparison then determines if a particular log record needs to be applied to the data page. If the LRSN in the log record is greater than the LRSN contained in the data page, then DB2 would apply the change.

What is the best method for implementing fail-safe disaster recovery for a data sharing sysplex?

GDPS (Geographically Dispersed Parallel Sysplex) is a way for DB2 to manage systems across multiple sites for maximum availability. The driving force behind the development of the GDPS was to improve disaster recovery capabilities. GDPS is a new automated environment with enhanced system management functions, including DASD configuration management and extended use of Remote Copy with peer-to-peer device dynamic switching. The GDPS technology builds upon the existing parallel sysplex technology and exploitation of DBMSs (namely DB2 for OS/390). By using this new technology, planned and unplanned outages become less painful and less risky. There is now a way to provide multisite environment support though the use of the GDPS technology to provide greater application availability.

Chapter 15

Accessing DB2

Answer Topics!

- ? Limiting the amount of data a QMF user can return
- ? Saving a result set from a query
- ? Moving queries or forms between DB2 subsystems
- ? What the alternatives to TSO or CICS QMF are

- ? Restoring a QMF object after it is erased by the user
- ? Using the Resource Limit Facility or the QMF Governor
- ? Changing the PF keys on the QMF panels

Accessing DB2 @ a Glance

In order to retrieve, manipulate, and report on data in a DB2 database, you must have a means of accessing and extracting the data. This chapter covers questions about the five most common and general methods of accessing DB2 on any of the DB2 family platforms.

CICS (Customer Information Control System) and IMS/DC (Information Management System/Data Communication) are both transaction processing monitors that have been around since the early 1970s. Today CICS is the most popular method of accessing DB2 data on the OS/390 platform. The interface between CICS and DB2 is controlled by the RCT (resource control table) and many questions arise about properly configuring the RCT for optimal access.

Other access to the DB2 subsystem is achieved through TSO (Time Sharing Option) or batch processing. In TSO, you can use facilities in ISPF (Interactive System Productivity Facility), such as SPUFI (Sequential Processing Using File Input), to input and execute SQL statements.

QMF (Query Management Facility) is an IBM query and reporting tool used to create simple or very detailed reports by defining and executing SQL queries associated with defined forms. QMF is also available in a Windows version for use against OS/390 or UDB.

There are also several options for reporting/querying GUI (graphical user interface) tools for the PC that can access either DB2 on OS/390 or DB2 UDB.

CICS AND IMS

What is the difference between SQLCODE –911 and –913 in CICS?

SQLCODE of –911 means that a rollback of all changes during a current unit of work has occurred (SQLSTATE = '40001') due to a deadlock or timeout. This SQLCODE applies to CICS if ROLBE=YES is specified in the RCT. An SQLCODE of –913 means a rollback was not issued (SQLSTATE = '57033'). The last SQL statement suffered a deadlock or timeout and was not executed. Locks are held until the program issues a rollback or commits the work. You can retry the statement, but generally you should not retry more than five or ten times. This strategy applies to CICS if ROLBE=NO is in the RCT. This is an option that is not often used.

What information is kept in the CICS RCT?

The information in the RCT is used to define the connection between CICS and DB2. CICS will only use one RCT at a time even though you may have several defined. The RCT describes the relationship between CICS and DB2 resources. You can define different types of threads (connections) in the RCT, and there are specific options to define for each. Many of these parameters can be tuned for optimal access to DB2.

The following represents a few lines of a sample RCT entry:

```
DSNCRCT TYPE=INIT,SUFFIX=Z,TOKENI=YES,DPMODI=EQ,
   SIGNID=CICSS, SUBID=DB2P,SNAP=T,THRDMAX=40
DSNCRCT TYPE=COMD,TWAIT=POOL,AUTH=(USERID,TERM),DPMODE=HIGH,
   ROLBE=NO,THRDM=1,THRDA=1,THRDS=1,TXID=DSNC
DSNCRCT TYPE=POOL,TWAIT=YES,AUTH=(USERID,TERM,TXID),
   THRDM=3,THRDA=3
*    Transaction Threads
DSNCRCT TYPE=ENTRY, TXID=DBT1,AUTH=(USERID,TERM,TXID),
   THRDM=1,THRDA=1, TWAIT=POOL,PLAN=DB2PLN2
DSNCRCT TYPE=ENTRY, TXID=DBT2, AUTH=(USERID,TERM,TXID),
   THRDM=1,THRDA=1, TWAIT=POOL,PLAN=DB2PLN3
```

In the above RCT, you can see in the INIT thread that there is a maximum of 40 threads allowed for connection from CICS to this DB2 at one time (THRDMAX=40). The entry threads, defined for the transactions, define the application plan to a CICS thread. The THRDA gives the maximum number of active threads allowed for that plan. The sum of all THRDA values on all threads, plus three, should be the number for THRDMAX. When the number provided in THRDMAX, minus two, is reached, CICS will terminate currently active subtasks if there are still requests being made for more subtasks. TWAIT specifies what to do when a thread is no longer available for an SQL request. In this example, the entry threads will use a pool thread if all the entry threads for its group are used.

What are protected threads, and how are they used?

There are two main types of threads defined in the RCT:

- Pool threads (TYPE=POOL).
- Dedicated threads (TYPE=ENTRY)
  - Protected threads
  - Unprotected threads

Protected threads are a type of dedicated thread and are the most exclusive type of CICS thread. They are recommended for high-volume transactions of any type or terminal-oriented transactions with several commit points in the unit of work. These threads will allow thread reuse for the same plan only, although any transaction bound to that plan can use the thread. It is possible for threads to remain active for about 45 seconds, allowing for other transactions with the same TXID to reuse the thread. At the end of the plan execution, the thread will be kept for a predetermined amount of time defined in PURGREC or it will be released if there are two consecutive 30-second periods.

Protected threads are defined as TYPE=ENTRY with THRDS and THRDA greater than zero.

What are some of the recommendations for tuning the RCT?

When developing a plan for creating RCT entries, you will first want to make sure the person in charge of administrating the RCT is knowledgeable in both CICS, the RCT itself, and DB2, and you will want to ensure that the performance is monitored

during the initial stages of rollout of the system so that additional tuning can be done if necessary. There are several parameters in the RCT that you can tune for optimal performance of your CICS/DB2 applications. A few recommendations for tuning the RCT entries are listed here:

- The sum of all the THRDA values for all threads types (COMD, POOL, and ENTRY) needs to be less than the value for THRDMAX – 2.
- Be sure to explicitly code pool and COMD threads.
- Be selective about which threads are defined as entry threads.
- The THRDA for pool threads should initially be set at the sum of all threads expected to be in the pool. The following are threads that will utilize the pool:

  - All plans/transactions defined in the RCT with TYPE=POOL.
  - Plans that are defined as TYPE=ENTRY, THRDA=0, and TWAIT=POOL will be forced to the pool.
  - Plans that were defined with protected threads may overflow to the pool if there are no more protected threads available for use (that is, if THRDA value is exceeded).

- If queuing is acceptable for high-volume transactions using protected threads (TYPE=ENTRY, THRDA, and THRDS greater than 0), then define TWAIT=YES, or allow the overflow to utilize the pool. You will want to avoid using too many of these.
- Define a plan as TYPE=ENTRY with THRDA greater than 0, THRDS=0, and TWAIT=YES in order to control the number of concurrent transactions, force serialization, and to avoid too many plans utilizing pool threads. These threads are known as high-priority unprotected entry threads.
- There should be at least one thread difference between THRDA and THRDM for tuning purposes.

- You can code ROLBE=YES so that changes will be backed out by DB2 rather than counting on the application program to perform this function. However, ROLBE=NO may be useful to maintain placement in a job and allow for retry logic in case a deadlock occurs in a CICS transaction. This is common in high-performance systems to avoid losing work that has been previously performed in the transaction.

- To help with performance tuning and debugging efforts, code TOKENI as YES in order to ensure that all threads will produce multiple accounting records.

What is pseudo wait-for-input in IMS?

The pseudo WFI (pseudo wait-for-input) option allows an IMS MPP (message processing program) region to remain scheduled until another input message appears. With pseudo WFI, unnecessary application program termination and rescheduling can be eliminated. Normally, if an MPP region is scheduled for a transaction, and no more messages for that transaction exist, the application program terminates. Frequently, another message appears for the same transaction after the program is terminated. Processing overhead is increased because of the unnecessary termination and rescheduling of that application program.

Pseudo WFI is specified with the PWFI parameter on the MPP region start-up procedure. Transactions using DB2 greatly benefit from the pseudo WFI because if another message can be processed, thread reuse will be applied. The locking involved with pseudo WFI is higher since the thread remains open and the plan stays allocated, as in thread reuse in CICS. With true WFI, the MPP region is dedicated to one program. With pseudo WFI, the MPP region is still able to schedule other work, but it acts like WFI if no work is remaining, hence the name pseudo WFI.

Can I check if DB2 is available in a CICS program?

Normally, a program will abend with the CICS abend code AEY9 when it tries to connect to DB2 and DB2 is not

available. You are able to check if the DB2 connection is running by issuing two EXEC CICS calls. For example, add a DB2-NOT-AVAILABLE paragraph in the program that will get control if the DB2 connection is down. This is shown in the following example:

```
WORKING-STORAGE
77 WS-POINTER   PIC 9(4) COMP.
77 WS-LENGTH    PIC 9(8) COMP.
PROCEDURE DIVISION.
EXEC CICS
    HANDLE CONDITION   INVEXITREQ(DB2-NOT-AVAILABLE)
END-EXEC.
EXEC CICS
    EXTRACT EXIT PROGRAM('DSNCEXT1') ENTRYNAME('DSNCSQL')
    GASET(WS-POINTER) GALENGTH(WS-LENGTH)
END-EXEC.
DB2-NOT-AVAILABLE.
    do some error handling stuff
```

How do I handle indoubt threads with CICS or IMS?

Indoubt threads exist if the DB2 connection is lost in the middle of a commit. Always let CICS or IMS handle indoubt threads by restarting them. You might get in trouble if you cold-start CICS or IMS and there are unresolved (indoubt) threads. You will see a lot of messages when the connection is made because DB2 remembers the thread and CICS or IMS do not. In this case you will have to dump the CICS or IMS log of the previous session (the one you should have used to restart). On this log you can see if CICS or IMS committed the transaction and determine the proper DB2 command to issue.

You can create problems if you clean up a thread before you restart CICS or IMS. The two transaction monitors handle this situation differently. If CICS thinks there is a pending commit and DB2 indicates there is not, CICS will issue messages and roll back the transaction. IMS will leave the transaction pending and the resources locked until you issue a /CHANGE command to resolve it.

Is it possible to add a transaction to the CICS RCT without recycling the entire system?

Yes, but doing so will still restrict DB2 access. You will have to stop and start the RCT in order to make it active. When the RCT shuts down, there is no DB2 access possible from any transaction.

Can a CICS region connect to multiple DB2 subsystems?

No, it cannot. The RCT interface is designed such that a CICS region can only connect to one DB2 subsystem. It is possible to set up a terminal region and multiple-process regions. Every process region can have a different DB2 subsystem.

How do I determine if I am getting CICS thread reuse for my DB2 threads?

In a performance monitor accounting report, you can view the number of commits per allocation of threads for a particular program. A thread may get some amount of thread reuse even if the threads are not defined as protected. If a non-protected thread is reused within 45 seconds, it will not have to be reallocated.

How can I determine how many threads are attaching to DB2 from a CICS application?

The number of threads attached to your application program depends on how you code your RCT and is not based on either the open cursor or the number of tables being used through cursor fetching.

The value in THRDS will define the number of protected threads. When the attachment is started, the number of threads available for each RCT entry is the value specified for THRDS. The value in THRDA will define the maximum number of active threads and can be dynamically increased or decreased. THRDM defines the maximum value to which

THRDA can be set. Other types of threads include command threads and pool threads.

You can monitor the CICS threads by using attachment facility commands. For example:

```
DSNC DISP STAT
DSNC014I    STATISTICS REPORT FOR 'DSNCRCT1'   FOLLOWS
TRAN  PLAN        CALLS   COMMITS  ABORTS    AUTHS     W/P HIGH     R-ONLY
DSNC                0        0       0         0        0   0          0
RYC1  RICHARD      12        2       0         1        0   1          0
RYC2  SUSAN        25        3       1         2        0   2          0
RYC3  SHERYL        8        1       0         1        0   1          0
```

This command will provide statistics on each of the entries in the RCT. In the output from that command, the column HIGH represents the maximum number of threads required by transactions associated with the entry at any time since the connection was started. This number includes transactions that were forced to wait on a thread, or that were diverted to the pool. The column W/P is the number of times that all available threads for this entry were busy and the transaction had to wait, or was diverted to the pool. The W/P value, compared to the total number of transactions using this entry, shows if there are enough threads defined for this entry.

What are some considerations for tuning the CICS DB2 interface?

There are a number of CICS tuning exercises that can be used to try and improve transaction throughput when using DB2. Even though some of these recommendations apply to both entry and pool thread use, entry thread use will generally achieve better effects. These are primarily for high-volume transaction processing.

Some of these techniques are related to each other. The result of combining all these related techniques together will not be the sum of the effects of each individual tuning technique. The tuning techniques are outlined below.

1. Reduce the Number of Threads per Region.
   The total number of DB2 threads in a system should always be only what is required. Never overload the region by defining unnecessary threads (TCBs) as they

will always cause extra OS/390 overhead due to task dispatching. Also, they use the processor cache inefficiently. The proper steps for tuning are:

A. Reduce the total number of threads.

- Merge the plans of infrequent transactions.
- Start with one thread per RCT entry.
- Increase the number of threads by one until the internal transaction response time is within acceptable limits.

B. Divide the threads across multiple CICS regions.

- Too many threads (for example, more than 15) inside one CICS region cause OS/390 dispatching overhead.
- Logically group and spread threads across regions using any CICS gateway.

2. Set DPMODE=HIGH.
   Set the DPMODE to HIGH. This will allow the batching of thread posts to CICS, which will reduce CICS wait time. The number of threads inside the CICS region will affect the dispatching overhead. Consider using a mixture of DPMODE values for a workload strategy.

   A. Set DPMODE to HIGH for the few transactions with the highest weighted average number of SQL calls by using the formula:

   weighted average = number of SQL calls per transaction × frequency of transaction

   B. Set DPMODE to EQUAL or LOW for all other RCT entries.

   C. Monitor the response times.

3. Use CMXT to Control Thread Waits.
   When entry threads are used, setting the TWAIT parameter to YES may produce better results than setting the TWAIT parameter to POOL, since this will generally use less CPU and virtual storage. Setting TWAIT to YES will likely cause a large number of thread waits and result in poor performance. Queuing will occur more frequently if you use CMXT to prevent

tasks from competing for DB2 threads and if you relieve overhead due to attachment queuing, as follows:

- Select the high-volume transactions or the ones with long thread occupancy time.
- Set the TCLASS to the number of threads + one.

4. Reconsider the Design of Inquiry Transactions.
   If the transactions are designed to be CICS read-only transactions, this will eliminate all CICS logical and physical logging. Proper use of CICS non-recoverable resources, such as user-maintained data tables and TS/TD scratch-pad facilities are recommended when designing such transactions.

What is dynamic plan selection?

CICS can dynamically select a planname. This is done by coding PLNEXIT=YES and PLNPGME=exit-routine in the RCT. IBM supplies a sample exit-routine called DSNCUEXT which assigns the planname to be the same as your programname. Using dynamic plan selection your program can call other programs (CICS LINK) or transfer control to any other program (CICS XCTL) without large binding implications. Your program should issue a CICS SYNCPOINT before transferring control otherwise the first SQL statement in the new program will suffer –805 SQLCODE. Dynamic plan selection has a planname of all asterisks in a DSNC DISP STAT command.

Why do I get strange abends if the first access is to DB2 and not to IMS in an IMS/DB2 program?

Refer to the answer to this question in Chapter 12.

TSO AND BATCH

Why shouldn't I develop applications for TSO/ISPF?

TSO is very inefficient compared to transaction servers like CICS or IMS. Every TSO user is an address space, which causes MVS lots of work in scheduling, paging, and

swapping. Large numbers of TSO users can quickly fill an OS/390 machine. Among the many other major reasons for this inefficiency is that TSO is a very dynamic conversational mode of processing, where locks tend to be held for a much longer time.

How can I get a return code or abend in DB2 batch?

Refer to the answer to this question in Chapter 12.

In SPUFI, how can I view a change made by a query without committing the change?

When using SPUFI (Sequential Processing Using File Input) under TSO, there is an option in the DB2I (DB2 Interactive) panel that allows you to turn the automatic commit process off. After you run a query, the results will be shown on the screen; however, the change will not have been committed. When you exit from the result screen, you will be asked if you would like to commit the change, defer the change, or rollback the change. During the period while DB2 is waiting for a commit or rollback to be issued, appropriate locks will be held on the uncommitted data preventing access to the data unless an uncommitted read is requested.

Is there a way to limit the TSO access?

There is an option in TSO to limit the maximum number of users that can log on to TSO at one time. But there is also an option in DSNZPARM called IDFORE that will limit the access from TSO.

Is there a way to run batch SQL commands, including SELECT, without DSNTEP2?

A normal procedure is to run SPUFI in batch mode under TSO batch. A code stream example follows our explanation of a few other alternatives.

One alternative is a shareware TEP program, which is a COBOL conversion of TEP2, available from the UK GUIDE Web site at http://www.gseukdb2.org.uk/. Try the URL http://www.gseukdb2.org.uk/darwin.zip, save the result to disk, and unzip it manually.

Another alternative is to use IBM's DSNTIAUL with PARMS('SQL').You can call this program in your REXX with DSN SYSTEM in online and batch mode.

And as we mentioned first, you can run SPUFI in batch mode under TSO batch. You will have to modify the following code by trial and error whenever DB2 changes, but the following JCL is capable of executing SPUFI. Your dataset names will all be different, but essentially you will be cloning your TSO LOGON PROC statements. Normally you will have to make changes in the VPUT area.

```
//* THIS IS VERY GENERIC PSEUDO JCL
//* TO EXEC SPUFI IN BATCH
//GENER03 EXEC PGM=IEBGENER
//* SPUFI INPUT
//* PUT SQL STATEMENTS HERE
//SYSUT1 DD *
-- EXAMPLE GETTING CURRENT DATE
SELECT CURRENT DATE FROM SYSIBM.SYSDUMMY1;
//SYSUT2 DD DSN=SPUFI.IN, etc…
//SYSIN DD DUMMY
//SYSPRINT DD DUMMY
//BLDCLST EXEC PGM=IEBGENER
//* SAVE CLIST COMMANDS IN PDS
//* SAVE SPUFI PARAMETERS ALSO
//SYSPRINT DD SYSOUT=*
//SYSIN DD DUMMY
//SYSUT2 DD DSN=&&TEMP(SPUFI), etc
//SYSUT1 DD *
/* CONTROL NOFLUSH */
CONTROL NOFLUSH SYMLIST
SET DSNESV15 = 'SPUFI.IN'
SET DSNESV16 = 'SPUFI.OUT'
SET DSNESV1A = NO /* CHANGE DEFAULTS */
SET DSNESV17 = NO /* EDIT INPUT */
SET DSNESV18 = YES /* EXECUTE */
SET DSNESV1D = YES /* AUTOCOMMIT */
SET DSNESV19 = NO /* BROWSE OUTPUT */
SET DSNEOV01 = DSN7 /* DB2 SUBSYSTEM */
SET DSNEOV04 = 50 /* LINES/PAGE (5-999) */
SET DSNESV2C = 400 /* LRECL */
```

```
SET DSNESV2D = 2000 /* MAX LINES SELECTED */
SET VPUT1 = &STR(DSNESV15 DSNESV16 DSNESV1A DSNESV17 DSNESV18)
SET VPUT2 = &STR(DSNESV1D DSNESV19 DSNEOV01 DSNEOV04)
SET VPUT3 = &STR(DSNESV2C DSNESV2D)
ISPEXEC VPUT (&VPUT1 &VPUT2 &VPUT3) PROFILE
ISPEXEC SELECT PANEL(DSNEPRI) OPT(1)
EXIT
//EFT01 EXEC PGM=IKJEFT01
//* EXEC SPUFI
//STEPLIB DD include any steplibs
//ISPPROF DD DSN=...
//ISPLOG DD DSN=...
//ISPLLIB DD DSN=...
//ISPMLIB DD DSN=...
//ISPPLIB DD DSN=...
//ISPSLIB DD DSN=...
//ISPTLIB DD DSN=...
//SYSEXEC DD DSN=...
//SYSHELP DD DSN=...
//SYSLBC DD DSN=...
//SYSPROC DD DSN=...
//SYSUADS DD DSN=...
//SYSPRINT DD SYSOUT=...
//SYSTERM DD SYSOUT=...
//SYSTSPRT DD SYSOUT=...
//* BDISPMAX(2) IN ISPSTART BELOW DO NOT CHANGE
//SYSTSIN DD *
PROFILE NOPREFIX
ISPSTART CMD(%ISPF) ...whatever else is needed and BDISPMAX(2)
/*
then some job to print output
```

Can I access DB2 from a REXX program?

Yes, but it requires a special interface that will not be
provided to the REXX language until sometime during the
summer or fall of 1999 (when IBM is scheduled to provide
REXX for DB2, including REXX stored procedures). Until
that time, there are many REXX DB2 products from
established vendors, and there are also many REXX DB2
products that are both shareware and freeware. Most of the
latter are available on the Internet.

QMF

 ### Should I run QMF under TSO or CICS?

If only a very small number of users (less than 10) will use
QMF, you could use CICS; otherwise TSO is the only
alternative. This is because QMF is an interactive program,
and it needs to be continually running. It uses many control
blocks to store the make-up information for your report, and
it has the sample data in storage so that it can create a
sample report for you. This is the reason that there is no
QMF for IMS—programs (even conversational ones) need to
terminate in IMS.

So what is the difference between CICS and TSO? In
TSO everybody has his or her own address space and this
uses a large amount of storage. In terms of storage, a TSO
user could be compared to a batch job, a started task, or a
complete CICS system. In CICS all users have to share
memory because they share the same address space. This
means that multiple QMF users represent a large drain on
the CICS resources. Large numbers (50 or more) would be
simply impossible in CICS.

 ### Why should I use one database per QMF user?

QMF has it own set of commands that are translated into
SQL statements (DML and DDL). If a QMF user does a
SAVE DATA, a new table is created (DDL) and the DBD
control block will be briefly locked exclusively by DB2. If
other users use the same database, this locking would not
be possible.

 Tip: *QMF also "replaces" data by doing a mass delete. For
good performance, make sure that your QMF user databases
only contain segmented tablespaces.*

 Caution: *Since tables are created and deleted by QMF, the
DBDs used by user databases tend to grow very quickly. Make
sure you use the MODIFY utility regularly in order to keep the
DBDs small and the performance of the EDM pool good.*

How can I limit the amount of data returned to a QMF user?

You can use the QMF Governor to limit the amount of data returned to a QMF user. After you have enabled the QMF Governor, you can set up resource groups by adding rows to the resource control table. One row (or resource group) could be defined to tell how many rows the users associated with that group can return. A value of ROWLIMIT in the RESOURCE_OPTION table and an integer value in the INTVAL column will define how many rows can be returned by the users in that resource group before they are cancelled. The following example will only allow users defined to the SMALLSET resource group to return 100 rows before they are cancelled. This feature would be of help in environments where there are ad hoc users.

```
INSERT INTO Q.RESOURCE_TABLE VALUES('SMALLSET', ROWLIMIT, 100)
```

Can I save my result set from a query?

Yes. You can use the SAVE DATA command to save the results of your query.

How can I move queries or forms between DB2 subsystems?

By using the EXPORT command you can move queries or forms out to a dataset, and then, after switching to another DB2 subsystem, you can use the IMPORT command to import the queries or forms into the subsystem.

What are the alternatives to TSO and CICS QMF?

There is a PC option to run QMF under Microsoft Windows (95, 98, NT, 2000). Everything you have done (forms, queries, and so on) are available to it. Your query still runs using DB2, but the formatting is done on the PC. Fortunately, GDDM is not a prerequisite to create graphs on the PC.

Can I restore a QMF object after it is erased by the user?

Yes, but it will take some work and disk space, and you need a full image copy from the moment the object still existed. You will have to define mirror tables of the Q.OBJECT_DATA, Q.OBJECT_DIRECTORY, and Q.OBJECT_REMARKS (remember there is an SQL statement CREATE TABLE LIKE). Find out the OBIDs of all objects and copy an OBIDXLAT table for DSN1COPY. Then restore the image copy with DSN1COPY using RESET,OBIDXLAT (this will only work if downlevel detection is off in Version 5). Once that is done, you can copy the objects from the mirror to the QMF tables using INSERT with the SELECT option.

Should I use the Resource Limit Facility or the QMF Governor?

The QMF Governor is gentler because it will allow for prompting to continue, up to a cancel limit. Also the QMF Governor can cancel a request when too many rows are pulled in for reporting or too much CPU time has been used for a query, so this is the best option for QMF. Remember that the QMF Governor only works in the TSO environment, not in CICS. The resource limit facility can only terminate a thread (SQLCODE –905) after a certain amount of CPU resource has been used. It works for every environment and can be used in conjunction with the QMF Governor.

Can I change the PF keys on the QMF panels?

Yes. The PF (program function) keys can be changed. You can change the settings for active keys, create new settings for inactive keys, and change the text explanations for keys. For each panel, the PF keys can be changed for everyone, a particular user, or a group of users.

Chapter 16

Performance

Answer Topics!

? Using dynamic prefetch when a package is bound with degree ANY

? Making the optimizer select a tablespace scan instead of using an index

? Influencing the optimizer to choose a different index

? Turning off list prefetch for a query

? How many predicates DB2 adds for transitive closure

? How SELECT DISTINCT affects query performance

? Improving prefetch performance in DB2 UDB

? Rebinding if an index is added for RI checking

? Understanding partition-range scanning

? Optimizing queries using correlation statistics

? Understanding performance of unions versus outer joins

? Improving SQL performance of distributed applications

? Resolving a query by accessing only the index in UDB

? Using access-path hints

? Forcing a partition-range scan of one partition

? When DB2 chooses access paths for RI relationships

? Performance disadvantage of using nulls

Performance @ a Glance

Perhaps the most important facet of DB2 is its ability to be highly tuned for any type of environment. Proper tuning will make your DB2 subsystem run with astonishing results, but on the other hand, lack of effort and knowledge in the performance area can have disastrous consequences. This chapter covers the most critical topics concerning DB2 performance.

First, you must be able to determine whether you currently have a performance problem or if you could potentially have problems. This involves continuous monitoring and tuning of the DB2 subsystems. Monitoring can be done in a variety of ways, including analyzing monitor reports, using various online monitoring facilities, or using commands to actively monitor current activities. However, even with proper monitoring, if the results cannot be interpreted and problems diagnosed and resolved, the tuning efforts will have minimal or no impact on the performance of the DB2 system.

Bufferpools are basically memory in DB2, but they play a crucial role in how the DB2 applications will perform. Bufferpools can be monitored through the means mentioned here; but, in order to properly configure a bufferpool, much additional information is required. Information regarding the application's use of the data will determine how the bufferpools are configured, and the size

and type of data play a role in how the bufferpools should be sized and where objects are placed.

Parallelism has many forms, but the concept is always the same: parallelism is the ability to execute multiple tasks simultaneously, instead of serially. DB2 has the ability to split up tasks and run them in parallel, in order to complete queries in less elapsed time; however, this option is not without its complications. Parallelism is not always the solution to all elapsed-time problems. Utilities can also take advantage of parallelism by running simultaneously against the same object. This has advantages for 24 × 7 shops, which require short windows for batch processing. However, if you don't use parallelism properly and don't tune the environment to handle it, you can become a victim of its excessive needs; not everything is well suited for parallel processing.

Query optimization is one of the most critical areas in performance tuning. Tuning a single SQL predicate properly may save up to 90 percent of a query's required processing time and resources. Not all tuning will return such extreme benefits, but many will have profound effects that can quickly add up if the query is executed frequently. Over the years, the DB2 optimizer has become very sophisticated, and many of the old rules of thumb are no longer valid. However, with the sophistication of the optimizer has come the sophistication of the user, and there are many new tricks and techniques to learn.

MONITORING AND TUNING

How do I minimize the overhead for a performance trace?

When using a performance trace, you can minimize the overhead by specifying the particular IFCIDs (Instrumentation Facility Component IDs) that you are most interested in. If you do not specify an IFCID, you will return all the IFCIDs for the particular performance trace. In order to do this, follow this example.

```
-start trace(perftrc) class(30) ifcid(60) planname(myplan)
```

How do I determine if I am getting CICS thread reuse for my DB2 threads?

In an accounting report you can view the number of commits per allocations of threads for a particular program. A thread may get some amount of thread reuse even if it is not defined as protected. If an unprotected thread is reused within 45 seconds, it will not have to be reallocated.

To get the most thread reuse, close cursors explicitly as soon as they are no longer needed. Thread reuse should result in a decrease in Class 2 CPU time that can be viewed through a monitor or an accounting report.

Where can I find a description of a DB2 trace and its corresponding IFCIDs?

In the SDSNSAMP library in member DSNMSGS, you can find a detailed description of each DB2 trace and its IFCIDs. This file can be easily loaded into a DB2 table to be conveniently referenced by SQL.

How can I monitor my DB2 logs to determine if the log buffers are large enough?

In a monitor statistics report, the field that represents the number of active log buffer write failures will indicate whether or not your log buffers are large enough. If this field is greater than zero, it indicates a probable log buffer size problem. The log buffers are buffers that hold writes before they are written to the active logs that will eventually be offloaded to the archive logs. The DSNZPARMs used to increase these buffers are INBUFF and OUTBUFF. The majority of increases will need to be made to the OUTBUFF DSNZPARM because the INBUFF DSNZPARM is used to ensure that there are enough log buffers available when reading the archive logs for purposes of recovery.

How can I improve the performance of operations against the DB2 log in UDB?

In DB2 UDB Version 5.2, there is a new configuration parameter called NEWLOGPATH. This new parameter is used to allow an administrator to change the log files' storage

location. You can now store log files on raw devices, and this will speed up read/write I/O to the log because there is less overhead in the code path length.

What is the difference between synchronous reads and asynchronous reads?

There are two different types of I/Os for reading DB2 pages: synchronous and asynchronous. A synchronous read reads a single page, and an asynchronous read reads 32 pages at a time into the bufferpool.

How can I control and monitor DB2 write activity?

In order to figure out how to optimally control the DB2 write activity in a DB2 subsystem, an understanding of what activities cause a DB2 write is needed. The primary drivers for the DB2 write process include

- The bufferpool parameters for the deferred write threshold (DWQT) and the vertical deferred write threshold (VDWQT) will determine how often the pages are written from the bufferpool to DASD. For more information on how to set these parameters, refer to the question "What is the difference between the horizontal deferred-write threshold (DWQT) and the vertical deferred-write threshold (VDWQT), and what are the optimal settings?" in the "Bufferpools" section of this chapter.

- The LOGLOAD DSNZPARM controls how often DB2 checkpoints. During a DB2 checkpoint, updated pages are also written to DASD. For information on setting the LOGLOAD parameter, refer to the question later in this chapter, "How do I control how often DB2 takes a checkpoint?"

- The number of closes performed on datasets will also have an effect on writes. Refer to the next question (How do I determine if values for PCLOSEN and PCLOSET are set appropriately?) for more details.

These are the parameters that are used to help control DB2 write activity; and, in order to set them correctly, you

must monitor various aspects of DB2 activity, such as the number of checkpoints taken per hour, the number of vertical deferred write thresholds reached, the number of horizontal deferred write thresholds reached, and the number of datasets open. You can monitor this activity through statistics reports and the –DISPLAY BUFFERPOOL command.

How do I determine if values for PCLOSEN and PCLOSET are set appropriately?

PCLOSEN and PCLOSET are DSNZPARMs set to control how often DB2 opens and closes datasets, which will also affect how often data is written to DASD. PCLOSEN is the number of checkpoints taken while the write claim count is at zero, before the dataset is switched to a read-only state. PCLOSET is a set amount of time in which the write claim count has remained at zero for a pageset prior to it being switched to read only.

The setting of these parameters is especially important in a data-sharing environment because the opening and closing of datasets will cause excess Coupling Facility overhead. Set the PCLOSEN DSNZPARM to zero in order to not have your dataset open state controlled by checkpoints. You can monitor how often datasets are opened and closed through a statistics report.

How do I control how often DB2 takes a checkpoint?

The LOGLOAD DSNZPARM determines how many active log records are written between DB2 checkpoints. The frequency will depend on the amount of update activity in the system, and it will help you determine how high to set the LOGLOAD parameter. A general rule of thumb is to have your DB2 subsystem checkpoint every 15 to 20 minutes. If your system is checkpointing too frequently, you may experience unnecessary wait time while the system is taking the checkpoint. You can see how often DB2 checkpoints by referring to a monitor statistics report. DB2 Version 6 will have a new option to set the logload parameter online.

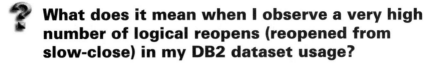 **What does it mean when I observe a very high number of logical reopens (reopened from slow-close) in my DB2 dataset usage?**

A high number of logical reopens of a dataset is good. This means that the datasets are not having to go through the overhead of physically opening when they are referenced. Make sure that your performance monitor reports a difference between open datasets and the DSMAX DSNZPARM.

How can I find out what real memory DB2 is supposed to be executing with?

One way to find out what amount of real memory DB2 can use is to look in the PROCLIB member for the DBM1 address space—the region parameter will show you the amount. This can also be done by viewing the address space in JES. If the amount is zero, DB2 can run with however much memory it needs and is available in the system.

The following code listing is an example of the PROCLIB member that contains the reference to the amount of real memory defined for DB2.

```
//DB5PDBM1 PROC LIB='SY.DB25P.SDSNEXIT'
//IEFPROC    EXEC PGM=DSNYASCP, DYNAMNBR=119,REGION=0M
//           PARM = 'ZPARM(DSNZPARM)'
//STEPLIB     DD DSN=&LIB, DISP=SHR
//            DD DISP=SHR,DSN=SY.DB25P.SDSNLOAD
```

What is the relationship between the number of LPAR definitions and the amount of CPU power DB2 determines it has to use for optimization?

During optimization, DB2 invokes the OS/390 macro SYSEVENT to obtain the MIPS available for optimization purposes. The information gathered regarding the CPU processor will affect the optimizer's cost estimation for I/O or CPU bound queries. When the optimizer is determining the

degree of parallelism, CPU bound queries will probably have a degree of parallelism equal to the number of online CPUs. I/O bound queries will get a degree determined from the number of partitions.

The SRM (system resource management) constant (su/sec), a defined OS/390 parameter, is *not* changed in response to LPAR or goal mode. It only depends on the uniprocessor speed and the number of processors defined to OS/390 (for an LPAR, this would be the number of logical processors). It will be adjusted when processors are varied online and offline. No adjustments to the su/sec value are made for LPAR capping, wait completion, LPAR weights, or shared/dedicated processors.

What should be the typical relationship between the number of GETPAGEs and the number of SELECTs?

Normally, GETPAGEs are only issued when the next row to be accessed by the application cannot be found in the current page being accessed. DB2 will only issue GETPAGE and RELPAGE (release page) for each row accessed when the data-management threshold (DMTH) has been reached, which means that 95 percent of the buffers are in use. It is possible to find many entries in the same page depending on row size and free space, and especially with indexes. Therefore, it is possible to see fewer GETPAGEs than SELECTs if the application is retrieving several rows on the same page, and if the page is still resident in the bufferpool.

What IFCIDs do I look at to find details on I/O for a tablespace?

You can obtain information from the IFCID 6, 7, 8, 9, and 10 records. You will have to correlate the internal DB2 database ID in these records with the actual tablespace and dataset names.

 Caution: *The overhead could be substantial for some of the traces that produce these IFCID records, especially for IFCID 10.*

How do I determine what is causing I/O spikes in my DB2 subsystem, and how do I resolve this?

It is not hard to determine whether you are experiencing I/O spikes. System I/O trending reports are the most scientific way of observing I/O spikes, but frequent slowdowns can be an indicator that I/O is spiking. In DB2, I/O spikes can be caused by improperly set parameters controlling the write activity in DB2. Refer to the question earlier in this chapter, "How can I control and monitor DB2 write activity?"

How can I determine how many sends and receives my DB2 UDB application is performing?

In order to determine the number of sends and receives performed by an application, use the DB2 UDB DB2DRDAT command. The information produced by this command will allow performance tuning in any client server environment using DRDA data streams.

What trace classes should I be running with at all times in DB2 for OS/390?

When a DB2 OS/390 subsystem is installed, it should have the SMFACCT DSNZPARM defined to run accounting trace classes 1, 2, and 3. The SMFSTAT DSNZPARM should be defined to have trace classes 1 and 3 running during normal DB2 execution. These traces will be started when the DB2 subsystem is started.

These trace classes will provide monitors with the necessary trace information to produce accounting and statistics reports for diagnosis and tuning efforts. If further detailed information is needed, the other trace classes can be started dynamically through the –START TRACE command. Having additional trace classes running all the time can cause unnecessary overhead for the DB2 subsystem and can affect application performance.

How do I tune the DB2 OS/390 sort pool?

DB2's relational system uses a special sorting technique that creates a kind of tree. The branches of the tree are called *runs*, and they can be compared to the SORTWKs you see in

OS/390 batch runs. At startup, DB2 allocates a sort pool in the private area of the DBM1 address space. If the sort pool is large enough, the complete tree is kept in storage. If the tree doesn't fit into storage anymore, DB2 will overflow the runs into the DSNDB07 database, and you will suffer performance degradation. So, make sure you assign an adequately sized sort pool to your system or avoid large SQL sorts in programs that have to run quickly. If you overflow to DSNDB07, this is reported in IFCID (traces), and your performance monitor can report on these events.

Can I ensure that updates are flushed without stopping the databases or quiescing tablespaces?

If you use the -ARCHIVE LOG command, DB2 will force a log switch and start the archive process. This process also forces a checkpoint, and the checkpoint will cause a write of all pending data. If data is updated during these writes, you might see a write immediately after the update is done.

Are there any negative effects of using the RELEASE(DEALLOCATE) bind parameter?

Yes, there can be some negative effects of using the RELEASE(DEALLOCATE) bind parameter. Many shops have found that the EDM pool will need to be increased when plans/packages are bound using RELEASE(DEALLOCATE). How much of an increase is necessary will depend on your applications. The EDM pool increase comes from the use of CICS protected threads or IMS WFI transactions—the plans/packages used will be kept alive in the EDM pool waiting for potential reuse.

Usually, a transaction has many different paths, and a single execution will only require a small percentage of all the possible packages. However, a different path through the transaction will use different packages; and, when you keep plans/packages active and waiting for the next execution, the result over time could be that you will have all of the possible packages active in the EDM pool for a particular thread.

Testing is recommended before doing a mass change of all programs from RELEASE(COMMIT) to RELEASE(DEALLOCATE). It is best to move a few programs at a time to RELEASE(DEALLOCATE) and monitor the EDM pool and IRLM memory usage before and after the change. In addition to the EDM pool issues, gross locks, such as tablespace locks, are retained, and this can cause problems with the IRLM.

How can I properly tune the DSMAX DSNZPARM in DB2 OS/390?

The DSMAX DSNZPARM tells DB2 how many open datasets there can be in the subsystem at any one time. The maximum is 10,000 through Version 5; and, although there have been some recent APARs that allow for more than this limit, it should be exceeded with caution.

There are advantages to setting the DSMAX limit high and advantages to setting it low. Here are a few general points to keep in mind when setting the DSMAX limit:

● Keeping the number of datasets low provides better restart times for DB2 in the event of an abnormal termination. If there are only a small number of datasets open during the failure, DB2 will require fewer dataset opens when it restarts, and thus will be faster.

● If datasets are constantly being opened and closed every few seconds or less, performance can be improved by increasing the DSMAX limit. There should also be enough margin in the value of DSMAX so that frequently used datasets defined as CLOSE YES will remain open even after they are no longer being referenced.

● One way to reduce the number of datasets overall, even before setting the DSMAX limit, is to use segmented tablespaces. This will also help to reduce open and close activity because there will be several tables in one tablespace. However, combining several tables into one tablespace can only work in some situations.

- Having too many open datasets can negatively affect the system, because this affects the log volumes and checkpoint costs. You will also need to set the PCLOSEN and PCLOSET DSNZPARMs appropriately to control how long datasets stay open in a read/write state. (For help with this topic, refer to the question "How do I determine if values for PCLOSEN and PCLOSET are set appropriately," earlier in this chapter).

How do I know if my DB2 OS/390 subsystem is paging excessively?

From a statistics report you can find how much paging is occurring. You want to keep the ratio of the number of PAGEINS for read I/Os to the total number of page requests below 5 percent. The following shows a sample calculation for determining your paging percentage:

```
PAGEINS FOR READ I/O / (SYNC READ I/O +
SEQUENTIAL PREFETCH PAGES READ +
LIST PREFETCH PAGES READ + DYNAMIC PREFETCH PAGES READ)
```

What is the difference between Snapshot and Event monitoring in DB2 UDB, and which one should I use?

The Snapshot monitor provides you with the ability to monitor database activities in real time (or very close to it), whereas the Event monitor captures information about database activities and logs them in a file for later evaluation. The information provided by the two monitors can vary due to the ways the data is captured, presented, and evaluated. With an Event monitor, you could have a record for every time a connection was made to a particular database, but only by using the Snapshot monitor would you be able to tell how many simultaneous connections there were to that database at a given point in time. Which you use will depend on the problem you are attempting to troubleshoot and the information you need to perform this task.

 Is there a way to quickly view the bufferpool activity for a particular database in DB2 UDB?

Yes. By using the GET SNAPSHOT command, you can actively monitor the use of a bufferpool by a particular database. The following is an example of using this command to obtain information on the bufferpools used by the Sample database.

```
GET SNAPSHOT FOR BUFFERPOOL FOR sample
Output:
Bufferpool name                            = IBMDEFAULTBP
Database name                              = SAMPLE
Database path                              =
/home/user/user/NODE0000/SQL00010/
Input database alias                       = SAMPLE
Buffer pool data logical reads             = 29
Buffer pool data physical reads            = 11
Buffer pool data writes                    = 0
Buffer pool index logical reads            = 51
Buffer pool index physical reads           = 20
Total buffer pool read time (ms)           = 362
Total buffer pool write time (ms)          = 0
Database files closed                      = 0
Asynchronous pool data page reads          = 0
Asynchronous pool data page writes         = 0
Buffer pool index writes                   = 0
Asynchronous pool index page reads         = 0
Asynchronous pool index page writes        = 0
Total elapsed asynchronous read time       = 0
Total elapsed asynchronous write time      = 0
Asynchronous read requests                 = 0
Direct reads                               = 32
Direct writes                              = 0
Direct read requests                       = 2
Direct write requests                      = 0
Direct reads elapsed time (ms)             = 1
Direct write elapsed time (ms)             = 0
Data pages copied to extended storage      = 0
Index pages copied to extended storage     = 0
Data pages copied from extended storage    = 0
Index pages copied from extended storage   = 0
```

 How do I find indexes that are no longer used?

Remember that it is often recommended that you query the SYSIBM.SYSPACKDEP catalog table to find such indexes. While this is a good way to determine if indexes are used by the queries in a package, there are some problems with this approach. For example, if you determine that there are five or six indexes in existence that are not used in any program, how do you know that they are not used by any dynamic SQL or used to optimize referential integrity checking? There is no exact way to determine this, and the only recommendation is to look very carefully before removing any index that "appears" to not be in use.

 Are there any negative effects of having only one plan for all packages?

The basic problems for having a single plan for an environment are the following:

● **Lack of ability to monitor and tune**   If you are getting an SMF record for every transaction in CICS (TOKENI or TOKENE), you might be able to manage using only one plan, but it will make the task much more difficult. If you are getting the rollup, then accounting data is not useful.

● **More storage in EDMPOOL**   If you specify RELEASE(DEALLOCATE) for plans with a large number of packages, the space in EDMPOOL is expanded greatly. This will generally take storage away from other potential uses.

● **More CPU to manage the storage; longer chains** This is probably less of a problem than the other items, but the EDMPOOL storage increases may force you to use RELEASE(COMMIT) when you could otherwise use RELEASE(DEALLOCATE). With only one plan and one set of parameters, some tuning options are precluded.

BUFFERPOOLS

What type of pages are contained in the DB2 bufferpools?

There are three types of pages contained in a DB2 bufferpool: *in-use*, *updated*, and *available*.

- **In-use**   These are pages that are currently being read or updated.
- **Updated**   These are pages with updated data that have not yet been written to DASD.
- **Available**   These are pages for new use and are to be overwritten by an incoming page of new data; both in-use pages and updated pages are unavailable.

How do I separate and allocate bufferpools for best performance?

When separating objects into bufferpools, there are some guidelines for optimal performance.

- All DB2 catalog and directory objects should be the only objects in BP0. The addition of other objects only introduces performance problems for all access against the catalog and directory. This bufferpool should be allocated accordingly and not oversized.
- DSNDB07 work file tablespaces need to be in their own bufferpool and have the thresholds set accordingly. For more information, refer to the question "Should the bufferpool supporting DSNDB07 always be defined as 100 percent sequential for best performance?" which falls later in this section.
- Always separate tablespaces and indexes—objects that are accessed randomly versus objects that are accessed sequentially. See the question, "How do I tune my

bufferpool if I have both random and sequential processing against the object in the bufferpool?" (later in this section) for information on how to deal with objects that are accessed in both ways.

● Separate read-only objects with a good deal of rereferencing from those that are not rereferenced. Similarly, separate objects with update activity that have heavy rereferencing from those with low rereferencing.

● Code and reference tables can be kept in a separate bufferpool and can be pinned in memory for better performance. See the question, "Is there any performance benefit to keeping an object in the bufferpool, and how do I do this?" (later in this section) for more information.

● Vendor objects that support software tools should be isolated in their own bufferpools.

● Large objects are better tuned when they are in bufferpools by themselves.

● Staging tables carry their own set of quirks and can perform better in their own bufferpools.

How do I determine the optimal size for my bufferpools to achieve the best performance?

In order to determine how large to make a bufferpool, you need to determine the residency time needed by the pages of the objects in the bufferpool. This is the time required for a page to be held for reference. The number of pages required in a bufferpool is based on the number of writes per second to the bufferpool multiplied by the number of seconds required for average page rereference.

What is the difference between the horizontal deferred-write threshold (DWQT) and the vertical deferred-write threshold (VDWQT), and what are the optimal settings?

The DWQT (horizontal) and the VDWQT (vertical) are probably the most important bufferpool settings, in terms of application and system performance. These thresholds control when and how DB2 writes out updated pages to

DASD. The differences between the two are briefly summarized below:

- **DWQT (deferred write threshold)**   This is the percentage threshold that determines when DB2 starts turning on write engines to begin deferred writes. The value is 0 to 90 percent.

- **VDWQT (vertical deferred write threshold)**   This is the percentage threshold that determines when DB2 starts turning on write engines to begin deferred writes for a given dataset. The value is from 0 to 90 percent. The value should normally be less than that of DWQT.

In order to set these parameters accordingly, you must first follow guidelines for appropriately separating bufferpools to account for the differences in object access. If you do not, you will never be able to set these parameters appropriately. For information on how to separate bufferpools for performance, refer to the question, "How do I separate and allocate bufferpools for best performance?" (earlier in this chapter).

How do I turn off prefetch in a bufferpool, and when would this be necessary?

In order to turn off prefetch in a bufferpool, you will need to set VPSEQT = 0 (virtual pool sequential threshold). You would need to do this when you have all the pages for an object (or several objects) stored in the bufferpool and there is minimal (or no) sequential access. For example, if a bufferpool is just holding code and lookup tables, set this parameter to 0 because most of the access to these tables will be random. By setting VPSEQT to 0, sequential prefetch is never considered and therefore never started unnecessarily.

What is the typical write time for a bufferpool write?

A typical time for a write from a virtual bufferpool on a 3990 storage controller is 10 nanoseconds per byte.

How do I know what to tune on OS/390 bufferpools?

There are many ways to monitor and trace bufferpools for tuning, but most of this can be accomplished at the macro level by using the DISPLAY BUFFERPOOL command multiple times over all periods of processing, and finding out how the bufferpools are used. See the next question, "What do I tune to make my DB2 OS/390 bufferpools more efficient in terms of parallelism usage" for an example of the DISPLAY BUFFERPOOL command.

The second way of monitoring bufferpools is to use the following DB2 Bufferpool tool. It offers many more options for fine-tuning the bufferpools.

BUFFERPOOL STATISTICS   Output from the DB2 Bufferpool tool (BPO):

```
Buffer size is.......................4K
 Number of VP Buffers is..........10,000
 VP sequential threshold is..........80%
 Number of HP Buffers is..............0
 HP sequential threshold is.........80%
 Hiper Space Castout is...............Y
 Vertical Write Threshold...........10%
 Horizontal Write Threshold.........50%


Number of GetP...............2,379,499
 Number of Sequential Access..1,429,246  60.1% of GetP
 Number of Random Access.......709,940  29.8% of GetP
 Number of RID_List............240,313  10.1% of GetP
 Number of Random Misses.......277,488  77.1 Misses/Sec
 Number of Misses (others)......149,291  41.5 Misses/Sec
 Number of No_Reads.................604   0.0% of GetP
 Number of Hits..............1,952,116  82.0% of GetP
                                         (Appl. HIT RATIO)
 System HIT RATIO.................34.7%
 Avg. Page Residency...............250 Seconds


Number of Pages Read........1,553,174    431.5 Pages/Second
 Number of Sync  Pages Read...393,989  25.4% of Pages Read
 Number of SPref Pages Read...999,889  64.4% of Pages Read
 Number of LPref Pages Read....14,853   1.0% of Pages Read
 Number of DPref Pages Read...144,443   9.3% of Pages Read
```

```
Number of Read I/Os...........442,966      123.1 IOs/Second
 Number of Sync  Read  I/Os...393,989   88.9% of Read I/Os
 Number of SPref Read  I/Os....32,127    7.3% of Read I/Os
 Number of LPref Read  I/Os....11,853    2.7% of Read I/Os
 Number of DPref Read  I/Os.....4,997    1.1% of Read I/Os
 Delay  of Sync  Read  I/Os........23    Avg. MSeconds (Max 249)
 Delay  of SPref Read  I/Os........36    Avg. MSeconds (Max 250)
 Delay  of Lpref Read  I/Os........43    Avg. MSeconds (Max 249)
 Delay  of DPref Read  I/Os........44    Avg. MSeconds (Max 243)

Number of SetW (Updates)...........170,158

Number of Pages Written........73,624      20.5 Pages per Sec
 Number of Sync  Pages Written ...100    0.1% of Pages Written
 Number of ASync Pages Written 73,524   99.9% of Pages Written

Number of Write I/Os...........45,719      12.7 I/Os per Sec
 Number of Sync  Write I/Os.......100    0.2% of Write I/Os
 Number of ASync Write I/Os....45,619   99.8% of Write I/Os
 Delay  of Sync  Write I/Os.........7    Avg. MSeconds (Max 66)
 Delay  of ASync Write I/Os.........4    Avg. MSeconds (Max 231)
 Average Number Pages/Write.......1.6
```

What do I tune to make my DB2 OS/390 bufferpools more efficient in terms of parallelism usage?

The VPPSEQT threshold is the percentage of bufferpool used for parallelism. This number is a percentage of the VPSEQT. The higher this threshold, the more space in the bufferpool that will be available for parallel operations. This threshold can be set to 0 in order to turn off parallelism when it is not necessary. In other cases, where parallelism is critical for query performance, the threshold can be set as high as 100 to allow for 100 percent of the VPSEQT to be used for parallel requests. By measuring the use of the VPPSEQT against the number of streams requested, the VPPSEQT can be adjusted to best fit the amount required.

The following is an example of the VPPSEQT found by using the DISPLAY BUFFERPOOL command. It is represented by the term "Parallel Sequential" in the output.

The VPPSEQT value can be changed by issuing the ALTER BUFFERPOOL command.

```
-DISPLAY BUFFERPOOL (BP5)

DSNB401I *DB5P BUFFERPOOL NAME BP5, BUFFERPOOL ID 5, USE COUNT 66
DSNB402I *DB5P VIRTUAL BUFFERPOOL SIZE = 5000 BUFFERS
ALLOCATED      =     5000              TO BE DELETED   =      0
    IN-USE/UPDATED  =      688
 DSNB403I *DB5P HIPERPOOL SIZE = 0 BUFFERS, CASTOUT = YES
            ALLOCATED       =       0      TO BE DELETED   =      0
            BACKED BY ES    =       0
 DSNB404I *DB5P THRESHOLDS -
            VP SEQUENTIAL     = 70    HP SEQUENTIAL         = 80
            DEFERRED WRITE    = 20    VERTICAL DEFERRED WRT = 5
            PARALLEL SEQUENTIAL = 80  ASSISTING PARALLEL SEQT= 0
```

How do I tune my bufferpool if I am experiencing parallelism fallback?

In order to tune a bufferpool to accommodate the amount of parallelism called for by SQL statements, you may need to first adjust the VPPSEQT threshold (use the ALTER BUFFERPOOL command) to allow for more of the bufferpool to be allocated for parallel operations. If this cannot be adjusted enough to support the required parallelism, you may need to increase the size of the bufferpool.

How do I tune my bufferpool if I have both random and sequential processing against the object in the bufferpool?

The VPSEQT threshold is the percentage of the bufferpool for sequentially accessed pages. This parameter was set in accordance with the type of processing occurring against the object(s) in the bufferpool. If the processing was more random than sequential, the threshold would have been lowered. The type of processing can be determined by evaluating the amount of sequential GETPAGEs as compared to random GETPAGEs. However, if at all possible, separate randomly processed objects and sequentially processed objects into separate bufferpools to best tune this threshold. Another option would be to dynamically alter the threshold to accommodate the bufferpool usage if the sequential and batch processes occur at different times, for example, if usage is sequential (online) during the day and random (batch) at night.

Should I be using hiperpools for better performance?

Hiperpools provide the ability to utilize hiperspaces as an extension of the bufferpools. Hiperpools allow you to keep large amounts of data in memory without increasing the OS/390 paging rate. The movement of pages to the hiperpool reduces the cost of data movement of a normal data page by approximately 8 percent, unlike the use of paging to back up the bufferpool.

The primary reason to use hiperpools is the OS/390 limit of 2GB for an address space. There is a maximum of only 1.6GB of "virtual" bufferpool space that can be defined; and, if you use all of the allotted space, it will normally cause the address space to hit the 2GB limit.

To improve performance when OS/390 paging is a problem and when extended memory is available for hiperpools, reduce the virtual pool buffers and increase the total pool resource by using hiperpool buffers. The paging rate can be lowered and application performance improved. It is important not to overallocate the hiperpool because this will eventually hurt the overall OS/390 environment if adequate expanded storage isn't available. Using the hiperpool to increase the memory hit ratio for data improves application performance without having an impact on the system-wide OS/390 paging rate.

How do I best size hiperpools for performance?

Hiperpools work best when sized at double the number of pages in the associated virtual pool. If the hiperpools are smaller that this, the system will spend a good deal of time working on moving pages between the virtual pool and the hiperpool, which degrades performance. It is important to determine the effectiveness of hiperpools and this can be done by using the following formula:

```
pages read from the HP ÷ pages written to the HP = hiperpool effectiveness rate
```

The information for this formula can be taken from any of the normal performance monitor reports and from the

DISPLAY BUFFERPOOL command output. As an example of effectiveness, if the ratio is 10%, meaning 10% of the pages written to the hiperpool were retrieved from the hiperpool rather than from DASD, that is good. If the pool is not effective, then don't use it. If the ratio is high, then the underlying buffer pool is probably too small or the VPSEQT is set incorrectly. These are starting points for further monitoring and tuning.

How do I determine if I have exceeded the sequential prefetch threshold (SPTH) in my bufferpools, and what can I do to resolve it?

The SPTH threshold is checked before a prefetch operation is scheduled and during buffer allocation for a previously scheduled prefetch. If the SPTH threshold is exceeded, prefetch will either not be scheduled or will be canceled. To see if you have reached this threshold, you can check the monitor Statistics Long Report for Prefetch Disabled—No Buffer. It will be incremented every time a virtual bufferpool reaches 90 percent of active stealable buffers, which disables sequential prefetch. The Prefetch Disabled number should be zero, or you will experience a degradation in performance.

To eliminate disabling prefetch you will need to increase the size of the bufferpool (VPSIZE). Another option may also be to have more frequent commits in the application programs to free pages in the bufferpool.

How do I determine the bufferpool hit ratio, and what does this mean?

By issuing the –DISPLAY BUFFERPOOL(BP*xx*)DETAIL command, you can gather the appropriate statistics to calculate the bufferpool hit ratio. The calculation is as follows:

```
(GP - (SIO + PfPgs + LpfPgs + DynPfPgs))/GP * 100
```

The abbreviations in the calculation are interpreted as follows:

- GP = random GETPAGE + sequential GETPAGE

- SIO = synchronous read I/O (random) + synchronous read I/O (sequential)
- PfPgs = sequential prefetch, pages read
- LpfPgs = list prefetch, pages read
- DynPfPgs = dynamic prefetch, pages read

The bufferpool hit ratio represents how often a GETPAGE needs to perform an I/O operation in order to be satisfied. The hit ratio is a relative value and will vary depending on the type of application that is executing. The hit ratio can also be found in a statistics report. Keep in mind that a high hit ratio is not always an indicator that a bufferpool is in optimal shape; it may just be repetitive SQL unnecessarily scanning the same pages.

Can pages still be in the bufferpool after I issue a --START DATABASE for a tablespace, or will an I/O be required to bring in the externalized pages?

Depending on the buffer activity, externalized pages still may be in the bufferpool. DB2 directory entries for the tablespace and its associated objects must be available for DB2 processing; therefore, additional reads to the DB2 directory may be required during the -START DATABASE command, if the required pages are not in the bufferpool.

Should the bufferpool supporting DSNDB07 always be defined as 100 percent sequential for best performance?

No. The bufferpool supporting DSNDB07 should not be defined as 100 percent sequential. You will want to at least set VPSEQT to between 95 and 98 percent to allow for some random access. You will want to set the VDWQT and the DWQT up to the sequential threshold of the bufferpool. The reason you will find random access in a work file bufferpool is due to activities such as sorting and the use of sparse indexes.

Tip: Always *isolate DSNDB07 in its own bufferpool.*

What are page cleaners in DB2 UDB, and can I use them to improve performance?

Page cleaners are agents that can perform the I/O for writing pages to disk that would normally be performed by database agents. By appropriately setting the number of page cleaner agents (NUM_IOCLEANERS in the database configuration), you can improve the performance of applications because they will write pages out to disk, and the applications will not have to wait for the database agent to perform this operation.

Should my DSNDB07 work files be backed by hiperpools for better performance?

About a 1 to 10 percent improvement in performance has been observed when backing DSNDB07 work files with hiperpools. Because all updated pages are written out to DASD before they go to the hiperpool, there will be no write I/O reduction. During a merge phase there may be a reduction in read I/O. It will depend on the size of the virtual pools and hiperpools and the amount of work file activity.

Should work files be on shared DASD in a data-sharing environment?

It is recommended that the work files be on shared DASD for the following reasons:

- DB2 will remain connected to its work files even in the event that you have to restart the DB2 on another processor in the data-sharing sysplex.

- You have the ability to create and drop a work file tablespace from any other member in the data-sharing group.

- Having work files on shared DASD is required for processing queries using sysplex query parallelism. Each assisting DB2 writes to its own work file.

Is there any performance benefit to keeping an object in the bufferpool, and how do I do this?

Yes, there is an advantage to pulling objects into the bufferpool and keeping them resident. The advantage will be seen mostly with objects that are sized to fit in the bufferpool and that are rereferenced. The following steps explain how to go about "pinning" objects in the bufferpools and keeping them there.

1. From the DB2 catalog, obtain the total number of pages needed to hold the object.

2. Define a single bufferpool based on that number of pages.

3. At the first opportunity, issue the appropriate following statement or a variation (the first statement is for a data object and the second is for an index object), and then start the application. This will "pin" pages of the object in the private virtual pool, where they will remain resident and available for use.

```
EXEC SQL SELECT COUNT(*)
FROM TABLE
WHERE Data-only column (non-index) = ' ' or something

EXEC SQL SELECT COUNT(*)
FROM TABLE
WHERE 2nd key column = ' ' or something
(non-matching index scan)
```

In DB2 OS/390, when do I set the VDWQT bufferpool threshold to 0?

Consider setting the VDWQT threshold to 0 when less than 10 pages are written to DASD by each I/O as an overall average (using the ALTER BUFFERPOOL command). This will cause a trickle effect—the updated pages will be written out whenever 32 pages are updated. However, even if this is done, the issue of page residency needs to be taken into consideration if these updated pages are going to be referenced within a short period of time. In Version 6, setting the VDWQT threshold to 0 will allow 40 pages to be the threshold, but will still trigger the updated pages to be output whenever they total 32 pages. This will allow heavily updated pages to stay resident and not be written out. Also, in Version 6, this parameter can be given a real integer number rather than using a percent.

 What are the optimal settings for the DWQT and the VDWQT thresholds for a bufferpool that contains the DSNDB07 work files?

DSNDB07 is the work area for DB2 for sorting, grouping, materialization, global temp tables, and so on. These primarily involve updated pages that are going to be referenced very quickly. Also, most of the work that is done in DSNDB07 is sequential in nature. A good starting point for the settings of DSNDB07 would be as follows:

 ● VPSEQT = 95

● VDWQT = 90

● DWQT = 90

This means that 95 percent of the use of DSNDB07 is sequential and that updated pages should only be flushed out to DASD when the pool is almost totally full. Of course, if the bufferpool is not large enough, these thresholds could be reached regularly, causing other problems. Monitor DSNDB07's use closely, and size the pool accordingly.

 Note: *Ignore the theory that DSNDB07 is 100 percent sequential, and use 95 percent as a starting point until you can measure it yourself. There is random use of DSNDB07 in most subsystems.*

What are the optimal settings for the BP0 bufferpool thresholds?

First of all, you must reserve the BP0 bufferpool solely for the DB2 catalog and directory. If you have any other objects in this bufferpool, it can degrade the performance of any process accessing the catalog and directory (which includes almost every process in DB2). In addition, the sequential use of the buffer pool versus the random use of the buffer pool in support of DB2 services (catalog access, authority checking, package/plan/DBD loaded, and so on) is normally quite different from that required for application object use (random access versus sequential access). This is so critical

for performance that in Version 6 there will be a way to set the default buffer pool for all objects that do not specify one during creation. This means that they will not default to BP0 and the buffer pool can stay clean. The thresholds for this bufferpool will be very different in each installation, but a good general starting point would be 2000 pages with a sequential threshold (VPSEQT) of 60 percent. After this, monitor it for a while and then adjust the horizontal write threshold (DWQT) and the vertical write threshold (VDWQT).

PARALLELISM

 Can I turn off parallelism for a single query in my program if it was bound with degree ANY?

No. For any static SQL, don't make the common mistake of using the EXEC SQL SET CURRENT DEGREE = '1' END-EXEC statement prior to executing the desired query. However, you should be able to use OPTIMIZE FOR 1 ROW, but keep in mind that it turns off many other things like prefetch, and so on.

Tip: *SET CURRENT DEGREE is only for dynamic SQL, not for static SQL.*

What kind of queries are best suited to take advantage of parallelism?

Queries with the following characteristics will be able to take advantage of parallelism:

- Long-running, read-only queries, both static and dynamic SQL, from both local and remote sites, and when using either private or DRDA protocols
- Tablespace scans and index scans
- Joins
- Nested loop
- Merge scan
- Hybrid without sort on new table
- Sorts

Can parallelism cause a strain on my CPU?

Parallelism is a method of reducing elapsed time by using more available CPU resources. If a system is already CPU constrained, parallelism would only add to the problem in most situations.

What can I expect the optimizer to choose as the optimal CPU parallel degree for a query?

The degree of DB2 parallelism is influenced by the largest partition. DB2 divides a tablespace into logical pieces (work ranges) based on the size of the largest physical partition of the table. For example, a table with 10KB pages, 10 parts, and a largest partition of 5KB would have degree 2. Another example is a large table with a total of 60,612,084 active pages, with a maximum partition of 691,050 active pages, giving

```
60612084 active pages/691050 maximum partition active pages = 87.710
```

or

```
DEGREE = 88
```

This number can be viewed in the EXPLAIN output of a query. However, at execution time, if the degree chosen cannot be supported (if there are not enough CPUs), a new degree will be used. In order to find out what degree is used at execution, you will have to run a trace using IFCIDs 221 and 223. The output of this trace provides the following:

- IFCID 221—Execution trace
  - Parallel group number
  - Planned (BIND) degree
  - PLAN_TABLE degree
  - Planned (RUN) degree
  - Start of execution considering host variables
  - ESA sort and ambiguous cursors
  - Actual degree

- What really happened, considering buffer pool resource
- Page ranges or key ranges of logical partition

● IFCID 222—Elapsed time trace

- Parallel group number
- Pipe (TCB) creation and termination time
- Rows processed per pipe (group)
- Subpipe (SRB) creation and termination time
- Rows processed per subpipe (I/O stream)

The output report from an analysis of IFCIDs 221 and 222 is shown in Figure 16-1.

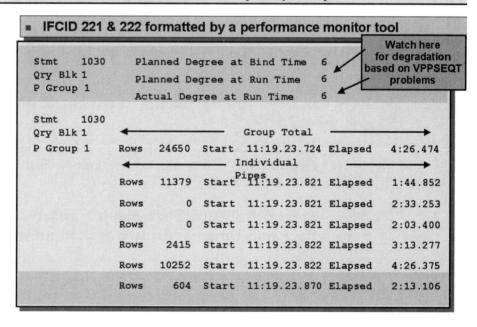

Figure 16-1   Trace output from IFCID 221 and 222 showing parallelism results

Why am I getting I/O parallelism instead of CPU parallelism?

There a couple of reasons that CPU parallelism is not chosen. One reason is if the optimizer estimates the ratio of I/O work to CPU work is 1:1; in this case, additional processors are not necessary. The second reason is that there may only be one processor configured to the subsystem or instance for the query.

How can I improve I/O operations by using parallelism in DB2 UDB?

One way to improve application response time is by allowing I/O operations for a query to be executed in parallel. You can enable parallel I/O for a database in DB2 UDB just by correctly setting the parameter in the database configuration file that controls the number of prefetch servers. This parameter is NUM_IOSERVERS.

You can define a number of I/O servers to improve query performance; and, if some servers cannot be used, it will not degrade performance—they will have their memory pages swapped out, and the servers will not be used.

How can I tell the optimizer to try parallelism for my query?

Try the BIND option of DEGREE = 'ANY' for the package or plan for static SQL. For individual dynamic SQL statements, use SET CURRENT DEGREE = 'ANY'.

What is the difference between intrapartition parallelism and interpartition parallelism in DB2 UDB?

Intrapartition parallelism is a simultaneous process within a single partition; interpartition parallelism is a simultaneous process in multiple partitions.

Intrapartition parallelism is used mostly with SMP (symmetric multiprocessor), where there are multiple processors sharing common memory and disks. Several threads will be created by the optimizer and will all be active during an SQL statement's execution. This number of threads is the *degree*.

Interpartition parallelism tends to involve several processors that all contain their own unshared memory and disks.

When should I use sysplex query parallelism?

First of all, in order to use sysplex query parallelism, you must be enabled in a parallel sysplex environment with DB2 data sharing. You should use sysplex query parallelism when you have long-running complex queries and are trying to achieve a reduction in the elapsed time in a data-sharing environment.

When is parallelism decided?

DB2 parallelism is decided at both bind time and run time. If parallelism is not chosen at bind time, there is no possibility of it being chosen at run time. Even if parallelism is chosen at bind time, it may not be used at run time due to several factors:

- If there is not enough space in the virtual bufferpool to support the requested degree of parallelism, the degree can be reduced from that chosen at bind time, or parallelism can be turned off altogether

- If host variables are used in the SQL query, this can prevent DB2 from determining which partitions will qualify in a query, and the degree chosen for parallelism will be decided at run time.

- If the machine on which DB2 is running does not have hardware sort at run time, parallelism will be disabled.

- If DB2 determines that a cursor is ambiguous, then parallelism will be disabled.

If parallelism is disabled, the query does not fail—DB2 simply uses a sequential plan for access to the data. In order to find out if your query has experienced downgrades in parallel degrees or fallbacks from parallelism, you can review DB2 accounting information.

If I create a tablespace with only one partition, can I still have parallelism?

Yes. Even if a tablespace is defined with only one partition, you can still achieve parallelism. In fact, it is recommended that you do this when you have a nonpartitioned table (by design) being joined to a partitioned table that is using parallelism. If the nonpartitioned tablespace were redefined to have at least one partition, it too could be made parallel during the join process.

Can host variables have an effect on the degree of parallelism chosen?

Yes, the use of host variables can have an effect on the degree of parallelism chosen by DB2 at run time. The parallel degree may depend on host variable contents of the cursor present at EXEC time. An EXPLAIN output will post a DEGREE = 0 in the PLAN_TABLE at bind time because the host variables are unknown and therefore their effects on the parallel degree would also be unknown. The only way you will know what degree was actually chosen is through a trace of IFCIDs 221, 222, and 231.

Can I have CPU parallelism when my cursor is defined WITH HOLD?

No. CPU parallelism cannot be used when a cursor is defined WITH HOLD, since this cursor's use is potentially interrupted by a commit, which causes a stoppage in processing.

How can I control the maximum degree of parallelism?

In DB2 OS/390, there is an undocumented zap to allow you to set the maximum degree of parallelism. This will set the maximum degree per parallel group. The zap is as follows:.

```
NAME V51AMDEG  DSN6SPRM
 VERIFY 000130 00000000 <- default of no limit
 REP    000130 0000000A <- sets MDEG to 10
```

In DB2 UDB, there is a configuration parameter called MAX_QUERYDEGREE, which specifies the maximum degree of intra-partition parallelism for a SQL statement. If this is not specifically set, the degree of parallelism will be determined by the optimizer.

In a random bufferpool, how can I define enough room to support parallelism in DB2 OS/390?

Parallelism is supported in a bufferpool by the setting of the VPPSEQT (parallel sequential) threshold. The VPPSEQT threshold is a percentage of the VPSEQT (sequential) threshold. In a random bufferpool, the VPSEQT would be set very low, allowing for the majority of the bufferpool to be used for random processing. This then leaves very little room in the bufferpool for the support of parallel operations against objects defined to this bufferpool. Often, the bufferpool will have to be inflated in size unnecessarily in order to have enough pages available to support parallelism.

How can I achieve parallelism on my non-partitioning indexes for SQL operations?

In order to have parallelism for SQL operations against non-partitioning indexes, you will need to take advantage of a feature introduced in DB2 OS/390 Version 5. This feature is called *pieces*. Pieces allow you to break a non-partitioning index into multiple datasets, or pieces. Operations can then be performed on the pieces in parallel. Pieces also help to eliminate bottlenecks caused by insert/update processes.

In CPU parallelism, will the degree chosen by the optimizer at bind time be the same degree chosen at execution time if I have a smaller number of CPUs than the degree chosen?

At execution time, DB2 will take into consideration the number of CPUs available; and, if there are not enough CPUs to support the degree of parallelism initially chosen by the optimizer, the degree will be degraded.

QUERY OPTIMIZATION

Should I give any consideration to the order in which my predicates appear in the WHERE clause?

Yes. The optimizer does take into consideration the order of the predicates when determining an access path. You should try to group your predicates together based on the following order:

- Indexable predicates—all matching predicates on index key columns
- Other stage 1 predicates
- Predicates that refer to columns in the index (index screening)

  - Equal type predicates, and IN lists with one element
  - Range predicates, and column IS NOT NULL
  - All other qualifying predicates

- Predicates that can only be applied to the data rows

  - Equal type predicates, and IN lists with one element
  - Range predicates, and column IS NOT NULL
  - All other qualifying predicates

- Stage 2 predicates

  - Equal type predicates, and IN lists with one element
  - Range predicates, and column IS NOT NULL
  - All other qualifying predicates

The optimizer will evaluate any remaining predicates in the order listed in the SQL statement, so list them in most restrictive to least restrictive order. This is especially true for subqueries.

What level of the DB2 UDB optimization simulates the OS/390 optimizer?

Level 3 is the rough approximation of OS/390 optimizer. The level is set in the Client Configuration Assistant or by manually updating the DB2OPTIMIZATION parameter in the DB2CLI.INI. Or, the level can be dynamically issued through the SET CURRENT QUERY OPTIMIZATION statement.

Is one join method better than another?

Each join method has its strong points. Generally speaking, the most appropriate join method is the one that provides you with the requested rows within the required response time. Here is a simplified comparison of the available methods with a brief explanation of how they work. (Note that *outer* refers to the outer table and *inner* refers to the inner table.)

1. **Nested Loop**   Filter outer, join to inner, filter inner, pass to result

2. **Hybrid** (OS/390 only)   Filter outer, join to inner RIDs and build intermediate table, sort RIDs and intermediate table, prefetch inner rows, swap RID with row values, pass to result

3. **Merge Scan**   Filter outer, filter inner, match merge to join, pass to result

4. **Hash** (UDB 5.2 only)   Filter inner, hash inner to memory, filter outer, hash outer one row at a time to join to memory, pass to result.

5. **Star** (UDB 5.2 only)   Filter small tables, Cartesian join small tables, join to inner fact table, pass to result.

The most important question to answer when analyzing the optimizer's join method decision is, "Is the entire result required?" If only the first n rows are required, the Nested Loop join provides the most streamlined path for joining n

rows. To strongly influence a Nested Loop join, add OPTIMIZE FOR *n* ROWS to the SELECT statement. If very few rows are participating in the join, any one of these methods is optimal. On the other hand, if large numbers of rows are participating, the subsystem or instance environment is a large factor in analyzing which method is optimal.

For example, a Hybrid join needs ample RID pool sort, Merge join needs ample SORT heap or DSNDB07, and Hash join works best with large memory allocations. These environmental factors affect which join method the optimizer chooses. If the environment is solid, table join order is more often the problem with a long-running join than the particular join method. See the following questions on changing the table join order for further details.

What is the difference between sequential prefetch and list prefetch?

Sequential prefetch and list prefetch are two methods for accessing DB2 data that are determined at optimization time. Sequential prefetch can be used when several blocks of data need to be read or when indexes need to be read. When using list prefetch, DB2 builds a list of RIDs, sorts them, and then uses the sorted list to retrieve the actual data. This method can help avoid duplicate I/Os, and it accesses the data in one pass.

How can I make the optimizer switch the table join order for inner joins?

There are several methods available for influencing table join order. Most do not guarantee absolute results, though; they are simply strong suggestions for the optimizer. Try one method at a time until you achieve your desired result, or use combinations of the methods.

The first method is the OPTIMIZER FOR *n* ROWS clause. Place it at the end of the SELECT statement to see if the optimizer changes the join order.

The second method uses special operations to discourage local predicates on the table you would like moved from the top of the join chain. For example, if the optimizer is choosing the larger table as the outer table for a Nested Loop join, and you would like the smaller table as the outer, use the following syntax:

```
SELECT columns
FROM LARGE_OUTER A, SMALL_INNER B
WHERE A.COL2 = B.COL1
  AND A.COL2 > 'X' CONCAT ' '
  AND B.COL1 BETWEEN 1 AND 900
```

The following expressions are the preferred discouragement operations because they disallow index access, but keep the predicate stage 1:

```
+0, -0, /1, * 1, ||' ', CONCAT ' '
```

The third method for changing join order uses table expressions or inline views to encourage a particular join order. In the following example, the inline view is requesting tables A and B to be joined prior to table C:

```
SELECT columns
FROM C,
    (SELECT columns
     FROM A, B
     WHERE A.COL1 = B.COL1)
WHERE C.COL2 = B.COL2
```

The fourth method uses bogus predicates to encourage a table to be moved up the join chain. For example, if the optimizer is choosing the larger table as the inner table for a Nested Loop join, and you would like the larger table as the outer so that it is only scanned once, use the following syntax:

```
SELECT columns
FROM LARGE_OUTER A, SMALL_INNER B
WHERE A.COL2 = B.COL1
  AND A.COL2 > 'X'
  AND B.COL1 BETWEEN 1 AND 900
  AND B.COL2 > ' '
  AND B.COL3 BETWEEN 0 AND 999999
  AND B.COL4 >= 0
```

You may have to use more than one bogus predicate in order to influence the optimizer. Each bogus predicate should be formulated on the next available index column. This method works by lowering the filter factor on the chosen table. The more bogus predicates added on different columns, the lower the filter factor.

How can I make the optimizer switch the table join order for outer joins?

You have much more control of join order with outer joins than inner joins. Changing table join order is as simple as placing one table prior to the other in the FROM clause. However, this may not achieve the desired answer set in multitable joins. A typical problem is having one large table left joined to several small tables. The following demonstrates a join of one large fact table, T1, to several small domain tables, whether or not they have qualifying rows for the join:

```
SELECT columns
FROM T1 LEFT JOIN T2 ON T1.COLA = T2.COLX
        LEFT JOIN T3 ON T2.COLX = T3.COLY
        LEFT JOIN T4 ON T3.COLY = T4.COLZ
```

In order to improve the performance of the outer join, the large fact table, T1, needs to be moved further down the join chain. The following statement moves T1 to the very end of the chain and preserves the required result set of all the fact table rows, whether or not the domain tables have qualifying rows for the join:

```
SELECT columns
FROM T2 FULL JOIN T3 ON T2.COLX = T3.COLY
        FULL JOIN T4 ON T3.COLY = T4.COLZ
        RIGHT JOIN T1 ON T1.COLA = T2.COLX
```

How do I know if my query is doing a Cartesian join?

A Cartesian join is basically joining all rows in the outer table with all rows of the inner table, algebraically A * B. The first symptom of a Cartesian join is the query response time. The query returns the correct result, but it takes too long. This

can happen in any production environment whenever a join predicate has been mistakenly eliminated on a table that is not returning columns to the result. The following query demonstrates this point:

```
SELECT A.columns, B.columns, D.columns
FROM A, B, C, D
WHERE A.COL2 = B.COL1
   AND B.COL1 = D.COL3
   AND local predicates
```

If columns were requested from table D, the result set would show the Cartesian join rows. This mistake is less evident when columns are not requested and the join predicates are mixed in with local predicates. Unwanted Cartesians can be avoided by simply grouping the join predicates separately from the local predicates so that they can be easily checked.

There are optimizer-chosen Cartesian joins that improve the performance of a query. These Cartesians are harder to spot because join predicates are accounted for; however, the optimizer has chosen to join two tables together that have no join relationship. The only way to detect this is to review the table join order listed in the PLAN_TABLE and compare it with the join predicates in the SQL statement. For example, when the PLAN_TABLE shows that two tables are involved in a Nested Loop join and there are no join predicates relating the two tables, then a Cartesian join is occurring. For further details as to why the optimizer performs this ritual, see the next question.

Why does DB2 force a Cartesian join in my query?

A Cartesian join is chosen by the optimizer when it deems that prejoining small tables, or a small number of filtered rows from a not-so-small table, prior to a join to a large table is more efficient than any other join sequence. For example, if one table has two rows that qualify after local predicates are applied, and another table has three rows, the Cartesian join would produce six rows prior to the join to another table. This could be faster than joining two rows to the large table, and

then joining the result to the three rows. Another example is if one table has one row that qualifies after local predicates are applied and another table has 12 rows, the Cartesian join would produce 12 rows prior to the join to another table. This would definitely be faster than joining one row to the large table, and then joining the result to the 12 rows. This eliminates one pass against the large table.

The optimizer may mistakenly choose to do a Cartesian join when host variables are used. In that case, the optimizer may be estimating the Cartesian to be 2×4 rows and the reality may be 20×40 rows, which yields 800 rows instead of 8. To correct the optimizer, see the earlier questions on changing table join order.

 ### How do I find SQL performance problems prior to migrating programs to production?

SQL performance analysis should start as early as possible in the development cycle. The sooner the performance issues are caught, the less unnecessary work inflicted on the system. Performance problems can reside within the SQL, as well as the access paths. In order to guarantee good performance in a large development effort (over 1,000 complex queries), analysis should be done on as many statements as possible using the following procedures:

Prior to moving to production, queries should be reviewed for valid indexable or stage 1 predicates. Any stage 2 predicates should be converted to stage 1 or indexable predicates, if at all possible. Any stage 1 predicate should be converted to an indexable predicate, if possible. For example, C1 NOT IN (1,7,12,15,18,21) should be converted to C1 IN (6,8,9,10,11,13,14,16,17,19,20).

All index and table catalog statistics in the test and acceptance environment should be updated to mimic the production environment for the purpose of validating the access paths. In addition to the statistics, the NUMLKTS DSNZPARM, RID pool, and hiperpool settings should be updated in order for the optimizer to react consistently between these environments. If the environments are inconsistent, the access path analysis is inaccurate.

EXPLAINs should be run on every program, and the access paths should be checked for possible performance problems. The PLAN_TABLE identifies where work is being performed within each access path. PLAN_TABLE queries can search for potential problems.

The following query will identify programs that have built-in functions that are evaluated in stage 2.

```
SELECT QUERYNO, QBLOCKNO, APPLNAME, PROGNAME, PLANNO, METHOD, CREATOR
     , TNAME, TABNO, ACCESSTYPE, MATCHCOLS, ACCESSCREATOR, ACCESSNAME
     , INDEXONLY, SORTN_UNIQ, SORTN_JOIN, SORTN_ORDERBY, SORTN_GROUPBY
     , SORTC_UNIQ, SORTC_JOIN, SORTC_ORDERBY, SORTC_GROUPBY
     , TSLOCKMODE, REMARKS, PREFETCH, COLUMN_FN_EVAL, MIXOPSEQ
     , JOIN_TYPE, PAGE_RANGE, CORRELATION_NAME, QBLOCK_TYPE
FROM PLAN_TABLE
WHERE COLUMN_FN_EVAL = 'S'
ORDER BY TIMESTAMP, QUERYNO, QBLOCKNO, PLANNO, MIXOPSEQ
```

The following query will identify indexes that are not being used.

```
SELECT NAME, CREATOR, TBNAME
FROM SYSIBM.SYSINDEXES   T1
WHERE T1.DBNAME = 'ABCD0001'
    AND NOT EXISTS
        (SELECT 1
         FROM PLAN_TABLE
         WHERE ACCESSNAME = T1.NAME)
```

The following query identifies indexes matching on fewer columns than expected.

```
SELECT QUERYNO, PROGNAME, index name, MATCHCOLS, &NUMBER
FROM PLAN_TABLE
WHERE ACCESSNAME = indexname
    AND MATCHCOLS <= number
```

The following query will identify programs that have SQL that uses list prefetch.

```
SELECT QUERYNO, PROGNAME, TNAME, ACCESSNAME, PREFETCH
FROM PLAN_TABLE
WHERE PREFETCH = 'L'
ORDER BY PROGNAME, QUERYNO
```

The following query identifies programs that have SQL statements that are accessing data using a multiple-index scan.

```
SELECT QUERYNO, PROGNAME, TNAME, ACCESSTYPE
FROM PLAN_TABLE
WHERE ACCESSTYPE LIKE 'M%'
    AND CREATOR    = 'AA'
ORDER BY PROGNAME, QUERYNO
```

The following query identifies programs with SQL using index access with no matching columns.

```
SELECT QUERYNO, PROGNAME, TNAME, ACCESSNAME, INDEXONLY
FROM OS.PLAN_TABLE
WHERE ACCESSTYPE = 'I'
    AND MATCHCOLS = 0
ORDER BY PROGNAME, QUERYNO
```

The following query ranks the queries from the least-matching columns to the most-matching columns.

```
SELECT IX.CREATOR, IX.NAME, IX.COLCOUNT, PT.MATCHCOLS
    , (FLOAT(PT.MATCHCOLS) / FLOAT(IX.COLCOUNT) * 100), 1
FROM SYSIBM.SYSINDEXES IX, PLAN_TABLE PT
WHERE IX.CREATOR    = PT.ACCESSCREATOR
    AND IX.NAME      = PT.ACCESSNAME
    AND PT.MATCHCOLS  > 1
ORDER BY 1, 2, 5
```

The following query identifies queries with sorts.

```
SELECT QUERYNO, QBLOCKNO, APPLNAME, PROGNAME, PLANNO,
    METHOD, CREATOR, TNAME, TABNO, ACCESSTYPE, MATCHCOLS,
    ACCESSCREATOR, ACCESSNAME, INDEXONLY, SORTN_UNIQ,
    SORTN_JOIN, SORTN_ORDERBY, SORTN_GROUPBY,
    SORTC_UNIQ, SORTC_JOIN, SORTC_ORDERBY, SORTC_GROUPBY,
    TSLOCKMODE, REMARKS, PREFETCH, COLUMN_FN_EVAL, MIXOPSEQ,
    JOIN_TYPE, PAGE_RANGE, CORRELATION_NAME, QBLOCK_TYPE
FROM PLAN_TABLE
WHERE SORTN_UNIQ    = 'Y' OR SORTN_JOIN    = 'Y'
    OR SORTN_ORDERBY = 'Y' OR SORTN_GROUPBY = 'Y'
```

```
     OR SORTC_UNIQ    = 'Y' OR SORTC_JOIN    = 'Y'
     OR SORTC_ORDERBY = 'Y' OR SORTC_GROUPBY = 'Y'
ORDER BY TIMESTAMP, QUERYNO, QBLOCKNO, PLANNO, MIXOPSEQ
```

The following query identifies the programs with SQL that access data by a tablespace scan.

```
SELECT QUERYNO, PROGNAME, TNAME
FROM PLAN_TABLE
WHERE ACCESSTYPE = 'R'
   AND CREATOR    = creator
   AND TNAME NOT IN (list of really small tables)
ORDER BY PROGNAME, QUERYNO
```

The "work" that is identified by these queries may or may not be a problem. Data volume and distribution statistics need to be applied to each situation and analyzed before tuning decisions can be made. Only then can you determine whether the access path meets the required performance objectives. For example, if sorts are identified in the PLAN_TABLE, and you determine that less than 50 rows will participate, tuning will not be necessary. On the other hand, if 25,000 rows will participate in the sort, and the required response time is less than a second, tuning will be necessary. In such a case, an index may need to be added or altered in order to eliminate the unwanted sort. If the sort is chosen by the optimizer as part of the Merge join method, other tuning options will be needed to change the join method.

There are several tuning options available in DB2. First, apply OPTIMIZE FOR n ROWS clause to the SELECT statement to see if the appropriate access path change was made. If that does not work, try adding CONCAT " (for character data) or + 0 (for numeric data) to the predicates for which you want to remove index access. These clauses demote a predicate from indexable to stage 1. More than one clause can be applied to each SELECT statement and may be needed to achieve the desired result.

For tougher tuning problems, like list prefetch that will not go away, the CLUSTERRATIO statistic may need to be

increased above 95 for the index. This technique is rarely used but may be necessary to eliminate the RID processing and materialization that can slow a query down.

The final tuning technique is to add bogus predicates that will not affect the rows retrieved to the SELECT statement, but that will change the access path (table join order). Examples of bogus predicates are C1 >= " for character data, and C1 >= 0 for numeric data. Each predicate that is added lowers the calculated filter factor for the table, provided the columns are different in each predicate.

Can one index be used multiple times in one query block?

Yes, one index can be used several times in one query block by invoking multiple index access, IN list access, self joins, and subqueries accessing the same table.

The multiple index access technique reuses indexes as follows:

1. Traverse the first index, applying matching predicates to locate the first leaf page.

2. Once the first leaf page is encountered, continue to scan the leaf pages, applying matching predicates as well as nonmatching stage 1 predicates (as of APAR PQ15670 in OS/390) to acquire RIDs from qualifying index entries.

3. Sort the RIDs in ascending page-number sequence.

4. Traverse the second index, applying matching predicates to locate the first leaf page. This step can optionally include accessing many different indexes or the same index many times.

5. Once the first leaf page is encountered, continue to scan the leaf pages, applying matching predicates as well as nonmatching stage 1 predicates (as of APAR PQ15670 in OS/390) to acquire RIDs from qualifying index entries.

6. Sort the RIDs in ascending page number sequence.

7. For OR predicates, combine (union) the RID sets and remove duplicates (referred to as index ORing). For AND

predicates, consolidate (intersect) the RID sets and remove duplicates (referred to as index ANDing).

8. Use skip sequential prefetch (which ignores duplicate page numbers and reads only the pages containing qualifying rows, even if they are not contiguous) to retrieve table rows, and apply additional stage 1 and stage 2 predicates. An additional sort may be required to satisfy an optional ORDER BY clause.

The IN list access technique reuses an index by issuing one probe to the index for each value included in the IN list, applying matching predicates until the first leaf page is encountered. The greater the spread of the values in the IN list, the greater the benefit. The next SQL demonstrates this type of IN list:

```
SELECT columns
FROM table
WHERE COL1 = 'X'
  AND COL2 IN('A', 'M', 'Z')
```

Self joins, or a table joined to itself, can use one index twice. The available predicates and chosen join method will determine the manner in which the index is used. The first index access may or may not use the same path as the second access to the same index.

Subqueries that reference the same table as the outer query can use one index twice. The available predicates and chosen access method for each query block will determine the manner in which the index is used. The first index access may or may not use the same path as the second access to the same index.

What are the benefits of index screening?

Index screening can be used for list prefetch and for multiple-index ANDing and ORing. It was released into DB2 OS/390 late in Version 5 and can be used with prior releases through APAR PQ15670. The benefits of index screening include a reduction in the RID (Row ID) list for RID list

sorting, a reduction in the RID list for data pages accessed, and quicker filtering of RIDs.

Index screening is the process of using columns that did not qualify for matching (due to a missing column value) in the index for RID selection. For example, if you have a four-column index (columns 1, 2, 3, 4), and the query's WHERE clause identifies 1, 3, 4 for the predicate, column 1 will be used for matching and with index screening, and 3 and 4 can be used for further screening even though column 2 is missing. If column 2 was identified in the WHERE predicate, it could have matched on 1, 2, 3, 4. This use of index screening can potentially reduce the number of qualifying RIDs for a query result by a large amount.

Can I join several inline views/table expressions together?

Yes, up to 15 inline views/table expressions can be joined together. They are most commonly used in outer joins and recursive queries (recursion in DB2 UDB only). The following example demonstrates the use of multiple inline views/table expressions, but it has one flaw:

```
SELECT     T1.COLA, T1.COLB, T2.COLC, T2.COLD,
    T3.COLE, T3.COLF, T4.COLG, T5.COLI
FROM (SELECT *  FROM T1 WHERE T1.CODE = 'SO')
LEFT JOIN
    (SELECT *  FROM T2 WHERE T2.CODE = 'MANY')
ON     T1.COLA = T2.COLC
LEFT JOIN
    (SELECT *  FROM T3 WHERE T3.CODE = 'COLUMNS')
ON     T2.COLC = T3.COLE
LEFT JOIN
    (SELECT *  FROM T4 WHERE T4.CODE = 'SO LITTLE')
ON     T3.COL3 = T4.COLF
LEFT JOIN
    (SELECT *  FROM T5 WHERE T5.CODE = 'TIME')
ON     T5.COL5 = T4.COL4
```

The one flaw is the number of columns that were requested within the individual inline view/table expression.

Since each one requested all columns (*) from the chosen table, many extra columns were gathered and placed in work files but were not needed in the final result. These unnecessary columns need to be eliminated within the inline view/table expression by explicitly requesting only the necessary columns.

When can I justify the overhead of using REOPT(VARS)?

In DB2 OS/390 only, the REOPT(VARS) bind option is justifiable when the host variable contents are volatile and the application can withstand an increased response time of 0.1 to 0.5 seconds. The reoptimization time depends on the complexity of the query: the more columns, tables, and predicates, the greater the increase in reoptimization time.

A good example of justifiable REOPT(VARS) is a long-running batch program with four queries containing host variables accessing several partitioned tables. These queries cannot qualify for a partition scan because of host variables usage. Instead, the queries do index and tablespace scanning. Significant reductions in run time (30 to 70 percent) are attainable by rebinding the program with REOPT(VARS) and incurring an extra 2.0 seconds (a worse case of 0.5 seconds per query) of reoptimization at execution time. This is easy to accept when one query is reduced from a 100 percent tablespace scan to a 34 percent partition scan. The optimizer can carve a precise path to the data within a partitioned table when the host variable's contents are known.

Further reductions in elapsed time can be obtained if the program is bound with DEGREE = 'ANY'.

When can I justify using optimization beyond level 5 in DB2 UDB?

Optimization levels 7 and 9 are justifiable for queries when the time to optimize the statement does not exceed the elapsed time of the query.

 ## What class of optimization in DB2 UDB enables query rewrite?

The minimum class for query rewrite is class 2 optimization. Class 5 is the default, with the range being from 0 to 9, where 0 indicates minimal query optimization and 9 indicates maximum optimization. There are three major categories of query rewrite:

- **Operation merging** DB2 will merge query operations so that the query has the fewest possible number of operations. For example: view merges, redundant join info, summary tables.

- **Operation movement** DB2 will move query operations to construct the query with the minimum number of operations and predicates. For example: DISTINCT elimination, predicate push-down, decorrelation.

- **Predicate translation** DB2 will translate existing predicates to more optimal predicates. For example, addition of implied predicates (predicate transitive closure), OR to IN transformations.

The category of rewrite that will occur will depend on the classes that are set for the query. The classes are listed here:

- **Class 0** Basic query rewrite rules are applied.
- **Class 1** Only a subset of query rewrite rules are applied.
- **Class 2** All query rewrite rules are applied except computationally intensive rules.
- **Class 3** Most query rewrite rules, including subquery to join transformations, are applied.
- **Class 5** All rewrite rules are applied, including routing queries to summary tables, with the exception of computationally intensive rules.
- **Classes 7 and 9** All rewrite rules are applied, including computationally intensive rules.

Why does DB2 not use dynamic prefetch when a package is bound with degree ANY?

The method of implementation of both query and CPU parallelism is based on predetermined access paths that are selected based on I/O and CPU overhead. If the selected type of parallelism is query I/O parallelism, the access path will already be using sequential prefetch. If the selected type of parallelism is CPU parallelism, the query has been rewritten to run on multiple processors and the method of implementation would be negated. Since dynamic prefetch is an execution-time selection, it is not allowed during parallelism.

How can I make the optimizer select a tablespace scan instead of index access?

To make the optimizer ignore all the available indexes for a query, you may need to add special operations to every predicate containing an index column. This is necessary when you know that more than 25 percent of the table will be qualified by the predicates, but the optimizer is estimating a much lower number. For example, if host variable usage is swaying the optimizer toward using a particular index, a special operation can be added to the predicate to discourage the optimizer from choosing that index. The following are the preferred discouragement operations because they disallow index access, yet they allow the predicate to be evaluated in stage 1:

```
+0, -0, /1, * 1, ||' ', CONCAT ' '
```

The following statement demonstrates how to discourage the optimizer from choosing the composite index A.B.C, and the single column indexes B and C, for the given query:

```
SELECT    columns
FROM TABLE
WHERE A = :hostvar1 + 0
AND B = :hostvar2 CONCAT ' '
AND C BETWEEN :hostvar3 + 0 AND :hostvar4 + 0
```

 ## How can I make the optimizer choose a different index?

There are several methods available for influencing the optimizer. Most do not guarantee absolute results, however; they are simply strong suggestions for the optimizer. Try one method at a time until you achieve your desired result, or use combinations of the methods.

The first method is the OPTIMIZER FOR n ROWS clause. Place it at the end of the SELECT statement to see if the optimizer changes the index choice. Keep in mind that when $n = 1$, the persuasion is stronger than any other number.

The second method uses special operations to discourage local predicates on the columns from which you would like index access removed. For example, if the optimizer is choosing an index on COL1.COL2 and you would like the COL5 index to be chosen, use the following syntax:

```
SELECT columns
FROM TABLE
WHERE COL1 = 400 + 0
AND COL2 > 'X' CONCAT ' '
   AND COL5 BETWEEN 1 AND 900
```

The following expressions are the preferred discouragement operations because they disallow index access, yet they keep the predicate stage 1:

```
+0, -0, /1, * 1, ||' ', CONCAT ' '
```

The third method uses bogus predicates to encourage an index to be chosen. For example, if the optimizer is choosing an index on COL5, and you would like the COL1.COL2.COL3 index to be chosen, use the following syntax:

```
SELECT columns
FROM TABLE
WHERE COL1 = 400
   AND COL2 > ' '   -- bogus predicate
   AND COL3 > 0     -- bogus predicate
```

You may have to use more than one bogus predicate in order to influence the optimizer. Each bogus predicate should be formulated on the next available index column. This method works by lowering the filter factor on the chosen table. The more bogus predicates added on different columns, the lower the filter factor.

 ## How can I turn off list prefetch for my query?

The first method is the OPTIMIZE FOR n ROWS clause. Place it at the end of the SELECT statement to see if the optimizer removes list prefetch from the access path. Keep in mind that when $n = 1$, the persuasion is stronger than with any other number.

For list prefetch that will not go away, you may need to increase the CLUSTERRATIO statistic above 95 percent for the index. This technique is rarely used but may be necessary to eliminate the RID processing and materialization that can slow a query down.

However, OPTIMIZE FOR 1 ROW will not turn off list prefetch for instances in which a final ORDER BY, GROUP BY, or DISTINCT sort cannot be avoided, because DB2 will have to materialize the full result set before a sort can occur. It also has no effect on subqueries, nested table expressions or views that materialize, subselects merged by UNION (ALL), and so on, and it cannot be used with a singleton SELECT.

Is there a limit to the number of predicates DB2 adds for transitive closure?

Yes. DB2 will add predicates to joins in order to achieve predicate transitive closure for better performance. Predicate transitive closure is when DB2 supplies additional predicates to the query during optimization of SQL with joins. There is a limit of nine predicates that DB2 can add to do this.

How does SELECT DISTINCT affect the performance of my query?

A sort of all qualifying rows is incurred when SELECT DISTINCT is used in a query without a supporting index. If the number of qualifying rows is small enough (less than 1,000), the impact will be minimal. If the number of qualifying rows is large (greater than 1,000), the impact is based on how fast the processor can sort the qualifying rows.

On the other hand, if a supporting index is available, the query can actually run faster with the DISTINCT than without.

How can I improve prefetch performance in DB2 UDB?

Using prefetch will allow for data and index pages to be copied from disk into the bufferpool before they are called for, allowing for I/O time to be minimized. If data is spread across separate devices, the performance of the prefetch operation will be more efficient, especially when tables are accessed by queries processing large quantities of data. This can be done if the tablespace was defined using DMS storage, and there are multiple device containers, and the containers are defined on separate disks.

If I add an index to help with RI checking purposes only, do I need to do a REBIND?

Checks done for referential integrity (RI) child relationships are not necessarily access paths as we refer to them for query optimization. These checks do not appear in an EXPLAIN and are not determined by the optimizer. RI checking can occur in one of two ways: by a tablespace scan of the table or by using an index if all foreign-key columns match the leading columns of the foreign-key index.

When DB2 performs referential-constraint checking, resulting from an UPDATE or DELETE action on a parent row, the access path to the child table will be determined dynamically at run time; and, if the delete rule is defined as RESTRICT, DB2 will stop scanning at first hit. There will be no need to rebind your programs when you add an index, if the sole purpose of the index is for RI checking.

What is partition-range scanning, and how do I take advantage of it?

Partition-range scanning provides data-page screening by only scanning the data partitions that qualify. It can access the data partitions that qualify through a non-partitioning index (NPI). Since DB2 OS/390 Version 5, partition scans for query parallelism can be enabled for both single-table access and joins. There is also support for LIKE and IN predicates, as well as for noncontiguous qualified partitions resulting from SQL using OR predicates.

The following pseudo-SQL example shows how you would code a query to take advantage of partition-range scanning. DB2 uses the partitioning index to determine which partitions need to be processed. In this case, that means partitions 2, 4, and 7. DB2 isolates only those partitions using the index tree. The index on COLUMN32 is an NPI. This index access is shown in the EXPLAIN output as INDEX ACCESS and PAGE RANGE SCAN. The index is used to determine where the COLUMN32 value is true. If parallelism is involved, these partitions can be processed in parallel. This technique allows a query to use an INDEX and process only a single partition.

```
SELECT ...COLUMNS,
FROM PARTITIONED_TABLE
WHERE (COLUMN1 BETWEEN 20000 AND 29999
OR COLUMN1 BETWEEN 40000 AND 49999
OR COLUMN1 BETWEEN 70000 AND 79999)
AND COLUMN32 BETWEEN '1997-01-01' AND '1997-05-12'
```

How do I optimize queries using correlation statistics, and when and how should I do this?

In DB2 OS/390 Version 5, key correlation statistics were introduced, providing DB2 the ability to gather statistics where one column's value is related to the value of another column. In previous releases, there were only the FIRSTKEYCARD and FULLKEYCARD columns with limited information, and the correlation was on columns for FULLKEYCARD only. This provided no second or third key cardinality, and multikey cardinality was considered independently, often leading to inaccurate estimation of filter

factors and inaccurate estimation of join size, join sequencing, and join methods, which resulted in inefficient access-path selection.

The new key correlation statistics are collected by RUNSTATS with minimal additional overhead, and could provide big CPU and elapsed-time reductions through improved cost and resources estimations. These key correlation statistics will play a major role in access-path selection by providing the optimizer new columns with information on multicolumn cardinalities and multicolumn frequent values. These new values used are in the catalog table and columns as follows:

Tables: SYSCOLDIST and SYSCOLDISTSTATS

Column: TYPE -- CHAR(1) NOT NULL DEFAULT 'F'
Type of statistic (cardinality or frequent value)

Column: CARDF -- FLOAT NOT NULL DEFAULT –1
Number of distinct values for column group

Column: COLGROUPCOLNO -- VARCHAR(254) NOT NULL WITH DEFAULT   Identifies the set of columns

Column: NUMCOLUMNS -- SMALLINT NOT NULL DEFAULT 1   The number of columns in the group

This new feature gives us the ability to specify the number of columns to collect statistics on (NUMCOLS) and to specify the number of values (COUNT). These new keywords are used in the RUNSTATS utility. The new KEYCARD parameter indicates that cardinalities for each column, concatenated with all previous key columns, are to be collected.

Using this RUNSTATS feature gives us the option to build the frequency values for critical concatenated key columns, such as the first and second columns, or maybe the first, second, and third columns.

For example, assume an index of state, city, and last name. Prior to Version 5, only the first key cardinality and full key cardinality were stored in the index, and the ratio of values between cities in New York State was not linear. There are many more New Yorkers in New York state than there are people from Utica. With that three-column index, the cardinality did not exist on only the first two columns. With the key correlation statistics, the first query following would probably result in a tablespace scan, possibly using page-range scanning, and the second query would probably result in index access. Without key correlation statistics, all DB2 can do is use the FIRSTKEYCARD or FULLKEYCARD column statistics, and it would probably use index access for both queries even though the first would be better as a tablespace scan, because more rows would qualify.

```
SELECT *
FROM USA
WHERE STATE = 'NY'
AND CITY = 'NEW YORK'

SELECT *
FROM USA
WHERE STATE = 'NY'
AND CITY = 'UTICA'
```

Is there a performance difference between a union and an outer join?

When using a union statement to code an outer join, the union will cause multiple passes of the tables whereas the outer join will not. If there are local predicates that need to be applied before the join, just use table expressions. Version 6 will change all this; but until then, use the table expressions for the local predicates and WHERE predicates for final filtering.

How can I improve the SQL performance of my distributed applications?

There are a few options for improving the performance of distributed applications. First of all, make use of all standard SQL performance tips and techniques. (See the other recommendations made in this section.) In addition to this, minimize the amount of data retrieved by the SQL statement

by using as much filtering criteria as possible (using WHERE, GROUP BY, and HAVING clauses). You would also want to minimize the number of parameter markers used because DB2 will be able to better execute the dynamic requests. Utilize the FOR FETCH ONLY or FOR READ ONLY options on the SQL statements to let DB2 take advantage of block fetch for optimizing data transfer between the server and the client.

How can I satisfy a query using only the index in DB2 UDB?

There is a new option on the CREATE INDEX statement that allows users to specify additional columns to be appended to the existing index-column keys. This new parameter, INCLUDE, will identify columns that are included in the index, but are not part of the unique key. The INCLUDE clause may only be specified if UNIQUE is specified; however, any columns included with this clause are not used to enforce uniqueness. The columns must be distinct from the columns used to enforce uniqueness.

The limits for the number of columns and sum of the length attributes apply to all of the columns in the unique key and in the index. A query will now be able to access only the index without having to make reference to the base table.

```
CREATE UNIQUE INDEX index-name
ON table-name(column-name)
    INCLUDE(column-name)
```

When should I use the DB2 OS/390 feature to provide DB2 with access-path hints?

DB2 Version 6 is introducing a feature called access-path hints, which is really a direct way of telling the optimizer what access path to use. This is a feature that should only be used in extreme cases. When the optimizer cannot pick a correct access path (and this is rare), the hint feature could be considered if all other techniques of SQL manipulation fail. A more appropriate place to use access-path hints is when a good access path has changed due to some change in the system.

 How can I force a partition-range scan of one partition of a tablespace with several partitions?

DB2 will not choose to use partition-range scanning for a single particular partition unless a second bogus predicate is added. This identical duplicate predicate must be ORed to the first predicate that specifies the clustering columns used to define the range. The following example shows how this is accomplished.

```
SELECT columns
FROM table
WHERE (clustering-index-column
    BETWEEN '1997-01-01' and '1997-02-01'
OR clustering-index-column
BETWEEN '1997-01-01' and '1997-02-01')
```

 When does DB2 choose access paths to account for referential integrity (RI) relationships?

DB2 optimizes access paths to account for RI relationships at execution time. The access paths chosen do not show up in EXPLAIN output, nor can they be determined by a trace. Because of this, you do not know what indexes are used for access to these tables, or if an index was used at all.

 Is there a performance disadvantage to using nulls in a query?

There is some overhead when retrieving nullable columns. Each null indicator that is returned does require additional code in DB2 and in the data transfer. There is extra processing in the application to check the null indicator variable. This is additional code length, which if used for a large result set, can be measurable. But there are other reasons to avoid nulls, except when they are absolutely required. There is a specific SQL syntax required to filter result sets for nulls:

```
WHERE COLUMN IS NULL
```

The null indicator testing that is required in the application code is not obvious and is often overlooked, which causes problems. This is especially true in COBOL programs on OS/390, since in normal use the field does not get cleared when a null value is returned for the column. If this is not the first select query, the field actually still contains the data from the previous select. There is also the one-byte overhead for each column that is nullable, and if there are several such columns and the table is large, this could be something to avoid. And finally, there is the hotly debated logic problem: the three-valued problem of true, false, and null. If something is null, is it true or false? Nulls cause problems with some of the newer SQL constructs, such as the CASE expression, if used for the primary test and certain aggregations. If performance is viewed as not only resource consumption but also the time and effort to find problems caused by using nulls, and the time spent in development, then there is a performance disadvantage to using nulls.

However, nulls do have their place in certain situations in which a default value would have no meaning.

Chapter 17

Backup and Recovery

Answer Topics!

Backup and Recovery @ a Glance

This chapter deals with some of the most common questions and problems encountered during the backup and recovery process. To ensure that your data is recoverable in the event of a failure, you must make backups on a regularly scheduled basis on both DB2 system objects and your application objects. The consistent base you establish for recovery must include all related objects that need to be in sync after a recovery is performed, and to accomplish this, the backups must be done in a timely and consistent manner. When designing your backup plan, several other things must be considered, such as image copy types (full or incremental), copy utility options, whether or not to use DSN1COPY, and the frequency and retention of image copies.

There are several types of errors that can occur in DB2, including subsystem loss, database object loss, and structure damage. Other types of failures outside of DB2 can cause a recovery to be necessary in DB2. The most common failures are application failures resulting in the need to back out changes in a particular unit of work. There are several utilities used in the backup and recovery process for the various failure scenarios, as well as utilities to help during the process of finding and diagnosing errors.

Although the concepts of backup and recovery are very much alike for both DB2 OS/390 and DB2 UDB, there are a few special UDB scenarios and features that will be discussed in this chapter. These will include such items as logging options, trigger usage, and obtaining recovery information.

GENERAL INFORMATION

What DB2 documentation should I read for backup and recovery information?

The IBM DB2 Administration Guide contains a detailed chapter on the backup and recovery processes. It is also important to have a full understanding of this chapter in order to successfully implement a backup and recovery process. Be sure to read material specific to your release of DB2, as changes in utilities involved with the backup and recovery process often occur between releases. Using material from a prior release of DB2 could result in incomplete or invalid recovery scenarios.

Does DB2 have a rollback in its recovery?

The only rollback that DB2 can perform is on a unit of work. Once a unit of work is committed, it cannot be rolled back in time. The best example of a unit of work that can't be rolled back is a mass delete that will only update the segment table (which is the only thing logged). In such a case, the data no longer exists and changes cannot be rolled back. The only information the log contains is the single update to the segment table; the freed segments can be reused by subsequent updates on the log.

What do checkpoints and recovery have to do with each other?

DB2 checkpoints and recovery are not related. Some people think that DB2 checkpoints are used in recovery also, but this is not true. The DB2 checkpoints are used by DB2 as a starting point when restarting a DB2 subsystem. For recovery, the checkpoint records are not used during the log apply process, and they are skipped.

What information is contained in the DB2 logs in regards to recovery processing?

There are two types of DB2 logs: active and archive. These log datasets contain all of the required information for recovery of the DB2 subsystem and database objects, as well as information required to recover from program execution

with incorrect results. The primary purpose of the active log is to record all changes (inserts, updates, and deletes) made to DB2 tables and indexes. The DML statements are recorded in the log as follows:

- Inserts: entire after image of the records is logged for redo processing
- Deletes: the before image is recorded for undo processing
- Updates: the before and after images are recorded for undo/redo processing

For more details on how the Data Manipulation Language (DML) changes are recorded in the log, refer to Chapter 6.

The active log records are written (offloaded) to an archive log when the datasets are full. DB2 can also use a dual logging mechanism to ensure there are two copies of the active log datasets; in the event that one is lost, the other can be used for recovery. During a recovery, DB2 applies the changes from the active log that are required to recover to the specified point in time. If the records needed to recover are not on the active log any longer, DB2 will call for the appropriate archive log(s).

The archive logs are the datasets to which the active log records are offloaded, and they can either reside on DASD or on tape. During the recovery process, it will take less time if the archives are on DASD.

 ## What recovery information is contained in the BSDS?

The BSDS (bootstrap dataset) is a VSAM dataset that contains information regarding the DB2 logs and the records contained in those logs. All of the current active log datasets are recorded in the BSDS during DB2 installation. When each new archive log is dynamically allocated during the offload process of the active log, the dataset name is then recorded in the BSDS, and a copy of the BSDS is also placed on the same volume as the archive log. During a recovery, DB2 will use the BSDS to find all of the available archive logs. The number of records that the BSDS can contain is determined by the MAXARCH DSNZPARM. You should have this number set high enough so that in the event of a recovery where you may have to go back through older

archive logs, these log datasets will still be recorded in the BSDS. If the dataset is not still recorded in the BSDS, but is physically available, you can place its entry in the BSDS by using the change log inventory utility (DSNJU003). However, this will require a recycling of the DB2 subsystem. The proper setting for the MAXARCH parameter will depend on how large your archive logs are and the oldest point in time an application is allowed to recover to.

BACKUP PROCESSING

 ## How frequently should I take image copies of my tablespaces?

The frequency with which image copies should be taken depends on the allowable downtime for the primary user of the application. This means that you should determine the clock-time needed if you have to recover your data. If an application cannot be unavailable for more than two hours, you will need to take image copies more frequently than if your application can be unavailable for a complete day. Also, depending on the currency of data required in a recovery, you will have to determine when image copies can be taken and what types of image copies need to be taken. You may need to have incremental image copies taken throughout the day, or you may only have to do one full copy at the end of the day's processing (during an available batch window).

There are also a number of technical considerations in image copy frequency. The bare minimum you should allow is half the retention period of the archive log, less one day ([retention period / 2] − 1 day). This will guarantee that at any moment there are two valid image copies of the tablespaces. You always want two valid copies because of possible media failure, or to reduce the risk of inconsistent data on the image copy. Remember that after a drop and re-create, all system retained image copy information is gone, so you also need dual image copies in case of problems with the first one. The same applies to utilities that will re-create the data (REORG, LOAD REPLACE) without the LOG YES option.

Should I make an image copy to cartridge or DASD?

The fastest recoveries occur when the input datasets reside on DASD. This applies both to recoveries using image copies and archive logs. However, since DASD space is more expensive then cartridges, there is a trade-off between the cost of an unavailable application versus the cost of DASD space. Remember that mounting and winding cartridges can take a very long time. If you use the cartridge method and stack the files, you should use the proper JCL options during image copy and recovery so that the cartridge stays mounted and positioned (see "Should I stack my image copies on cartridge?" later in this section).

Can I use the DF/HSM migration to migrate my image copy datasets?

Use the DF/HSM migration for image copies only if the clock-time for recovery is not crucial. This option will work, but you will need to wait for the recall of the image copy dataset, if the dataset is migrated. Some vendor software will do a mass recall for you before the recovery starts. DF/HSM will optimize the recall process in such cases. The standard recovery utility will recall one dataset ahead during execution, and therefore the recalls will not be optimized.

Caution: *Remember that if DF/HSM is reorganizing its datasets, you cannot recall the datasets! This means that there are moments when you cannot recover. Be careful!*

How many image copy versions should I keep?

The minimum number of full image copies you should keep is two. This is because if there are errors in your data (logical damage to the tablespace structure), you can go back in time and find, hopefully, that this error doesn't exist on the previous image copy. Physical damage to an image copy would then not be a problem because the dual copies taken of the same data would provide a backup. The more full image copies you have, the further back in time you can recover. The recovery time needed to recover from such old image

copies can be astronomical, but it can be your lifesaver. Remember, though, that you always need the DB2 log in order to roll forward. If the archive logs do not exist anymore, the only use you can make of old image copies is a RECOVER TOCOPY, because you will not have the logs necessary to complete the recovery from the old image copy.

However, under normal circumstances the retention period (the period of time you keep data) should never be longer than the retention period of the archive log.

Incremental image copies are based on full image copies and cannot be used without an initial full copy available. Therefore, incremental copies should never be kept longer than full copies. A common problem many database administrators experience is keeping SYSCOPY, the ICF catalog, and the tape management system in sync. Normally, tape management system procedures remove expired tapes or cartridges from the ICF catalog. However, cleaning SYSCOPY is up to you. (For information on this topic, refer to Chapter 4.)

Caution: *You should take some special care if you use a job scheduler and have advanced restart procedures or software in place. Sometimes these procedures will remove datasets from the ICF catalogs during restart, or return cartridges that were used in the original job to the scratch pool.*

When do I take an image copy of my catalog/ directory?

Because you start a DB2 systemwide recovery by first recovering the catalog and directory, and no other recoveries are possible before this process is completed, the catalog and directory need to be image-copied often, so that the recovery process for these objects is as fast as possible. Also, if you loose your catalog and/or directory, you will not have an operational DB2 subsystem.

The time required for the recovery of the catalog and directory are crucial and needs to be kept to a minimum. Because DB2 performs the log apply for the catalog and directory, it does not matter when you take the image copy of the catalog. However, it helps if you take a share-level reference image copy just before you cut your last archive,

and take both this image and the archive logs to the vault or offsite. This way you make sure that the DB2 catalog contains all updates and that it is also valuable without the archive logs.

It is also important that the ICF catalog be kept in sync with your DB2 catalog. For example, if the ICF catalog has yesterday's image in a disaster recovery scenario, your DB2 catalog will reference datasets (such as image copies and/or tablespaces) that do not exist, according to the ICF catalog. To avoid this problem, make sure that the recovery procedures of the ICF catalog match the DB2 catalog.

When are incremental image copies useful?

Incremental copies of your data are always useful, and because the procedures involved in taking incremental copies are more complex than those for full image copies (for example, how often to take incremental copies, and when to run the Merge Copy utility), many database administrators choose only to take full image copies.

There is also a slight danger of losing data with incremental image copies, in that incremental copies are a possible substitute for the log. DB2 will try to mount the incrementals to skip large parts of the log during the log apply phase. But if, for whatever reason, this fails, DB2 notes the RBA or LOGPOINT of the last successful incremental and uses archive log from that point on.

Some administrators use the incremental copy utility for its speed, and then run the MERGECOPY utility to merge the last full copy and latest incremental into a new full copy. This procedure combines the best of both worlds: ease of recovery and the speed of incremental image copies.

Caution: *You don't want to use incremental copies if the data is very volatile and has more than 15 percent of the pages updated between copies. Starting from Version 5 of DB2, the image copy utility has parameters to switch from incremental to full image copies through the use of the user-defined thresholds. You can use the thresholds in the image-copy utility to control subsequent steps, depending on whether an incremental copy or a full copy was done.*

 Should I stack my image copies on cartridge?

Stacking image copies on a cartridge means that you write multiple, sequential files to a tape or cartridge—you could say that the files are *stacked* on each other. This procedure is probably a good idea for image copies, since tape mounting, dismounting (including rewinding), and possible tape silo handling can take a great deal of time during recoveries. Stacking the files will not require as many mounts, because a tape would only need to be mounted once.

Also, cartridges are expensive, and if you use only a small percentage of each one, you'll have to put many cartridges into use to store your files. A possible limitation can also be involved when storing tapes in a tape silo that can only hold a "limited" number of volumes (*volume* is the OS/390 MVS term for one physical cartridge). Some system administrators are surprised at how fast they run out of volumes in a silo. Optimizing your cartridge usage is key, but do not span volumes, because the JCL becomes complex, and finding the correct file can take a very long time.

You need to take extra care during recovery so that the tape does not get (re)wound continuously and/or dismounted. You can do this by putting the recovery statements in the same order as they are on tape, and preallocate the files in the JCL. For example:

```
//SYS00001  DD  DSN=IMAGE.COPY.TS01,UNIT=CART,
//  DISP=SHR,VOL=(,RETAIN,,,SER=012345),LABEL=(1,SL)
//SYS00002  DD  DSN=IMAGE.COPY.TS02,UNIT=CART,
//  DISP=SHR,VOL=(,RETAIN,,,SER=012345),LABEL=(2,SL)
//SYS00003  DD  DSN=IMAGE.COPY.TS03,UNIT=CART,
//  DISP=SHR,VOL=(,RETAIN,,,SER=012345),LABEL=(3,SL)
etc.
```

In general, you could say that you will have to spend some time on creating the statements and JCL for recovery, but the time required more than pays for itself during a recovery. Recoveries that are not optimized can spend over 70 percent of the total recovery time on media handling. There is ISV software (JCL generators, and replacements for the recovery utility) that does optimizing and that will create the best possible recovery.

 ## Can I use Generation Dataset Groups (GDGs) for image copies?

Generation Dataset Group, or GDG, is an OS/390 concept in which the same dataset exists multiple times. The operating system adds a version number to the dataset and keeps track of the versions. You can use GDGs for image copies, but you have to be extremely careful because GDGs can have some strange behavior.

First of all, GDG datasets are catalogued at job termination time and not at step termination time, the latter being normal. This means that if a job doesn't go through job termination, all GDG datasets from previous steps are not cataloged, but DB2 still records them in the SYSCOPY table as already being cataloged. Not only does this mean that a polluted SYSCOPY exists, but restarts can also fail because the utility process can encounter duplicate datasets on disk. (Tapes and cartridges normally do not have this problem. Most tape management systems will return tapes and cartridges to the scratch pool when a job fails.)

Also, job schedulers often use complex procedures during job restarting (such as adjusting the GDG version numbers) and DB2 is unaware of these changes. If you are not very experienced with the GDG concept, you may need to get help from a system administrator with knowledge of how GDGs are handled in your environment; if you have a job scheduler with restarting procedures, be careful.

 ## How do I know that an image copy is usable?

The image copy that you create does not check, in detail, the logical integrity of a tablespace it is copying. There is an IBM service aid utility delivered with DB2 called DSN1COPY. The DSN1COPY program has a CHECK option that does some verification on image copies, though it does have some limitations. For instance, it does not check for errors across pages (segment table to segments, off-page rows, etc.). ISV vendors have created software that does full checking during the copy itself.

 How can I speed up the image copy process?

Here are some options you can use to speed up the image copy process:

- Give the utility as much memory as possible, by setting the region parameter (as follows) so that the utility optimizes the number of BSAM buffers:

  `REGION=0M`

- Create image copies on DASD—some SMS (System Managed Storage) options and hardware options can help to speed up the process even more
- Use incremental image copies whenever applicable
- If files are stacked on cartridge, use the correct JCL options so the tape stays positioned.
- Use the standard (BUFNO) parameter on the utility JCL (for example, `BUFNO=50`) for the image copy files. Note that each defined buffer increases the storage required.

Tip: If you are using DB2 Version 3, the BUFNO option default is 8 buffers; for DB2 Version 4, the BUFNO option default is 20 buffers. In DB2 Version 5, if SMS is being used, a calculation considering SMS options is performed with the BUFNO option defaulting to a minimum 20.

- If you using an earlier release of DB2 (Version 3 or older), consider upgrading to Version 4 or higher. Starting in Version 4, DB2 does not turn off the dirty bit in every modified page, which speeds up the image copy process significantly.
- Using compression on the tablespace will result in fewer pages to be copied because DB2 does not decompress the data for the image copy utility.

Caution: Remember that compression is not always the best option because queries and other utilities might take longer to run and may not actually save you any time.

What share level option (SHRLEVEL) should I specify for my image copies?

Most DB2 utilities have a keyword called share level, or SHRLEVEL, as it is abbreviated in the utilities. The share level option controls if and how other programs can access the tablespace. If you plan to use the RECOVER TOCOPY option, you should use SHRLEVEL REFERENCE because it is the only valid input for such a recovery.

In all other cases you can use SHRLEVEL CHANGE. If you're using DB2 Version 5, and if space availability is an issue, you can use the inline copies option on a concurrent reorg. This way, you create a SHRLEVEL REFERENCE copy with minimal unavailability.

Should I use the QUIESCE utility before and/or after an image copy is taken?

The QUIESCE is a utility that will drain all activity on a tablespace. If there is no activity any more—that is, if the tablespace is quiesced—DB2 will flush all buffered data that still has to be written, and then it will record the position of the log (RBA—relative byte address) in SYSCOPY for this tablespace.

There are several reasons to perform a quiesce of a tablespace before and/or after an image copy. The main reason to use this utility before an image copy is made is that with a SHRLEVEL REFERENCE image copy, you want to flush as much data as possible from the bufferpool to the tablespace. By doing so, the log apply during a recovery will be minimal. The primary reason to use this utility after an image copy is made is to maintain the synchronization of all related data by establishing a log point (RBA) for recovery of both DB2-defined RI (referential integrity) relationships and application-defined relationships.

 Caution: *Make sure that all tablespaces that are part of a DB2-defined referential integrity chain, or that are logically related, are quiesced in the same statement—otherwise the quiesce will be useless.*

 Do I need dual image copies?

Yes, it is strongly advised that you create dual image copies. If there is an error on the primary image copy and there is no secondary copy of your data to rely on, then the recovery will fail. Even when it is possible to fall back to a previous image copy, substantial time is needed to perform the log apply from the previous image to where the failed image copy was taken. A previous image copy should be regarded as a safety net, in case there are errors in the pages. By uncataloging the most current image copy, you can force a fallback. This, of course, only works if you catalog your image copies (which is a very good idea, in general).

In addition to using dual copies, it is ideal to make two sets of copies so that there are two copies onsite and two copies offsite. Using just the second copy of a dual copies for offsite backup is not the best choice, because if your onsite copy is bad, then obtaining the offsite copy after a failure may be inconvenient, depending on where your offsite disaster recovery location is. Keeping two copies on the primary site will ensure that you have an immediate backup to use if a copy is bad; the same concept applies when recovering from image copies at the disaster recovery site, where two copies should also be maintained.

Note: *Recovery site copies should not be considered to take the place of dual copies because they are not immediately usable. You will have to specify the RECOVERYSITE keyword in the recovery utility if you need to be able to use them. Also, remember that these image copies will not be available for immediate use if they are at the remote recovery site.*

 Can I restart image copies that failed?

Yes, the image copy process can be restarted. However, remember there are a number of JCL complications, such as UNIT=AFF and label processing. Most people who use stacked tapes or cartridges prefer to rerun the job completely rather than to restart the image copy process.

Tip: *If you do restart the image copy process, don't forget to terminate the "executing" utility before you resubmit the job by issuing the* -TERM UTILITY *command with the appropriate corresponding utility ID.*

An extra complication of restarting an image copy is that your GDG datasets may not be cataloged. If the failing job didn't go though job termination, these datasets are not recorded in the ICF catalog, so they exist in SYSCOPY but not in the ICF catalog. This situation gets worse if the image copy datasets reside on disk; if the rerun you specify encounters the duplicate datasets on disk, the utility will fail. This is a prime example of why GDG datasets are mainly popular for use with stacked file cartridges.

Also, if you are going to restart an image copy, be careful when you use job schedulers and tape management systems. Job schedulers can sometimes scratch datasets when you restart, and tape management systems sometimes free volumes or change the retention period of datasets when jobs fail. You can use a special dataset naming pattern to alter this behavior.

Should I use the DB2 recovery site option on my image copy?

The recovery site option is a feature of DB2 that can be used for an offsite recovery scenario. All image copies that are created for a recovery site using the RECOVERYDDN option should be transported as quickly as possible to the other computer site (the recovery site) so they are as current as possible in the event of a needed remote recovery.

These image copies can normally not be used by DB2 unless DB2 is in recovery mode or you specify the RECOVERYSITE keyword in the recovery (available in DB2 Version 4 and higher). When DB2 is in recovery mode, it will use all the image copies intended for the recovery site. Using the recovery site option requires complete planning for offsite scenarios, although setting up an offsite scenario is not essential.

 ## When do I need to use the MERGECOPY utility?

The MERGECOPY utility can merge a full copy and one or more incrementals to create a new full copy, or merge one or more incremental copies into one incremental. Remember that during a recovery the RECOVER utility will attempt to use the last full copy plus all necessary incrementals to complete the recovery to the specified point in time.

If this fails, the recovery will fail or it will fall back to log processing, which can take enormous amounts of time, depending on the number of log records required to complete the recovery. DB2 may also need tape drives to be available in order to allocate any archive logs that exist on tape or cartridge. During recovery you can easily run out of available tape drives. Using the MERGECOPY utility to limit the number of incremental image copies necessary for a recovery can help in this situation.

! ***Caution:*** *The MERGECOPY utility cannot merge image copies that are from different share levels. It also allocates all copies at the same time (like the RECOVER utility). So, if you create more incrementals than you have tape drives, you will have a problem.*

 ## How can a tablespace get into copy pending status when no updates have been performed?

DB2 keeps a record of every activity performed against a tablespace in the SYSCOPY table (which stores information about utilities performed), SYSLGRNGX table (which records log ranges that contain updates to the tablespace), and the BSDS (which records the existence of archive logs). It is possible, especially with the -START DATABASE () ACCESS(FORCE) command, to disrupt DB2's recording mechanism.

Consider the following scenario: You perform a LOAD utility with the LOG NO option, which means that DB2 does not log every row you load. However, there still are some changes occurring to the physical structure, which are logged by DB2. This would result in only SYSLGRNGX knowing

about changes to the tablespace. After the utility execution, you force the tablespace into read/write (RW) mode by issuing a -START DATABASE () ACCESS(FORCE) command. DB2 would not be aware of the last archive that contains updates (the load) of this tablespace. DB2 will then redetect a non-recoverability and force the tablespace to an image copy pending status.

> **Caution:** *Only issue the* -START DATABASE () ACCESS(FORCE) *command if you are a very experienced database administrator or systems programmer.*

Is a recovery site image copy usable on the local site?

Yes, you can use a recovery site image copy at the local site, starting with DB2 Version 3. This is controlled by the recovery process using the LOCALSITE and RECOVERYSITE keywords in the RECOVER utility.

Can I use hardware compression on image copies?

Yes, you can use hardware compression on image copies, but be careful that under all circumstances you are able to read the media again during a recovery.

> **Caution:** *Many people used special hardware options and found that in their offsite scenario they didn't have the proper devices to read their image copies, and so could not complete the offsite recovery.*

Is there a way to create an incremental or full copy depending on change activity?

If you are using DB2 Version 5, there is a new keyword called CHANGELIMIT used by the image copy utility. This new feature allows you to specify a threshold for determining when an image copy will be taken, depending on the volatility of the data. For example, you can specify that an incremental image copy be taken if no more than 20 percent of the data has been changed.

✛ ***Tip:*** *If you use this CHANGELIMIT option along with the REPORTONLY option (also new in Version 5, allowing only a report to be returned from the utility without the copy being physically taken), you can view whether a full or incremental copy will be needed during the image copy execution based on the specified CHANGELIMIT, and this may help determine if there is time enough to perform the necessary image copy. Also, another use for the combination of the CHANGELIMIT option and the REPORTONLY option is auditing. This provides a quick way to view if any changes have occurred against a table.*

Why do I need an image copy after executing a utility with the LOG NO option?

If you specify the LOG NO option in a utility (REORG or LOAD for example), DB2 does not log changes to the data, but the utility will still be modifying the data (a reorg will move rows from one page to another, or a load will add or replace data). Since DB2's recovery mechanism is a roll-forward process, whereby it restores an image copy and applies the log to the data, if it picks up the log used after a LOG NO utility, the logged data will not match the current data structure. To prevent this, DB2 sets the Image Copy Pending flag to force you to create a new starting recovery point—this is the newly required image copy. You should not avoid making the new image copy by using the REPAIR utility with the SET NOCOPYPEND option, or even worse using the `-START DATABASE () ACCESS(FORCE)` command. For information on the implications of using the REPAIR utility to perform such an action, refer to Chapter 8 and to the next question.

How do I resolve an image copy pending situation?

If you execute a LOAD or REORG utility using the LOG NO option, or the utility detects a non-recoverable situation, the Image Copy Pending flag will be set. You can turn this flag off by executing the copy utility, by executing the REPAIR utility using the SET NOCOPYPEND keyword, or by executing the `-START DATABASE () ACCESS(FORCE)` command. Using an option other than taking an image copy can lead to unrecoverable data. Actually you should never use the −START DATABASE () ACCESS(FORCE) command unless you are not concerned about the recoverability of the data. This command forces a tablespace into read/write mode, no matter what state the data is in. You could easily bypass other conditions as well (like check pending) and create inconsistent data. By executing the REPAIR SET NOCOPYPEND, you tell DB2 that you accept a non-recoverable situation or a non-DB2-controlled recovery scenario.

Caution: *Every release adds more safeguards to ensure data integrity. Many non-DB2-controlled recovery scenarios will not work or will have to be changed in the future.*

What are inline copies?

Inline copies, introduced in Version 5, are simply image copies that are taken during another maintenance process or utility, such as during a REORG. An inline copy starts as a share-level change (fuzzy) incremental image copy, but at the end of the utility process, it contains the pages that were updated during the execution of the utility containing the inline copy.

The same changed pages can occur multiple times at the end of the incremental copy; the recovery process will overlay all these multiple images of the same page during execution. The last image is a consistent one, so in effect the inline copy is a share-level reference copy. That is also how they are recorded in the SYSCOPY table.

RECOVERY PROCESSING

Do I always need a quiesce point to do a point in time (PIT) recovery?

If the tablespace you are recovering is part of a DB2-defined referential integrity (RI) chain or application-enforce relationship, you must recover all related tablespaces to the same quiesce point. Otherwise DB2 will put the tablespaces (using DB2 defined RI) in the CHECK PENDING status, and you will have to run the CHECK utility. Application-enforce relationships could potentially get out of sync.

You could choose an arbitrary point in time, and run the DSN1LOGP service aid to verify that there were no units of work active that involved any of the tablespaces in the RI chain. If the log shows no units of work active and you can use this point in time to recover, you still will get the CHECK PENDING condition, but you can turn it off by executing a `REPAIR SET NOCHECKPEND`.

Caution: *This is not an IBM-supported scenario, and can only be done by experienced users.*

How do I know which resources are needed for a recovery?

You can get a listing of all resources needed for a recovery by using the REPORT utility. This utility will show you all of the image copies (full and incremental) and all archive logs needed by the RECOVERY utility. The REPORT utility is not very popular because its output is not very easy to read (especially for new users). Some ISV recovery tools have their own report options.

How do I synchronize the DB2 catalog with the ICF catalog?

If you catalog your image copies, you become very dependent on the ICF (Integrated Catalog Facility) catalog. It is best to have one ICF catalog per DB2 subsystem that records the physical objects used by DB2 (tablespaces and indexspaces) and the non-VSAM dataset related to this DB2 system. If you image copy your SYSCOPY, you should *always* dump the related ICF catalog(s), too; otherwise it is possible to lose entries during a disaster recovery. Updates to user catalogs should be logged on SMF (System Management Facility) datasets and recovered separately. The SMF offload data should be handled in the same manner as archive logs. Recovering the ICF catalog is difficult and should only be performed by system specialists.

> ! **Caution:** *Many people have good procedures for their DB2 subsystems, but forget that the ICF catalog is also critical.*

How do I ensure synchronization of system objects with application objects during a total system recovery?

In the event of an offsite disaster recovery scenario, the active logs will be lost, meaning that you cannot recover your catalog and directory up to the moment of error but only to a prior point in time before the disaster. If this time difference is very significant, it is possible you may lose entries in SYSCOPY needed for application recovery. You should always attempt to create all application image copies first, and then your system object image copy.

If you frequently create application image copies, regardless of whether or not they are scheduled, you should also frequently take system-object image copies. The system-object image copies are very important. These image copies should be kept with the archive logs, and be transported as soon as possible to the vault or offsite building to ensure that the most current copy of the system objects is available for a recovery.

How do I select a proper point of consistency (POC) for my recovery?

Any type of recovery, other than a recovery to the end of the log or a quiesce point, will result in DB2 enforced RI checks (setting the check pending flag). If you need to do a point in time recovery, and do not want to do the RI checks, you can dump the log (using DSN1LOGP) and then find a point in the log that is near the point in time where there was no unit of work active on the objects in the RI chain. This point would be a valid point in time to recover to, and you could then safely turn off the check pending flags using the REPAIR utility, after you have finished the recovery.

Other valid points in time are starting or ending points of utilities. Refer to the chapter on backup and recovery in the IBM DB2 Administration Guide for details.

 ## Are disk dumps usable for database recoveries?

Yes, disk dumps can be used for database recoveries; however, you should not use them for your standard DB2 recovery procedure because disk dumps require that DB2 be unavailable. If the disk dump was taken with DB2 executing, you can restore one or more tablespaces from the disk dump and use the RECOVER log apply feature to bring the tablespace to its current state or to a point in time that you like. The only problem is setting the starting point for the log apply. It should be before the start of any unit of work active at the time the disk dump was taken, so all updates are applied. You could think of the disk dump as a share-level change copy created without DB2's knowledge.

 Caution: *If you run DB2 Version 5 and downlevel detection is on (DLDFREQ DSNZPARM), this scenario does not work. DB2 will detect that the tablespace that comes online (gets started) to do the log apply is not in the same state as DB2 left it in (a downlevel has been detected). The tablespace will be rejected and cannot be started.*

 ## How do I deal with referential integrity (RI) in recoveries?

RI-related tables should always be recovered to the point in time where there is no activity on the related tables (better known as quiesce points) or to the end of the log. Recovering to any point in time will force DB2 to set check pending flags on the related tablespaces. Make sure that you include all tablespaces in the RI chain in your QUIESCE utility. It will not protest if you forget one, but if you do, RECOVER will set the check pending condition.

 Tip: *You can find the RI-related tables / tablespaces using the REPORT utility.*

 ## Can I predict my recovery clock-time?

Yes, you can predict the clock-time required for a DB2 recovery, but you have to accept that the answer has a rather

large margin of error (30 percent or more is not unusual). However, you can get a good estimate or average (whether the recovery will take 30 minutes, 60 minutes, 120 minutes, and so on). A formula that has worked for many database administrators is as follows:

$$0.7D + 0.1C + 6V + 0.15D + 2X$$

where:

D = Gigabytes of data in the tablespace
C = Number of archive logs to be processed
V = Number (in millions) of updates to this data on the archives
X = Gigabytes of indexspace

In the formula, 0.7D is for the restore of the data from the image copies, 0.1C is for reading the archive logs (200MB archives, reduce if archive logs are smaller), 6V is for the random log apply, 0.15D is for scanning the data for index keys, and 2X is for the sort and index build. The result is in hours (multiply everything by 60 to get minutes).

This formula assumes that all data required for the recovery is immediately available. Normally this is not true. Archive and image copies often are on tape or cartridge. An average mount of these media normally takes between 30 seconds and 2 minutes (unfortunately, silos are much faster than operators). Positioning the media (winding) can take also take up to 2 minutes.

For example, the calculation of estimated clock-time for restoring a system with the following specifications is given in Table 1.

● 13 segmented tablespaces with a total of 130,000 pages totaling 0.5GB

● Indexspaces totaling 0.4GB

● 13 archive logs (size 85MB/log)

● 270,000 updates done over these 13 archives

Restore Step	Time Calculation	Time
Restore	0.7 * 0.5 * 60	21 minutes
Log read	0.1 * (85/200) * 13 * 60	33 minutes
Log apply	6 * 0.27 *60	97 minutes
Index scan	0.15 * 0.5 * 60	5 minutes
Index build	2 * 0.4 * 60	48 minutes
Total		204 minutes (3.4 hours)

Table 17-1   Calculation of Restore Clock-Time

You can see where the margin of error comes from. Can you mount and read 13 archives in 33 minutes? Probably not! If the log apply is not totally random, it takes less than 97 minutes (perhaps 65 minutes). The idea is to get an estimate—this particular recovery could not occur in 1 hour, and even 3.4 hours is unlikely, since 13 archives can probably not be processed in 33 minutes.

 Note: *This formula will work for DB2 Versions 3, 4, and 5. DB2 Version 6 introduces a much better and faster recovery procedure, and the formula will need adjustment.*

 ## When do I need the DSN1CHKR service aid utility?

The DSN1CHKR program is a service aid utility that verifies the integrity of the DB2 catalog and directory. It cannot verify SYSUTILX and SYSLGRNGX. It works directly on the tablespaces and can only be run if DB2 is unavailable. Also, in a complex environment it can use a great deal of CPU and I/O. Due to its demands and limitations, it is not a very popular program, and many database administrators do not use it very often, if at all (though, it is required during a subsystem release migration).

Despite the drawbacks, it is still a good practice to run DSN1CHKR on a regular basis—once every month or every few months is a good idea. It is especially good practice to run this service aid just before you upgrade your software (before you apply fixes). This can prove that subsequent errors did not exist before installing the new software. If DSN1CHKR finds error(s), you generally need help from IBM to diagnose the problem.

If DB2 cannot be down long enough to run DSN1CHKR, consider using DSN1COPY to create a "shadow catalog" and run DSN1CHKR on this shadow. You can also use a DSN1COPY share-level reference copy of the catalog as input, but in this case DB2 does have to be brought down. Some ISV image copy utilities provide the same functionality as DSN1CHKR at minimal overhead, and the check is done at every image copy of the catalog/directory.

How can I use DSN1COPY for detecting page errors?

Remember that all programs that start with DSN1 are so-called service aids, and are not guaranteed to be fully compliant with the current level of your software. Their purpose is to be a helpful tool for the system programmer or system administrator. This means that you should not use these service aids in normal procedures. Of course DSN1COPY has value (for example, with dropped tablespaces).

There is one special case of using DSN1COPY. If you use this service aid with the CHECK option, it can verify that the input (tablespace or image copy) does not contain errors. Keep in mind that the CHECK option cannot verify intrapage errors (for example, if the segment table in the space map claims that segment x belongs to table y (using OBIDs), the CHECK option cannot verify whether this is true). Also, DSN1COPY will only detect one error at a time per page, and fixing one error can result in other errors. Many ISV image copy utilities have built-in support for page verification (including intrapage and special hash checks for the catalog, as found in the DSN1CHKR program).

How do I find the earliest roll-forward recovery time for a tablespace in DB2 UDB?

The earliest point in time that a tablespace can be recovered to is any point in time after the last tablespace backup. To find the earliest point in time that can be used, the recovery history file can be queried using the LIST HISTORY command (Figure 17-1), or the LIST TABLESPACES SHOW DETAIL command.

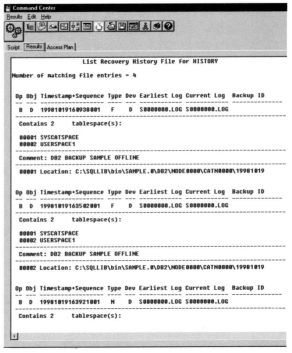

Figure 17-1 LIST HISTORY to show earliest forward recovery time

SPECIAL RECOVERY SCENARIOS

Can I recover my catalog/directory to a prior point in time?

No, you should *never* recover your catalog/directory to a prior point in time. This is a very dangerous process that might result in loss of data or inconsistent data. Also, in full system recovery it is not possible to recover the catalog/directory to a point further back in time than one or more of the application tablespaces.

Can I recover a dropped tablespace?

No, there is no official way to recover a dropped tablespace. But there are ISV tools that will help you recreate a dropped tablespace. When using tablespaces defined using STOGROUPS, DB2 cleans all related data regarding the tablespace, including the underlying VSAM dataset, when the tablespace is dropped. However, if a tablespace is user defined, DB2 will clean the catalog information but leave the tablespace on disk. You can attempt a manual recovery of a dropped tablespace, but this is not an easy process and can only be performed by database administrators who have knowledge of DB2.

You would need the following resources and information to perform a recovery:

- the last full share-level reference image copy
- the DDL (Data Definition Language) CREATE statements of the tablespace, tables, and indexes
- the old OBIDs (Object IDs—hex numbers that DB2 uses to identify objects)

To perform the recovery, you would have to follow these steps:

1. Recreate the tablespace, including tables and indexes.

2. Look in the DB2 catalog to determine what the new OBIDs are.

3. Create an OBIDXLAT (OBID Translation) table for the DSN1COPY service aid.

4. Execute DSN1COPY, using the OBIDXLAT option, filling in the appropriate OBIDs for the new objects, so that these IDs reflect the dropped objects.

5. Use the RECOVER utility to recover (or in Version 6, rebuild) the corresponding indexes.

There are a number of problems with this approach, however. First you need to know the old OBIDs—you would have to have saved them after (re)creating the table. Second, there might be more involved, such as RI chains, plans/packages, and so on. And last, but not least, all original updates made after the time of this copy are lost, because you cannot use a log apply with a DSN1COPY.

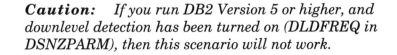 **Caution:** *If you run DB2 Version 5 or higher, and downlevel detection has been turned on (DLDFREQ in DSNZPARM), then this scenario will not work.*

 Tip: *If you don't know the old OBIDs, and the tablespace is segmented, you might find them by looking at the segment table in a formatted print of the space map (using the DSN1PRNT service aid). By printing some pages of every table, you might recognize which OBID is which table (look at the row length, for example).*

 Tip: *DB2 Version 4 introduced the WITH RESTRICT ON DROP option of the CREATE TABLE statement. This option should prevent accidental drops of tables/tablespaces or databases. See the IBM DB2 SQL Reference manual for more details.*

Is there a way to recover an image copy on another DB2 subsystem?

Yes, you can recover an image copy on another DB2 subsystem; however, this is a very complicated process and should only be attempted by an experienced database administrator. This process requires the use of the DSN1COPY service aid with the OBIDXLAT and RESET options in order to copy an image copy from one DB2 subsystem to another DB2 subsystem. In both DB2 subsystems, the tablespace structures must be exactly the same. You should query both DB2s to locate the OBIDs necessary to construct the OBIDXLAT table.

Caution: *Starting with DB2 Version 5, there is an option in DSNZPARM (DLDFREQ) that will detect if a dataset is downlevel, and if it is, DB2 will reject the tablespace. This downlevel detection works systemwide and cannot be turned on or off at a tablespace level.*

How can I recover only a few units of work (undo updates)?

The standard recovery techniques for DB2 do not allow for a more granular recovery than full tablespaces recovered to a point in time. Some ISV vendors have built tools that analyze the log and can create SQL DML statements to selectively undo changes. Some organizations (especially banks and insurance companies) have indicated that they can never do full tablespace recoveries, since they are 24 × 7 shops.

However, if a batch job does incorrect updates, an SQL undo program will need to be written to back out the changes. The only assistance DB2 provides here is the DSN1LOGP service aid that can format the log, so you can see the before values. This can be an extremely time-consuming process that can create an enormous amount of data, and it requires in-depth DB2 knowledge, because the printed data is displayed in the DB2 internal format.

How do I know what was on a lost disk volume?

If you loose a complete disk volume, you would have to know exactly what was contained on the volume in order to know what objects need to be restored. DB2 OS/390 records this information in the VTOC (volume table of contents). It helps if you have a very current VTOC snapshot of the volume.

Tip: *Many people run a VTOC listing utility every day, and store the output in a dataset on another volume.*

There is, of course, the possibility that new datasets have been created or datasets are gone due to DDL and/or utility activity between the time the VTOC listing was taken and when it is viewed. Other sources for finding out what datasets were on the disk include:

- The ICF catalog (requires special utilities and can be very slow)
- The DB2 catalog (only if STOGROUPS are volume driven, not SMS driven)
- The -DISPLAY command (tablespaces that cannot be opened get the OPENF status; if they were open during the failure, they will get I/O errors)

After you find out which tablespaces were on the disk, you have the difficult task of constructing one or more recovery jobs. This whole process can take several hours (10 or more is not unusual). This means that if the data is critical, it is a

good idea to have RAID-5 disks installed, so the impact of losing a disk would be minimal. There is also ISV software that deals with lost volume scenarios.

> ❗ ***Caution:*** *Many people think they are completely protected if they use RAID-5 disks. This is not true—software failures can destroy data, for example—and all RAID-5 will do in that case is make sure that the invalid data is mirrored.*

❓ What is the difference between recovering to current versus recovering to an image copy when NPIs are involved?

If you do not recover a tablespace to the current point in time, any NPIs (non-partitioning indexes) will need to be recovered, because there is the possibility that the data and the indexes have become out of sync. When a recovery is done TOCOPY or TORBA and there are NPIs on the table, DB2 will place the indexes in recover pending status, and this will cause those indexes to be unavailable for query processing.

❓ What is the difference between circular logging and archival logging in DB2 UDB?

In circular logging, the log files are used in sequence and tablespaces are therefore only recoverable to the point at which the last backup was taken. Circular logging only works well for query-only databases. Archival logging archives log files when they become inactive, and this allows for a roll-forward recovery, which applies transactions recorded in the log files.

> ❗ ***Caution:*** *When a database is first created, circular logging is the default logging method. If your database requires roll-forward recovery, be sure to enable archival logging.*

> ❗ ***Caution:*** *If you change a database to enable roll-forward recovery through archival logging, you must take an offline backup of the database before it is usable.*

What are the implications of performing a recovery when the tablespace includes tables with defined triggers in DB2 UDB?

If a roll-forward recovery is performed on a tablespace containing tables defined with triggers, the changes made by the use of the triggers to tables in other tablespaces would be repeated. In other words these changes would be made twice, which may or may not be appropriate for that point in time.

HANDLING ERRORS DURING BACKUP AND RECOVERY

 How do I handle an unavailable image copy?

If DB2 cannot use an image copy, it will attempt to use the dual copy. If this fails, it will do a fallback to the previous image copy. If this is undesirable (for example, if you have a more current recovery site image copy), you will have to cancel the recovery at the next copy request. By simply replying "no" to a request to use a fallback copy, you only make the situation worse, since it will continue to go back further in time. Commands following this recovery in the same batch job will not be cancelled when you cancel the one recovery command.

Tip: *You could keep replying "no" until DB2 detects a non-recoverability (no more image copies to fall back on), thereby forcing the batch job to continue with the next command.*

How do I handle VVDS (VSAM volume dataset) and/or ICF failures?

This is not a DB2 problem, although DB2 requires the VVDS and ICF catalog to be in good condition. If you get error messages that indicate VVDS or ICF catalog failures, contact the person responsible for DASD management. The IBM DB2 Administration manual contains a detailed section on VVDS and ICF failures.

   Caution: *Remember that recovery of ICF catalogs requires that changes to the ICF catalogs are being logged (via SMF).*

 How do I deal with invalid DBD structures?

A DBD (Database Descriptor) is a kind of shorthand DB2 uses to deal with databases and all objects that exist inside databases. DB2 doesn't use the catalog but has its own internal control block (the DBD). There is a `REPAIR DBD TEST/DIAGNOSE` utility that will verify that DBD matches the structure according to the DB2 catalog (which is preferred). The trouble with the DIAGNOSE option is that it produces a great deal of output with several warnings. It requires a DB2 specialist to interpret the output of a `REPAIR DBD TEST/DIAGNOSE`. Whenever you get messages indicating an error with a DBD, or you suspect a DBD error, contact IBM support. Only do a `REPAIR DBD REBUILD` when you receive instructions from IBM to do so.

Chapter 18

Network Connectivity

Answer Topics!

Network Connectivity @ a Glance

Network connectivity technologies have come a long way since their inception. We now have several options for connecting our application interfaces to database servers. Of course, with flexibility comes complexity.

For applications needing to connect to any DB2 servers, there are several options and methods to follow. While the facilities for UNIX, Windows, and NT have been commonplace for years, the need for applications to connect to the DB2 OS/390 database server is growing rapidly. No longer are expensive middleware solutions required to accomplish the task of connecting the desktop with the mainframe. With options such as direct TCP/IP support through DRDA, connecting and communicating with DB2 OS/390 has become much easier.

ODBC protocols, CLI (Call Level Interface API) and SQL in Java through JDBC and SQLJ are used heavily in the client server world. There are many questions concerning the setup and tuning when using ODBC connectivity, and interfacing to the database through SQL either generated through CLI or hard coded with JDBC or SQLJ.

GENERAL CONNECTIVITY

What is the difference between DDCS and DB2 Connect?

DB2 Connect provides a means for users (either stand-alone or LAN) to access data from DRDA servers. It is a follow-on product to the DDCS (Distributed Database Connection Services). The access to the DRDA servers, such as DB2 OS/390, is transparent to the client.

Can DB2 for OS/390 retrieve data from DB2 for Unix or NT?

Yes, the other DB2s can be set up as servers. If all settings are correct and the definitions in the communication database (CDB) are correct, you can issue a CONNECT TO statement in SQL that opens the connection to the smaller DB2, which acts as a full two-phase application server. DB2 Connect and DDF play an important part in managing the communication, doing translation, and providing services for maintaining integrity.

What is the CAE and why do I need it in Windows?

Any client workstation that is in a Windows environment, or an OS/2 environment, for that matter, needs software installed on it to provide a connect service. The very lowest level of software that is required is the CAE (Client Application Enabler). You will not see an icon for this, nor will you find anything in the menus. The CAE is nothing more than a series of DLLs that enable the Windows client applications to talk to DB2. The server always has CAE installed on it, and when you run any of the UDB tools from the server, it is using the CAE that is on the server.

How do I connect DB2 OS/390 to the Web?

The better question is how do I connect a Web client to DB2 since it is the Web-client function that will be accessing data in DB2. The answer, however, is the same. DB2 now comes with a product called Net.Data. Net.Data allows you to retrieve data from DB2 and put it in Web pages. It also

allows you to retrieve data from several other sources, including IMS.

Net.Data is a follow-on product to the original DB2 WWW. It is a product for creating dynamic HTML pages using information from various sources, such as databases, flat files, scripts, or executable programs. Net.Data is normally called from a Web server. Building Web applications is fairly easy when using a Web server and Net.Data. There are also several other solutions on the market that will help provide Web access to DB2 servers.

How do I connect to a DB2 host from a single Windows-based PC?

This is a very common request and it may be the most common connection in the DB2 world. IBM has a product called DB2 Connect, which can provide this kind of connection for several different configurations. For a single Windows client to connect to a DB2 host, there is the DB2 Connect Personal Edition.

DB2 Connect allows clients to access data stored on database servers through DRDA (distributed relational database architecture). The most common of these connections is for a Windows client (95, 98, NT) to connect to an OS/390 DB2 server. DB2 Connect supports APPC connections between DRDA clients and the DB2 servers. DB2 on OS/390, as of Version 5, also supports TCP/IP in a DRDA environment. DB2 clients, through the appropriate CAE (Client Application Enabler), can use many supported protocols to establish a connection to the DB2 Connect gateway. This does require the proper CAE to be installed on the client. However, the CAE is not a DRDA Application Requestor but DB2 Connect does provide DRDA application requestor (AR) functionality.

Besides the DB2 Connect product from IBM, there are other middleware products from other vendors that also provide this type of functionality.

Can I remove the DB2 CAE login Window?

Often it is required or desired to remove the CAE login window. It is possible to set a default userid and password to be used with ODBC applications to access any particular database. You do this by using the Client Configuration

Assistant and specifying a User ID and Password that will be used as the defaults when connecting with ODBC applications. This procedure makes a change in the db2cli.ini file which could be edited directly instead of using the CCA.

Where do I begin when I have a connection failure between an application and DB2 OS/390?

If a distributed connection fails, there are several places to begin to look for the source of the problem.

First of all (and this may sound silly), make sure the remote system is started, and then look next to the communication pieces: Is DDF active? Is VTAM active, or has VTAM experienced any path errors or failures? If you are using TCP/IP, have there been any failures there?

Then check the information in the DB2 CDB (communications database) to ensure that it is still correct. Follow the path from server to receiver and check the stability of all involved components. After checking all of these components without finding any answers, you may want to also consider the possibility of user error.

In DB2 UDB, what processes are created at CONNECT time?

The processes that are created at DB2 CONNECT time are:

- **DB2AGENT**   The agent handles all SQL processing that the application requests. It is a process that is subtasked (spawned) by the System Controller if the application is local, or the Communication Manager if the application is remote.

- **DB2DLOCK**   The database deadlock detector looks for and resolves deadlocks on a particular database.

- **DB2LOGGR**   The database logger handles all of the logging required for a particular database.

Every subsequent DB2 CONNECT from each distinct application to the same database will result in one additional agent process. The database deadlock detector and the database logger serve all applications connected to the same database.

If I am in a data-sharing environment and I lose a member, do I lose total connectivity?

No, in a data-sharing environment, if a connection is lost (caused by a quiesce or failed member), all requests are routed to the remaining active members of the data-sharing group.

Can I retrieve data from DB2 and non-DB2 databases in one unit of work?

Not from DB2, but there is a special product from IBM called Data Joiner that can query DB2 and non-DB2 (including non-IBM) databases in one query, and it does two-phase commits as well. In addition, it will allow heterogeneous joins between tables from differing databases.

When debugging connectivity problems in DB2 UDB, how can I find out if the problem is with the protocol used for communication?

In DB2 UDB, there is a tool that can be used to help you to determine whether or not a particular LAN protocol is functioning and whether communication can occur using a given protocol. This tool is called Protocol Communications Test and it works independently of UDB. It is helpful to use this tool when trying to solve connectivity problems by eliminating or verifying that the protocol is a contributor to the problem at hand.

Protocol Communications Test is found in the MISC subdirectory of the SQLLIB.

DRDA

What is DRDA?

DRDA (distributed relational database architecture) was designed and published by IBM to meet the requirements for open client/server data access in an unlike, or heterogeneous, systems environment. DRDA provides the conventions and protocols that allow for connectivity among relational database management systems.

 ## How does DRDA process work for static SQL?

DRDA processes SQL by prebinding the statements into packages that reside on the database server, and during execution the server location is either determined by the commands issued by the DB2 bind process or through a CONNECT statement in the application program. This allows you to have either static or dynamic SQL statements, because the required information for execution already resides on the server.

When using DRDA protocols for statement execution, DB2 will not send the entire SQL statement to the remote DBMS; rather it will identify the statement and then send only the required information for execution of the statement to the remote location, allowing for static execution of SQL statements.

 ## How can I determine the VTAM log mode in a DRDA environment?

In order to determine the VTAM log mode in a DRDA environment, you start by issuing the command:

```
DISPLAY THREAD(*) LOCATION(...) DETAIL
```

You can then obtain the VTAM session ID (except that the first byte of the session ID is not totally accurate) by issuing the following VTAM command:

```
D NET,SESSIONS, LU1=db2lu,LIST=ALL
```

By scanning the resulting list of session IDs (SIDs), you can identify the correct session ID (match bytes 2–8 in the result set of the DB2 -DISPLAY THREAD command). Then issue the following command:

```
D NET,SESSIONS,SID=correct_session_id
```

This will give you the LU names, class of service, and the log mode entry being used.

Can I access DB2 OS/390 using DRDA through dependent LU?

Both dependent and independent LU6.2 are APPC connections, and DRDA can be used with either type. While independent is recommended, either will work.

What is the difference between DRDA and DB2 OS/390 private protocol?

Which method you use will depend on the application requirements. The following points explain the differences between the two.

- Both DRDA and DB2 OS/390 private protocol can read and update at remote locations from CICS, TSO, IMS, batch, or CAF, and both can only have one location specified per SQL statement.

- Private protocol can only go from one DB2 subsystem to another DB2 subsystem, whereas DRDA can connect DB2 to any server.

- DRDA allows you to bind SQL statements before execution, and private protocol does not allow remote binding.

- Any DRDA server can be explicitly connected to by an application; however, using private protocol the DB2 requester can find the remote data by its object name.

- With DRDA you can issue any SQL statement supported by the subsystem executing the statement. When using private protocol you are limited to SQL DML (SELECT, INSERT, UPDATE, DELETE) and statements supporting SELECT.

In Version 6 of DB2 OS/390, DRDA will support all the features of private protocol (including three-part names as defined by aliases), and private protocol will cease to exist sometime after Version 6 is released.

 ## Do I have to use DRDA in order to execute stored procedures?

No, you do not need to use DRDA in order to execute stored procedures. You would need this connection to the server if the SQL executing the stored procedure is from a remote client. A client running on the server (for example, a COBOL program running on OS/390) directly executes the stored procedure without any network connectivity issues.

ODBC, CLI, AND JDBC

 ## How do I connect my Windows client to an ODBC DB2 database?

The first step is to install the CAE on the client. After this is installed and the client is rebooted (as required), the CCA (Client Configuration Assistant) should start automatically. This tool gives you three options for defining the ODBC data source:

- **Access Profile** This is a text file containing all the required information. You can create it, but it is normally given to the client.

- **Searching** This searching of the entire network for ODBC data sources can be time consuming if the network you are connected to is large.

- **Manual** These screens will enable an experienced user to set all the necessary parameters.

No matter which option is selected, the purpose of the whole process is to define the ODBC data source that this particular client can connect to. All front-end tools have their own unique ways for you to define the ODBC database that you want to work with.

 What are some tuning options for improving performance with DB2 CAE clients and CLI ODBC use in UDB?

There are some values in the DB2CLI.INI file that can be set to help with performance. These values can be changed by either manually updating the DB2CLI.INI file or by using the DB2 Client Configuration Assistant. The follow options are in order of most performance benefit gained.

- **DeferredPrepare=1** By using this option, you will gain the most benefit in terms of performance because you will save line turnarounds by combining flows. This defers sending the PREPARE request until the corresponding execute request is issued, combining the two requests into one command/reply flow instead of two.

- **Autocommit=0** If you set Autocommit to 0, you can save the overhead of the additional message otherwise required to perform the commit. The default is 1, which provides a turnaround message for the commit for every message sent. Be careful with this option, and ensure that your application programs are performing commits where necessary.

- **Txnlsolation=1** This parameter sets the isolation level. If possible, set it to 1 to allow for uncommitted reads. This will eliminate the overhead associated with acquiring locks.

- **OptimizeForNRows=x** This will set up the number of rows to be returned in a block. By making this value greater than 0, OPTIMIZE FOR N ROWS will appear on every SQL statement.

- **EarlyClose=1** This option will allow for any open cursors on the server to be closed after the last row of the result set has been sent to the client, without closing the cursor on the client. Turning this option on can help to

speed up applications that have small result sets. This will save the ODBC/CLI driver a network call, because it will not have to issue a call to close the cursor.

- **Cursorhold=0** Setting this option will allow for cursors not to be maintained across a unit of work, and will therefore result in fewer line flows. This can help as long as your application is not dependent on the cursor being held open through units of work.

- **KeepConnect=4** This option represents the number of connections to cache. By setting this number greater than 0, you can speed up applications that are continuously connecting to, and disconnecting from, the same database using the same connection information. The value represents the number of connections.

- **KeepStatement=6** This value represents the number of statement handles to cache. In order to improve performance for applications that allocate and then drop large sets of statement handles, you can increase this number from the default of 5. The number of handles available will be dependent on memory.

Why can't I update my DB2 table from ODBC?

The main reason why people run into trouble updating tables from an ODBC environment is because the ODBC interfaces require a primary key to update the data. Because the interfaces want to be at a compliant ODBC level, they allow for a scrollable cursor in both directions. To implement this, the interface reads the complete result set from an SQL query into storage. Therefore, there is no longer a current cursor to do the update. In order to make sure that the correct row will be updated from the program, these interfaces ensure that the primary key is in the result set, and when an update is done, they add a WHERE clause to the update identifying the key. These implementations restrict a result set to browse only, if the table has no primary key.

 What is the DB2 ODBC catalog?

The DB2 ODBC catalog is a set of pseudo-catalog tables designed to improve the performance of ODBC applications that access DB2 databases. These catalog tables contain data that represents objects in the real DB2 catalog; however, the data kept in these tables is only the necessary data required to support ODBC operations. The tables in the ODBC DB2 catalog are indexed specifically to support access to the catalog by ODBC applications, and they are prejoined for faster access. Views are also supported in the DB2 ODBC catalog to further limit the information required by the ODBC application.

What are the advantages and disadvantages of using ODBC vs. CLI?

ODBC and CLI are both standards that are based on a set of APIs (application programming interfaces) that access data sources. ODBC was originally based on an early version of CLI. DB2 provides both ODBC and CLI drivers.

	CLI	ODBC
Installation	CLI applications will only need the DB2 CAE installed.	The ODBC driver will have to be installed only if ODBC applications are used.
Portability	CLI can port to environments other than Windows. However, a CLI application can only access DB2-family databases as data sources.	ODBC is used for Windows or DOS applications only. However, an ODBC application can access several different databases from multiple vendors.
Standards	CLI is a standard controlled by the X/OPEN standards body, and any changes made to CLI will be made by all vendors on all platforms.	ODBC is supported by Microsoft and can be changed by them to better support their products.
SQL Performance	Both ODBC and CLI use dynamic SQL, supported by several vendors, and performance is similar.	Both ODBC and CLI use dynamic SQL, supported by several vendors, and performance is similar.
Use with DB2 UDB	Changes to CLI are implemented in UDB quickly because IBM is involved in the standards-creation process for CLI.	There typically is a longer lead time for changes made to ODBC to be implemented in DB2 UDB.

What functions of ODBC does DB2 UDB support?

The current versions of UDB support all of the level 2 functions and several of the level 3 functions in ODBC 3.0.

What can I use to help diagnose a problem when accessing DB2 UDB from an ODBC application, such as Powerbuilder or Microsoft Access?

If an ODBC or CLI application is having problems accessing DB2 UDB, you may want to start a trace on the ODBC/CLI function calls. The trace will log the function calls to a file in ASCII format. To activate an ODBC/CLI trace, you can either use the DB2 Client Configuration Assistant, or you can manually activate the trace by adding the following statements to the COMMON section of the DB2CLI.INI file:

```
Trace=1
TraceFileName= (name of trace file)
TraceFlush=1
```

You can deactivate the trace by setting the value of Trace to 0.

What is JDBC?

JDBC (Java database connectivity) is an API that provides a uniform SQL interface to a large selection of relational databases and a common base on which higher-level interfaces and tools can be developed.

On the sever side, JDBC supports both fenced and unfenced UDFs and stored procedures in Java. Of course, on OS/390, all stored procedures are fenced to protect the environment (why give user code capability to corrupt the environment?).

On the client side, JDBC is considered to be an "equivalent" to ODBC. JDBC is a dynamic SQL interface that has become a standard interface for Java applications needing to access several different relational database systems. Although not as simple as static or embedded SQL, it does provide a perceived level of portability.

What are JDBC applets, and how are they used?

A JDBC applet is a program written in Java that can be invoked by any Java-enabled Web browser when a page is displayed. By using the facilities of JDBC, the applet can connect to the database, and retrieve and display data. Use of JDBC applets can allow computers that can access the Internet to access your data on DB2 UDB.

Does JDBC provide any advantages over CLI?

JDBC is very similar to CLI and is actually built on top of it. JDBC has the same features as CLI, with a few more advantages. First, by using JDBC you can code Java applets to be executed by a Java-enabled browser, allowing your data to be accessed from the Web without additional client software. Second, you can access relational databases by using an object-oriented interface, because JDBC is integrated into the Java language.

TCP/IP

What is needed to access DB2 OS/390 via TCP/IP?

DB2 OS/390, from Version 5 on, can be a native TCP/IP DRDA server. The TCP/IP address comes from the BSDS (bootstrap dataset). All that is needed is TCP/IP support enabled in OS/390. When properly set up, Java applets can access DB2 using JDBC or SQLJ without using DB2 Connect or a gateway.

Can I cancel a DDF thread that has a distributed TCP/IP connection?

A DDF thread using TCP/IP can be canceled using the same method for canceling normal DB2 threads. This is done by using the -CANCEL DDF THREAD command.

 How is TCP/IP enabled in a sysplex environment?

TCP/IP is not sysplex-enabled in the same way VTAM is enabled. There is no support for generic resources and no support for multinode persistent sessions, so the notion of automatically routing TCP/IP work to another system in the event of a system failure won't work.

This is not to say that TCP/IP does not have any support for sysplex. TCP/IP 3.2 supports IP over XCF connections through shared support with VTAM. One simple definition will enable this support. The domain name system (DNS) server on OS/390 has been enhanced to communicate with the workload manager (WLM). The DNS server obtains workload information from the WLM and uses this information to calculate the best system on which to place a new connection. It returns a weighted list of systems in response to the client get host name or host address calls.

If the zone records to the DNS server have been defined correctly and the applications have been placed on the systems in your sysplex in a balanced way, DNS will distribute new connections in the sysplex based on workload and capacity. The new DNS functions require OS/390 2.4. Where it makes sense, IBM has said that TCP/IP will be enhanced to support more sysplex strengths.

 How do I enable TCP/IP in DB2 UDB?

In order to enable TCP/IP on the DB2 UDB server, you will need to set the DB2COMM profile variable to TCP/IP as shown below:

```
db2set -i  DB2COMM=TCP/IP
```

The service name must also be defined in the services file on the server. This is done through the database manager configuration file with a parameter called SVCENAME, which is the name assigned to the main connection port for the instance. This is done as follows:

```
UPDATE DATABASE MANAGER CONFIGURATION USING SVCENAME service-name
```

Index